Wholesale MBA

How to sell consumer goods to distributors, retailers, and consumers

Written by Jorge S. Olson & Sandro Piancone

ISBN: 978-1-945196-33-1

Manufactured in the United States of America

Edited and Produced by Cube17, Inc.
Cover by Jacqueline Gonzalez De Leon

Table of Contents

Introduction

"Your goal should be to get your products into the hands of consumers over and over again."

"Snoop Dogg doesn't like that photo," Tiffany tells me on a video call. I better keep looking. We're two months behind schedule with our Dogg lbs launch, a company we created with Snoop Dogg. Tiffany Chin is the CEO of Snoop Dogg and Death Row Records, hemp and Cannabis companies. The pressure is on, and we must formulate, develop, and manufacture gummies, smoking paper, hemp blunts and tubes, vapes, candy, and chocolates. We have two million dollars in orders for the first product, gummies, and I can't even get Snoop's photo approved to start on my packaging concept. Tiffany had already shot down two of my art concepts, which I thought were brilliant, but Snoop and Tiffany disagreed. This project might collapse before it even begins.

When you want to launch a product, you need to think of the entire equation, solving for the consumer, because at the end of the day, the consumer will decide to buy it or not. So, the team gets on the phone, calling Snoop photographers from all over his appearance, including red carpets, concerts, and television interviews. I don't like any of the photos, plus they were quite expensive. One photographer wanted fifty thousand dollars up front, plus royalties, for using one of Snoop's photos. The stress level in the company was increasing; we couldn't order the gummy bags from China because we didn't have artwork ready, and I was still stuck on the main image.

I decided to call my old friend Gustavo Mayoral. We go way back. Gustavo is an award-winning artist, professional photographer, and recovering programmer. I met Gustavo when I was fourteen years old, and I knew he could help me, but not in the way you think.

"Gustavo, how are you doing with Artificial Intelligence?" I asked over the phone.

"I'm up to date with the visual aspect of it," he said.

"How far in are you in image AI?" I asked.

"I already started programming to develop my artistic photography style using my intellectual property and tools," he said.

I knew I had the right guy. So, I met with Gustavo and asked him to start working on an AI model that could program Snoop Dogg for our packaging and Augmented Reality, as the packaging on our products would talk to you using your phone. The problem was that Snoop didn't want to use AI for anything. Good luck convincing him that this was the way to go.

The team got on the phone with Tiffany, and I explained how I knew Gustavo from back in the day in Tijuana, that he was an artist, and that he would get paid for his work. Snoop is big on paying artists and thought AI would steal from artists. After Snoop and Tiffany understood that there was a real artist behind the image, they agreed to make this AI image the official product image of Dogg lbs, and we were out to the races. From that day, it has been craziness day in and day out, trying to develop an entire portfolio of products simultaneously.

Snoop Dogg is not the only product development on the agenda. Next on the list are Wiz Khalifa and Death Row Records, after finishing a portfolio of products for Rick Ross, Cheech and Chong, Hemp Bar, The Real Stuff, and Lucky To Be. Our goal is to develop and sell our products in one hundred thousand convenience stores, supermarkets, and pharmacies, not to mention online sales. What is your goal?

I spent the month developing artwork, labels, point of sale material, speaking with distributors, planning for tradeshows, printers, our sales team, and management meetings with my partner Sandro Piancone, the captain of the ship. In the time it takes to develop, formulate, and manufacture one product, we created an entire line with our partner, Snoop Dogg. We even sold two truckloads to our master distributors for a million dollars; the product is not officially out yet. What does it take to add this kind of speed to your product development and sales? We'll cover every step of the equation in the book and take you behind the scenes on how Sandro and I develop products, sell them, and manage our companies. Our companies are publicly traded, so you can follow our sales and stock price in real-time as you read this book.

Create products and place them in the hands of consumers; that's the goal. This book aims to help you sell products, specifically consumer packaged goods like beverages, beauty and cosmetics, nutritional supplements, snacks, CBD, Cannabis, Cannabinoid products, electronics, food, novelties, pet supplies, and other Fast Moving Consumer Goods and Durable Goods.

We aim to sell your products to retailers, including online and brick-and-mortar retailers like supermarkets and convenience stores.

We reach the end consumer and the retailers that sell to them through wholesalers, distributors, category buyers, brokers, direct sales, and other strategies I've used successfully to sell my products into these retail channels.

How you get your product into the hands of consumers and keep them coming for more is the name of the game! I am referring to supply chain, wholesale distribution, and consumer marketing. Gaining this knowledge is the purpose of this Wholesale MBA book.

How you get your products into the hands of consumers will depend on you, your company, and your business model. Maybe you want to sell your product online using Facebook, Instagram, or Amazon. Perhaps you want to create and sell a brand to a Fortune Company or take your company public. You must think of placing your products in convenience stores or supermarkets. The above are just channels, a part of the entire Wholesale MBA system that goes from your product idea to repeatedly selling and reselling to the consumer.

Please pay special attention when I say, "sell repeatedly." The idea of reselling your product in your channel is what builds a brand. For example, if you sell a beverage into one hundred 7-Eleven convenience stores in your hometown and then conduct in-store promotions, merchandising, and sampling events, you'll get new customers walking into the store to purchase your beverage. Maybe many people will taste your drink, and a quarter of them will buy it because your team is there promoting it. But what happens after you leave? What happens when your sampling team is not there to help push the sale of your drink? Will that customer still buy your product, or will they revert to their favorite beverage? Their decision is the making or breaking of your brand.

Without knowing how your brand is faring, you move your team to the next city, opening one hundred more stores. A few months later, when you return to your distributor or your original one hundred stores in your hometown, you notice your product is no longer on the shelf. The store managers and the distributor tell you they will discontinue your brand. Wow! This loss is a real hit to your business. Does this happen often? Does it happen to start-ups or Fortune companies? The answer, unfortunately, is yes. It happens to everyone. It has happened to me many times with many different products. Distributors carry a portfolio of products because they can't solely rely on one or two products to survive. They must protect themselves by testing different products, delivering multiple products at one store, and increasing sales per store. I like to call this the store drop.

You may be thinking, "What happened? I was doing so well opening new stores in a new territory. I already invested in the previous region. Now I must remove my product from those stores or the distributor's warehouse and start again, opening new stores and territories."

Don't worry about the doom and gloom scenario I just described above. From the beginning, I want to assure you that we will not do this. We know this can happen and will avoid it at all costs. The same scenario can occur if you sell directly to consumers, for example, if you sell online, say from your website or on Amazon.

The concept of a Wholesale MBA is the entirety of your business model. Don't worry if you don't already have a set business model. You will if you follow this guidebook. Once you complete your business model, it will have a clear, step-by-step formula for getting distribution, retailers, and selling your product to consumers.

The job of reaching the end consumer and selling to them is the same for a start-up entrepreneur, distributor, or Fortune company dominating the shelf space. Now more than ever, the internet, social media, Amazon, Google, and online retailing have shortened the product and consumer gap. You needed to place your product on a shelf a few years ago to reach many consumers. The other alternative was a massive direct-to-consumer sales force. Now, an entrepreneur can sell products online and outsell Fortune companies in the same category. Look at Amazon's best-selling list to find small companies competing with large multinationals.

As we advance through the book and your business model, don't forget that the end goal is to reach the consumer. I'm going to repeat that over and over again. It's your job to sell to the consumer, retailer, distributor, wholesaler, sales broker, salespeople, bartenders, chefs, merchandisers, and everyone in your supply chain.

The world of consumer goods and wholesale distribution is more than creating and selling new products through distribution, online, and retail strategies. The wholesale trade represents the creation of modern wealth worldwide. Imagine transporting yourself to the Middle Ages, when they measured wealth in land, and only kings and royalty could own land. In those days, if you were not born into royalty, you had a tough life, and creating wealth was almost impossible. The trading of goods altered this, along with our civilization, culture, communication, and the very definition of wealth, trade, and capitalism.

Within the pages of this book, you'll discover everything related to finding and creating new products and selling them directly to the consumer by using contemporary and traditional means of distribution into wholesale and retail channels. More importantly, you will understand how to find your perfect consumers or alpha consumers, captivate them, communicate with them, and make them your brand ambassadors.

We will explore the traditional wholesale distribution and product development forms in detail. However, there are innovative ways to find and sell to consumers your competition will most likely not use. You'll incorporate those into your strategy, using resources like social media, articles, landing pages, Amazon, direct response, direct sales, and other marketing techniques.

Some of the Goals after reading this book:

- Develop & launch a new consumer product
- Sell to wholesalers, distributors, and retailers
- Find, market & sell products
- Become a Wholesaler or Distributor
- Sell to retailers and consumers
- Export to new markets

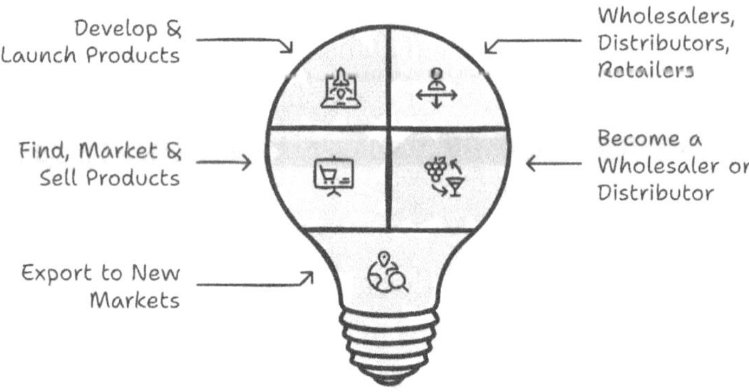

Figure 1 - Pathways to Market Success

This book is for entrepreneurs and executives who make, sell, and distribute products. The ones that make them, the manufacturers, are visionaries who create products of all kinds to sell in stores or directly to consumers. The distributors and wholesalers look for such products and want to increase sales, find great products, new accounts, export markets, new channels of distribution, and maybe even create a product of their own.

Some of the questions you should ask about your business include:

1. *Do you have an excellent idea for a product and would like to bring it to market?*

2. *Do you want to find and establish relationships with buyers and consumers?*

3. *Do you want to sell products in convenience stores, supermarkets, and pharmacies?*

4. *Do you prefer to concentrate on selling directly to consumers online or through other direct-to-consumer strategies?*

With the help of this book, you'll know the wholesale business inside and out – from product development to testing, opening new stores, sales, distribution, consumer marketing, and how to be successful in the wonderful world of wholesale distribution. This guide is genuinely an MBA program in one book. It's an MBA with twenty years of experience, mistakes, and triumphs. It summarizes working with hundreds of executives and launching over a thousand consumer packaged goods. It's a synopsis of distributing over five thousand SKUs into traditional retailers such as supermarkets, superstores, pharmacies, convenience stores, restaurants, hotels, and bars. It reviews how to sell online using direct sales and other out-of-the-box alternative distribution methods.

But wait, there's more! You'll benefit from my experience as a Chief Marketing Officer, VP of Sales and Marketing, Chief Operating Officer, product development, direct response, and online marketing Consultant. I will share stories of my continuous work with other consumer goods companies worldwide and how I have helped companies grow to $100 million in sales. You'll also benefit from the serial entrepreneurial brain of my partner and co-founder of two public companies and a portfolio of products, Sandro Piancone, CEO of Green Globe International, Inc. (Ticker Symbol GGII) and Hempacco, Inc. (Ticker Symbol HPCO).

Sandro is an expert on starting and scaling multiple companies simultaneously. He's the elbow grease that allows our companies to expand and grow. His last wholesale distribution company scaled from zero to $200 Million in sales. Sandro will show you how to grow your brand or distribution company. He'll guide you in this book through starting a company and scaling it quickly, including the mindset you need, and he used to grow multiple companies selling over a billion dollars.

To get started and continue with our MBA theme, you don't get an MBA degree from this book; you do know that, right? But stay with me as we follow the example of a university learning program. Following the school example, you'll need your undergraduate degree in product development, sales, distribution, wholesaling, and retailing. Don't worry; you won't have to read another five books or spend four years at a university. I have a summary for you in the first chapter. You'll read a real-life program's "cliff notes" in only one chapter. After the first chapter, we'll jump into the MBA program, exploring products, distributors, marketing, sales, and everything entrepreneurs, CEOs, wholesalers, or retailers need to know about the wholesale industry. The first chapter will not cut corners. It will provide all the information you need to start or improve your business. The rest of the MBA program goes over all aspects of the business. Here, you'll learn big-picture strategies and precise ways of marketing, testing, exporting, selling, and more. This MBA will be enlightening even to the most veteran executive of a consumer packaged goods company.

The New World Order of Sales & Competition

Entrepreneurs are entering a new world order. Gone are the days when you had to compete with Fortune 500 consumer companies for a place on the refrigerator door or shelf or pay sixty dollars per store to place your product next to the company, spending $100 million per year on advertising.

In the New World Order, you can appeal directly to consumers, sell your products without a distributor, and have large retailers begging you to have your fabulous product in their stores. Sounds too good to be true? It's happening daily, and if you're not part of it, your competitor is, so you better join the club. Of course, this will not happen to every product, just the good ones!

You'll know more about the industry than most manufacturers and distributors combined with this book. This knowledge will allow you to make sound decisions, find the niche that works for you, develop new products, market, and sell them correctly. In product development, you'll learn to invent a new product, look for holes in the marketplace, fill them, and market your original idea. There is no singular way to develop an idea for a product, but there are formulas and shortcuts for product development without spending all your capital before you have a product to test.

In sales, you will apply the top methods of distributing and retailing your product. You'll learn how to sell to the trade and consumers, know what buyers want, where they get it, and how to reach them. I'll share some stories of trade shows gone wrong and sales campaigns that went right. Sales are an integral part of your business. We'll cover it in detail, examining every wholesaler, distributor, and retailer type, from convenience stores to supermarkets, club stores, etc.

For marketing, you'll discover how to make it the driving force of your new product, not just how to advertise or have a good-looking label and package. After all, selling is only one of the different parts of marketing, even though many companies separate the two into distinct departments. Some companies see marketing as the creative department, publicity, or advertising. Indeed, all of these include sales, consumer awareness, and even customer service. Use marketing to steer your product development, sales, distribution, customer relationships, and distributor relationships. This is how we'll treat marketing in this book: as the all-mighty law of consumer goods.

This Book Is About Selling Your Product

The book is about creating products, finding hidden market niches, and creating new, exciting distribution channels. Still, more than anything, it's about selling your products. If you don't sell any products, it won't matter if you have the best-tasting or the best-looking product. You'll be stuck with your inventory; it will be the best, but you'll be stuck with it. Being stuck with loads of merchandise happens more than you would imagine to new companies and entrepreneurs, even companies with large budgets. This guide will help you overcome this mega mistake before going into production.

There are many ways to sell products, and we'll cover the most important ones, including the most popular method of reaching consumers. You'll also discover why your marketing plan starts with your consumer. Yes, I said your consumer, not your product; this will be a recurring theme throughout the book. The consumer will tell you what they want and how they want it, how to price your product, how and where to sell it, who the distributor will be, and how to make it. If you start with the product instead of the consumer in product development, it will be a fatal mistake (I'm getting dark now), and your product will fail. So avoid it and give the consumer all the credit; they'll give you their money after all.

Today, you can do things you couldn't before because the methodology and technology were unavailable or too expensive. Now, you can establish consumer relationships, not through expensive market tests, sampling, and pilot programs. Instead, I'm talking about fundamental interactions and conversations with hundreds, thousands, or millions of consumers. Social media platforms, blogging, videos, and other forms of modern communication allow you to interact with consumers unprecedentedly; the key will be how you use these tools. Will you push information or advertising, as everyone else does, or will you invite consumers into your home, converse, and become part of your product? That, my friend, can be the holy grail of product success –you'll find out quickly if your product will sell and who will buy it.

The distributor, wholesaler, and category buyers from convenience stores, supermarkets, and pharmacies are significant. Still, ultimately, the consumer is making the buying decision, and you need to market to them.

Make an emotional connection with your consumer. This is the holy grail of marketing, and I'll say it countless times in this book because it's that important.

If you could get your consumer emotionally attached to your product, or at the very least hook the consumer in some way, they will look for your product everywhere and buy it. However, you need help finding the consumer and making your product available to them in various locations. Let's call this help your sales or distribution channel.

I spend a lot of time explaining how the consumer rules the world, and now that you're on board with this concept, let's move on to the tools you'll need to grow your company exponentially. After all, we don't want you selling your products one by one using only direct sales. So, let's talk leverage. How can you leverage your distribution channels to grow exponentially into every retail channel available in the USA and worldwide? No, this is not just for new consumer product entrepreneurs. It's for $100 million companies and Fortune companies alike.

When choosing your sales or distribution channel, you must have your goals and strategy. You need to know what you want from your business, product, and budget. Your high-level, long-term goal could be to sell your company. If this is your goal, your strategy differs from just cash flowing your business or leaving it to your children. In other words, **you need to establish clear goals**.

For example, your goal might be to sell your company in five years. A different plan can be to sell your product in five thousand retail stores by year two. Your goal doesn't have to be measured in dollars or cases sold. It can be personal, related to stores, or exporting to other countries. Just make sure you have clear goals for both you and your business.

Most of the people I work with want to sell their companies. It doesn't matter if they're just starting or are veterans of consumer goods. Most of them started their company with an exit strategy in mind. A few want their kids to inherit the business, especially if they're distributors. In this case, many are already in the hands of the second or third generations. Let's take the example of wanting to sell your company in five years. Companies looking to buy a brand want a specific distribution channel, whether retail or direct response. If you sell your company to Coca-Cola, your distribution strategy differs from selling it to Amazon. Coke would look for beverage distributors and convenience store penetration. If you're not there, you at least need to be selling to the natural channels. Amazon would want direct response sales, maybe through social media or an e-commerce store selling your products directly to consumers.

Your budget is another crucial consideration when following the examples and strategies of this book. If you're the CEO of a company selling $100 million per year and want to penetrate convenience stores, your budget and goal differ from a start-up with your first production run in the warehouse. You will have many strategies, each with a separate budget and various types of staffing needed to execute.

Who should read this book?

This book is for people who want to produce and market consumer goods, including Impulse Buy, Consumer

Packaged Goods, Perishables, Beverages, Nutraceuticals, and any other Fast Moving Consumer Goods type. It can also apply to different categories, such as durable goods, clothing, auto supplies, toys, pet supplies, tools, electronics, and even books. I've created, distributed, merchandised, and sold most of the products on the list online.

The above definition is straightforward, encompassing many people, but that's who it's for. It includes new entrepreneurs looking to launch a new product. It also includes veteran entrepreneurs and CEOs with an existing product who aspire to grow their company. It's also for prominent Fortune company executives who would like to penetrate new distribution channels, such as convenience stores, the most challenging channel for these large companies and one they do a poor job of servicing. But the book is not just for what we call "Manufacturers," the creators and owners of brands. It's also for distributors, wholesalers, retailers, and employees of these companies, such as merchandising managers, salespeople, category buyers, and others who want to figure out how to sell more products.

Many readers want to be wholesale distributors. For you, I have unique content and many specifics on how to start a business, find the best products, open new stores, and grow your business. I will explain the numbers behind wholesale distribution, how much money a distributor makes per product, store, and day, and how to start, grow, and run your business from your warehouse to your deliveries.

Learning from readers was the first influence in deciding what to include in the book. When I wrote the book "Build Your Beverage Empire," now in its third edition, my goal was to teach new beverage entrepreneurs how to start their beverage companies, develop their beverage and packaging, and produce their drinks. I also included beverage marketing, sales, and distribution information for new entrepreneurs. To my surprise, the book landed on the desks of CEOs and VPs from the largest beverage companies globally, and they not only read it but also bought it to discuss with their employees. I learned a valuable lesson about selling a book. You should know who can benefit from your product besides your target market. I thought only new entrepreneurs would benefit, and many others read the book and benefited from it. Surprisingly, the beverage book is used in graduate and undergraduate programs in the USA and worldwide. I applied those lessons in this book, including information for newcomers to the business and old wolves. The result is a book that will allow you to launch and sell products whether you're the new kid on the block, a distributor, a retailer, or a veteran executive from one of the big firms.

How To Use This Book To Sell More Products

"Keep a notepad handy as you read, and re-write or update your sales and marketing strategy."

We already established that this book aims to help you sell more products, but I don't know what type of products you have or what retailers you want to target. I also don't know if you are the CEO of a new business or a VP of Sales of a hundred-million-dollar company. I want to make sure you get the most value from this book. Please get in touch with me if this book changes your business. I'm dedicated to sharing my experiences and knowledge with you, including your approach to the book, how you read it, share it, take notes, and apply the knowledge.

How to read this book? I recommend taking notes as you go, not just thinking about a concept or strategy; take notes based on how it applies to you, and then keep reading. You'll find I build on those concepts as the book continues, so you can return to your original notes and fill in the gaps. If you see something that's extraordinary, page mark and highlight it. I like to use a yellow highlighter and sticky notes. I write on the sticky notes what I got from the highlighted area. This way, I can read my short notes and reference the concept.

Here are some examples of who can benefit from this book:

- Product Manufacturers
- New Consumer Goods Entrepreneurs
- Importers and Exporters
- Brand Managers
- Sales Managers
- Consumer Goods Incubators
- Wholesalers

- Distributors
- Wagon Jobbers
- Retailers
- Sales Brokers
- Executives
- Salespeople
- Foodservice Companies
- Beverages Companies
- Existing Brands
- Investors
- Analysts

As you read this book and start your MBA in the wholesale industry, I will not address you as a wholesaler, distributor, or manufacturer. I'll give examples and address you as if you are all of them; if you're devoted to this business, you must learn the intricacies of the broker, manufacturer, importer, wholesaler, and salesperson. Yes, I'll give plenty of examples, case studies, and information on business methods. It is much easier for you, the reader, as you don't have to listen to the information you might think doesn't apply to you.

What is Your Business?

The advantage of knowing how each person is involved in the creation, sales, distribution, and product retailing is that you'll appreciate how they think, what they want, how they make money, their gross margins, and the internal operations of their enterprise. With this information, you can market to them, service them better, and make new alliances in every aspect of the business.

If you're a distributor or sales broker, you will learn how brand owners think, what they want to accomplish, the inner workings of their cash flow, and how they need to support you in your marketing efforts. You'll also learn how to sell more products to your clients and get more retailers to buy more often. You'll even discover how to develop your private-label products, adding another fifty percent to your gross margin. Imagine making seventy or eighty percent on a few products instead of only twenty or thirty percent. How would that change the outlook of your business?

If you are a manufacturer, you will learn to be a brand manager and sell more products throughout the wholesale and retail supply chain. You will get inside the minds of all your clients, from brokers to distributors to retailers, and learn what they want, how they buy, and what they expect from you. You will understand how to launch new products if you don't already have one. You'll also establish relationships with consumers, distributors, and wholesalers in the USA and other countries. Your goal may be to service retail channels, but you'll also learn the advantages of direct channels. You never know; maybe your best channel starts with internet sales, and after an informational trial, you will find your product in every store in the nation.

Your Current Businesses

If you have an existing business, this book will help you grow your business by discovering new distribution channels, using better merchandising and sales best practices, and getting to know your customers better.

Don't think you're supposed to know everything because you are already in business; that rarely happens. About half of my projects are with existing companies, not new ones. Maybe you don't know how to acquire more customers or distributors, perhaps you're spending your time at trade shows and not getting any additional sales, or you need cash flow to maintain the sales you already have. You'll learn to reach your goals (remember, you need to set them first) and pivot your company when you're going the wrong way.

Pivoting is a part of doing business. You must adapt to changing conditions, competition, technology, or opportunities. Here is an example: I oversaw procurement for a wholesale company with my partner, Marshall. Marshall had thirty years of experience buying, selling, and manufacturing products in the USA and China. We distributed our products to seventeen thousand stores and made private label products for several chains around the USA, including Target, Rite-Aid, and Walgreens. I assessed about two hundred products we were selling and drove from San Diego to Los Angeles to speak with some of our suppliers. These suppliers had a thirty-year relationship with my partner, Marshall. Marshall told me I was wasting my time, "I've been doing this for thirty years," he said. "I already know the prices for all those products." As you can imagine, I went anyway. Not only because I thought I could lower our costs but also because I wanted to learn the business, speak with more people, learn from them, and make new wholesale connections. Imagine visiting another five business owners, some of the largest importers on the West Coast, each with over thirty years' experience, and learning from them. I wasn't about to miss that opportunity.

Before I started negotiating new prices, I needed more information. After all, I was a newcomer to the industry with only two years of experience buying wholesale products. I decided to go to the general merchandise trade show in Las Vegas, known today as the ASD show. I attended this and many other shows. In this particular year, many of our suppliers had booths. I visited them and other importers around the show, taking a one-page document describing my business and operation. It was a straightforward document stating how many stores I had, my buying needs, and what products I was looking for. I learned the wholesale lingo and approached the owners of new importing companies with the following questions: "Do you have a buying office in China or India? Do you own your brands? How many do you have in stock?" I wanted to determine if they were resellers or the actual producers of these products. If they were resellers, I thanked them and moved on to the next supplier, manufacturer, and product importer.

What was the result of this exercise? I managed to lower the price of an auto-visor CD holder, used to store your CDs on the go, from $0.74 to $0.20 for the same quality and quantity I had previously purchased. I then resold the product to other wholesalers for $0.65, to my retail accounts for $1.65, and it sold for $2.99 to consumers. Imagine that, from $0.20 to $2.99. Let me remind you about the point of the story. It doesn't matter if you've been in business for 30 years; you can save money or make an extra 60% using some of the strategies in this book.

Business Start-ups

If you're starting a business, this book will save you a lot, and I mean A LOT of time and money, even the occasional headache. You will shave at least two years from your wholesale learning curve, more if you read the book twice! You'll save money when buying products, make more when selling them, and get paid quicker. You'll get new products to market for a fraction of the cost and ten times faster than I've seen others do.

If you're a farmer, manufacturer, co-packer, brand owner, distributor, or retailer, you must understand each supply chain step. It doesn't matter where you are in the supply chain. We talk a lot about the consumer, but you must also thoroughly understand the business models for distributors, manufacturers, brand owners, and retailers. Failure to understand their business model means you'll fail when you sell your products or try to support them.

Here are a few examples of distributors, manufacturers, and retailers.

You are a Distributor

- Wagon Jobber
- Wholesaler
- Foodservice
- Private label
- Importer or Exporter
- Find new products
- Merchandising
- Impulse buy
- Route management
- Racks and Displays

You are a Manufacturer

- Product Development
- Find co-packers and manufacturers
- Find distributors
- Find retailers
- Direct response
- Exporting
- New channels
- Consumer interaction

You are a Retailer

- Private label products
- Find new manufacturers

- Import products
- Negotiate better prices
- Merchandise better
- Find trends
- Communicate with consumers

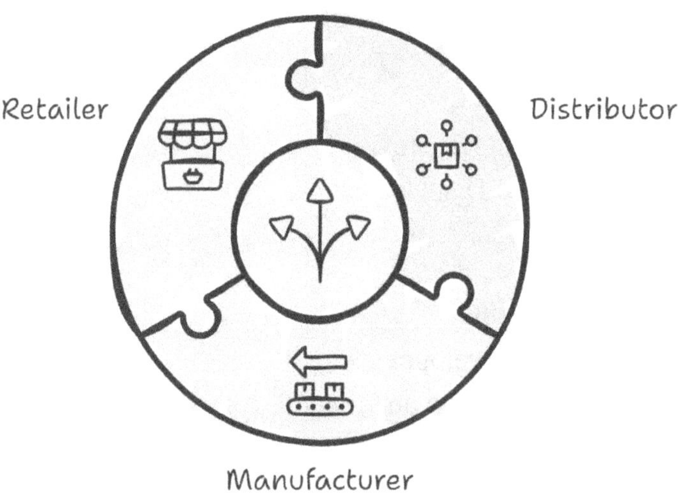

Figure 2 - Business Roles and Strategies

If you're starting, you must also know the right business for your personality. I sold my first wholesale distribution company business because it didn't fit my personality. I didn't realize it then; I just wanted a business and worked hard every day to make it work. After a fourteen-hour workday in the warehouse, my wife asked me, "What are we doing here? Is this what you want to do with your life?" We sold the business immediately. I didn't leave the wholesale world; I just pivoted to something more in tune with my personality. Since then, I've incubated new businesses and launched new products for myself and others. I do it as a consultant, mentor, and coach for large, medium, and small companies and start-ups alike.

You'll also determine what type of personality and goals are best for each business. Not all companies are for everyone. Maybe you don't have fifty thousand or five hundred thousand dollars to start your business; maybe you do. Perhaps you're a Hedge Fund looking to launch new consumer goods products. You may enjoy managing employees, or maybe you prefer to work alone. What if you learn that you need special trucks, a lot of inventory, and a sales team to run a beverage distribution business, and you don't like to manage people? Then, a beverage distribution company is not a good fit. These traits are essential when deciding the type of business you want to start or how you want to distribute products.

Wholesale businesses come in different shapes and sizes. You can sell your private label products, import products, manufacture products, buy products from others, and sell them. In many instances, you don't even need to purchase products. You can sell them to other larger companies and let them deal with shipping issues and collecting the money. Or maybe you're just the manufacturer and only want to sell to four or five master distributors without dealing with sales, stores, or marketing. That's also a possibility. It all depends on your.... (you guessed it) your goal!

Keep Learning

Different people learn in various ways. Some learn by reading; others are visual, auditory, or kinesthetic. Reading this book does not end our "Wholesale (Distribution) MBA" relationship. As part of this book, we have a learning series consisting primarily of videos, audio, and webinars. To join the party, go to www.WholesaleMBA.com and start by watching a special wholesale distribution video accompanying this book.

Consumer Packaged Goods, or CPG, and Wholesale Distribution are accessible businesses when you have the correct information. Fresh out of college, I was an executive at software and Internet technology companies. I loved the industry, but selling software is nothing like selling consumer products. As an executive (CEO and VP) of these technology companies, I assure you the software sales cycles are lengthy. The software is usually costly, and customers require changes, bug fixes, training, and updates.

When I sold enterprise software, the sales cycles took about a year, and the software installation took several years. Yes, in the end, you have a "big bang" of a sale worth up to several million dollars. I loved that, and I did not mind the long sales process. When I discovered consumer goods and wholesale distribution for the first time, I could not believe how fast and easy it was to sell. Even if you have a small one-person business, you can buy some products and quickly sell up to $2,000 the same day. Imagine coming back with that kind of money every day. Imagine if you have five, ten, or twenty distributors doing that every day when you're a manufacturer. Even if you do it over the phone or online, you can still get that kind of bang quickly.

PART 1 -

Do You Have a Winning Product?

Chapter 1 - You Are the Brand Manager, Go and Create a Brand

As a brand manager, you're responsible for everything that has to do with your product.

We were all sitting around the conference room table: Sandro, Alfredo, the production director; Gerardo, our procurement manager; Chris, our compliance director; and Eduardo, one of our graphic designers. We all had a twenty-pack of our hemp cigarettes called The Real Stuff™ in our hands. The box was packed in our factory just moments ago, and we joyfully analyzed the finished product.

Everyone in that room—including the printers, tipping paper suppliers, and hemp suppliers—played a role in every decision to develop, print, and produce the finished product we held in our hands.

The room was silent as everyone carefully examined the pack in their hands. Some snapped a photo or two, and others tested the QR code to ensure it worked and directed them to the certificate of analysis. It was crucial to verify that the product contained less than 0.03% THC to remain compliant—in other words, to confirm it wouldn't make anyone high. One person pulled out a Pantone color chart to compare it with the colors on the box, while another opened a pack to assess its aroma. The production manager removed a hemp cigarette from its package, placed it on a large sheet of white paper, and performed a meticulous inspection. Using his pocket knife, he sliced the cigarette lengthwise, exposing its contents. He carefully examined the hemp inside, checking its color and ensuring it was free of seeds and stems.

I was quiet, secretly sighing to myself, looking around at everyone. I had already found two big mistakes in the package. I usually can't spot a spelling mistake, typo, or any other thing that's out of place; however, if it has to do with marketing, a sales letter, landing page, or, in this case, packaging, I can spot all the mistakes in just a glance.

"How many did we print?" I asked Gerardo, the production manager. "Ten thousand," he said. I took a deep breath. "How many did we produce?" I asked Alfredo, the production manager, "All of them," he said, shrugging his shoulders. "Oh no," I said between my teeth. At least one of these mistakes was a huge deal. Will we have to scratch the entire batch and start from scratch?

Sandro looked up after a few minutes, "looks fine to me," he said, and pointed at the person next to him, "it's fine," he said, then Sandro pointed at the next person, "good," he said, and Sandro continued around the table starting from his left side, I was on his right side, the last one to speak. When it was my turn, I said, “Houston…” and everyone said in chorus, “We have a problem.”

“I’m afraid it’s a big one,” I said. Gerardo asked, “Who’s the brand manager?” everyone in the room pointed at me in unison. So what was this big problem? I’ll go over my mistakes in detail and give you the solution so you don’t make the same mistake. First, let me tell you how I got to be sitting at that table that day, launching a brand that would go against Big Tobacco with our Disrupting Tobacco™ business model.

The Brand Manager

In Guadalajara, Mexico, I was with my partner Carlos Lopez at the ANTAD, Latin America's largest supermarket and convenience store trade show. Carlos and I became partners after I sold my first distribution company. We co-authored the first edition of the book Build Your Beverage Empire, developed beverages, and did sales consulting together for a few years. Carlos and I had a booth at the show and sold Jolly Rancher soda and California wine. Our booth was facing the Hershey’s booth by coincidence, as Jolly Rancher is a brand owned by Hershey’s.

The first exciting thing that happened that day as we spoke with buyers and passersby was that Hershey’s executive team came over to see and taste the soda. The vice presidents and directors asked us, “Where do you sell the soda? Is this already selling in Mexico? Do you have the exclusive rights to sell it?" and on and on. Carlos and I thought nothing of it until we got a call. Carlos answered and chuckled a few times, then shook his head. When he finished, I asked, "What is it?" "That was Joe," he said. Joe was the brand manager for Jolly Rancher Soda and worked for Honickman Group, the largest beverage distributor in the USA at the time. Honickman also owns extensive production facilities, including the Pepsi bottling company for New York, among many others. Joe made us brokers through our company, Liquid Brands Management, Inc., offering five percent of all sales from Jolly Rancher Soda.

I met Joe that same year, and my former wholesale distribution mentor and partner, Marshall Shields, introduced me to him as I was doing beverage consulting. It turns out Marshall and Joe have known each other since they were five years old, as they grew up on the same block and went to the same school. As soon as Marshall called Joe and told him about me, Joe took me under his wing and treated me like family.

That day, Joe called us because Hershey's VP of Sales in Mexico called the International VP for Hershey's corporate to tell him a couple of youngsters claimed they had permission to sell Jolly Rancher Soda in Mexico. As you can imagine, we caused an international scene that day as the VP of International called his boss, who explained that Honickman had licensed Jolly Rancher from Hershey's and bottled the soda. When Joe called us, he described the issue and answered the questions of the Hershey executives.

This was not the first time I had problems exporting or selling products in Mexico, and it wasn't the last. The funny thing is that I accidentally started exporting consumer goods to Mexico when people in the United States learned that I grew up in Mexico and spoke Spanish. They always asked for my help exporting to Mexico, even though my expertise was selling in the USA. By now, I'm a veteran in exporting and dealing in Mexico.

Our ANTAD booth was very popular, and we received buyers from the largest Mexican chains and several distributors. When a booth at a trade show has action, everyone notices it, and they all want to talk to you. That day, another gentleman strolled by our booth and stopped when he saw the soda and California wine. He had an entourage trailing him. We started chatting; his name was Sandro Piancone, and he lived near my house in San Diego, but we met in Guadalajara. He gave me his mobile phone, and we met for coffee a week later. He invited me to participate in a roll-up strategy for wholesale distributors in Mexico to go public in the USA. I joined Sandro as VP of Marketing and Director of Acquisitions. We had a lot of fun building a hundred-million-dollar company until the crash of 2008 left us broke, but that's a story for another chapter.

Sandro and I remained friends through the hard and the more challenging times, and we always met for coffee. We had other businesses together, including an investment fund, where I was appointed the manager. It was a small investment fund called the Mexico Franchise Opportunity

Fund. The fund managed six hundred "smart" vending machines valued at eight million dollars. A couple of years later, Sandro sold these assets to a new company called Hempacco, Co, Inc., a manufacturer of Hemp Cigarettes. I ended up as a shareholder in the hemp cigarettes company. Sandro invited me to join, and I became a Co-Founder and Chief Marketing Officer of Hempacco and Brand Manager of The Real Stuff™ hemp cigarettes.

Now, I found myself staring at a pack of hemp cigarettes that weren't the ones I approved of. The mistake seemed so small that nobody dubbed it a mistake because it was a merchandising mistake. What was it? The top front of the pack, the opening part, included the text 100% Organic Hemp. No big deal; however, the writing was illegible from more than two feet away. It was embossed in gold and printed with hard-to-read font [*100% Organic Hemp*], which is a big problem.

It's a big deal in merchandising because we're using a traditional tobacco cigarette box to sell something that's not a tobacco cigarette. Still, you can't easily see or read it's not a tobacco cigarette, so it flunks my merchandising test. A consumer should know what a product is at first glance and from six feet away. I failed my criteria for product development, and I was the brand manager, so the mistake was mine, even if I had approved a different artwork. When manufacturing private labels, we adopted a more efficient workflow to avoid errors in our and our customers' brands. I now use project management software with workflows to approve the artwork and assign due dates and priorities.

When we started Hempacco, the most valuable asset was our hemp vending machines. Our process and manufacturing patents grew in value as we grew and expanded. The Real Stuff™ hemp cigarettes have the most value, especially after the wholesale distribution matures. When investors visited us a few months ago, their interest was around our value in manufacturing and vending. Now, more investors are interested in the brand because they know the importance of wholesale distribution in maturing a brand. The brand manager must focus on wholesale distribution more than the package, formula, social media, or manufacturing.

The value of a product-related company is the brand, the product itself. Owning a brand allows you to raise capital, own intellectual property, sell your company in the future, or take it public. Wholesale Distribution gives your brand value; your brand might be worthless without it. But who is responsible for the actual product? Who is the godfather of the brand? I call the responsible party the Brand Manager, in other words, you! Yes, you're accountable for creating and developing the product, the vision, and the execution of the idea.

The execution of your vision will be your business model. It will be how you market to the consumer and the wholesale distribution supply chain. At the end of the day, when problems arise, you have a manufacturing problem or a sales mistake, it is all your responsibility because, as a brand manager, you're responsible for everything that has to do with your product.

Let's not confuse branding with the brand manager. Branding is only a part of what a brand manager does, and it has little to do with traditional branding, especially for a small business. Branding is not advertising, and it's not the colors or package of the brand; it's everything about the brand, in and out of the company.

In creating my brand, I drew from all my experiences as a distributor, broker, and CMO to create a product that consumers wanted, with the materials and the feel they wanted. I spent two years testing the manufacturing process and gaining a dozen patents. Still, the brand's real value will be the wholesale distribution channels. In the case of the hemp cigarettes, that's convenience stores first, but it also includes other retailers such as supermarkets, pharmacies, and smoke shops. Second, we will focus on online sales as hemp cigarettes become more popular.

As a brand manager, you're not only responsible for the brand and wholesale distribution but also for consumer marketing and communicating and influencing consumers over the long run. Imagine how you'll affect the consumer as they walk the store, stand in line, and at checkout. Consider how you'll influence the consumers outside the store before they decide to act and buy your product. It doesn't matter if this is a brick-and-mortar or an online store. Consider how you'll communicate, befriend, and influence your perfect consumer.

It's time to ponder how the brand manager pushes and pulls the brand or product through the wholesale distribution supply chain. In other words, it's time for you to develop your Wholesale Distribution Business Model.

Chapter 2 - Develop a Winning Wholesale Distribution Model

"An Executive Summary of Your Entire Wholesale Distribution Business Model."

Do you have a winning business model? How about a winning Wholesale Distribution business model? Before we jump into the content, write down what you want to do with your product and company. In other words, what is the goal? Determining your destination or your investors' team goals is essential before jumping into what you want to do; otherwise, how will we measure success? Let's not go in blindly and leave it to chance. Let's develop an ending, a goal, and start from there.

Our ultimate goal is to sell the company in my current Hemp Cigarette company, either by going public or selling it to another company. That's the goal. That's our ending. When I drafted our business model, we started with the end goal in mind. You don't start with the product, production, or even research and development. You start with the end in mind and work backward to determine how much money you need to succeed, identifying your Avatar, Unique Selling Proposition, Unique Value Proposition, etc.

"Money gives you speed!"

What is your goal? Do you want to sell your company? When? For how much? Will you ask for investment to achieve your goal in your timeframe? My partner Sandro and I believe in funding companies to be first to market and quickly execute. Yes, we give away equity but rarely give away control.

Now is an excellent time to chat a bit about funding. If you've been following me, seen my videos, or listened to my podcasts, you know one of my favorite sayings is "Money Gives You Speed." Don't be afraid to ask for funding. You just need to decide how to structure your company and what percentage you want to offer investors, board members, and other stakeholders. Speaking with a securities attorney before deciding would be best, as they will significantly help.

You may prefer to grow organically without investors; that's fine. Don't assume you can grow nationally with a few hundred thousand dollars. Do your research and determine how much money you need per metropolitan area to open, support, and market to your target audience or Avatar.

I've launched and helped plenty of bootstrapping businesses, and let me tell you, it's a lot more fun with money. You need to do most of the work without money, even in things you don't master, like design, online marketing, or trade sales. You can hire the best and achieve your end goal faster with money. Be clear when writing your goals. Specify how many consumers you need, how many retail accounts, how much will be spent on direct or internet sales, how many distributors you need, how much inventory you will carry, and how much marketing support you will offer. Investors will recognize your ability to plan if you enumerate everything well and the numbers jive. Next, you must show them you can execute.

Let's jump into creating your business model and understanding why it is so crucial you have one. Remember, you don't need to be a start-up to work on your business model. You can be a ten-year-old company and just now learn how to craft a targeted business model. That's fine; it's never too late to do it right.

What's a Business Model? Is it Essential for my Product?

A business model is a formula you use to run your entire business. This book will focus specifically on the business model pertaining to your product development, marketing, sales, and distribution throughout your supply chain. If it seems that's your complete business model, it's not. We will not explore manufacturing, accounting, human resources, or team leadership. Instead, we'll dissect your sales, distribution, and marketing models. We'll take deep dives into how to market your products to the distributor so they can carry your product and how you market to retailers in convenience stores, natural stores, supermarkets, pharmacies, online, and other alternative forms of retailing. We'll also explore the many ways you can market to the consumer, from online sales to social media and in-store promotion through push and pull programs.

Your business model is the most critical information you have about your business. In it, you'll know how much money to spend to acquire a distributor, a store, or a customer. Your business model will tell you the type of customer you need and how to advertise to them on Facebook, magazines, television, or any other media you choose. Before you advertise, your business model will tell you where your perfect consumer hangs out and where they shop. Maybe they buy at Whole Foods or only shop at Walmart.

One of my clients has a functional beverage, "Breezzo," that we initially decided would be sold in high-end stores for $2.50. This is a high price as the competitors sell their drinks from $1.49 to $1.99. We came up with an Avatar for the product; the Avatar is an example of your perfect consumer. The Avatar was a female between 25 and 45 with a six-figure family income. Months later, when we started advertising online to potential customers, my client told me, "My product is for everyone." This change in strategy presented a big problem at several levels, the first being that advertising to "everyone" requires Coca-Cola-type money. I suggested we return to our consumer marketing model and see who our Avatar was and how much we could spend to acquire every consumer. Once my client saw the numbers, it all clicked. "We have to be laser-targeted to make each dollar count," my client said. Bingo! This is your business model. It will keep you honest and focused and save you time and money.

This chapter is a fast overview, the equivalent of an Executive Summary of your business plan or business model. The Executive Summary is where you convey the entire story and the outline and show the forest, not the trees. Later, we'll dissect every aspect of creating products, the operations, and the channel you need to sell those products. You'll read the basics of what makes a wholesaler and the differences between a wholesaler and a distributor. In the following chapters, you'll read in detail about wholesalers and distributors, including types of wholesalers and distributors, how they sell, how much money they make, how to become a distributor, how to sell to them, and much more.

Let's recap:

This chapter = Your Executive Summary

All other chapters = Your Business Model

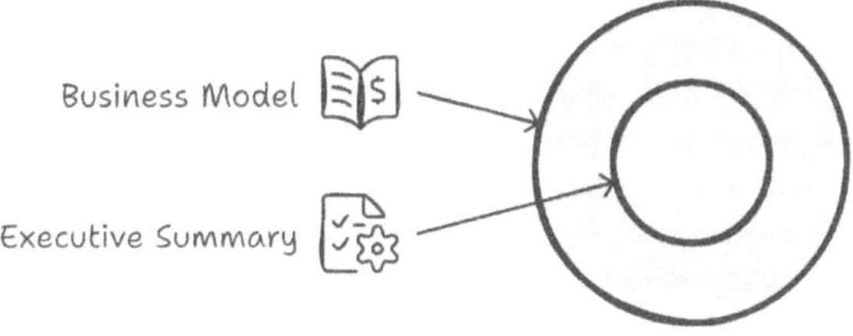

Figure 3 - Business Model Structure

As I'm updating this book, I find myself in the middle of launching not one but a portfolio of products that include a functional beverage portfolio for one of my clients. The product will soon go into mass retail and natural channels and be sold by DSD beverage distributors shortly after. Another client has another complete portfolio of liquid vitamins, including 10 SKUs, going into Natural Stores before going into supermarket chains and selling through wholesalers in the USA. I'm also helping a dozen clients launch their CBD, CBG, and THC brands, some in California and others nationwide. They sell in channels, including online sales, social media advertising, selling at malls with kiosks, and direct sales. To top it all off, I'm launching my brands of CBD-rich Hemp Cigarettes under the banner of Disrupting Tobacco™, together with my long-time friend and partner Sandro Piancone.

As I train CEOs, large wholesalers, and distributors, I'm constantly taking notes of the great questions they ask me to include in this book. Yes, I started in the wholesale business twenty years ago; however, I've never worked with so many talented and intelligent brand owners as I do today. This is why I'm so excited to add and update the book with all these new brands, case studies, adventures, funding occasions, Mergers & Acquisitions, and fabulous trips I'm taking with them.

As it turns out, there's so much information and goodness to share that I want to keep you updated on all the changes. So, I offer you this at no cost: go to WholesaleMBA.com/book and sign up for the newsletter. I'll email you the information you must have to continue selling more products. It could be a LinkedIn strategy, a must-do campaign, new marketing software I'm using, or even a tradeshow I'm attending where we can meet up. Again, just go to WholesaleMBA.com/book and subscribe to the newsletter.

When I ventured into the wholesale distribution industry, I had to learn things the hard way. Yes, I had a few mentors who helped me initially, but I could not find the information I wanted for the most part. Not in books, not in school, not anywhere. Even people I spoke with holding C-level executive positions in large companies did not know what I needed. Maybe they knew how to sell to brokers, merchandise products in the store, keep store scorecards, or sell advertisements on television. But nobody knew the other person's job or impact in the industry; nobody knew how to open new stores, launch new products, or look for venture capital.

Example: Even the big boys don't know it all

One of the largest vitamin companies in the country asked me to show them how to penetrate the convenience store channel. My first surprise was that a company with national coverage and advertising was not already selling in convenience stores. I visited their headquarters and met with the CEO and the VPs of sales and marketing. After an initial conversation, it was evident I had to give them the entire overview of the convenience store business. You will get the same information in the convenience store section of this book.

What was the sales channel situation? The company sold to every natural store, supermarket, and pharmacy nationwide but did not sell in convenience stores. Unlike the other chains, the problem with convenience stores is that you need distributors. The more significant issue was they priced themselves out of the convenience store channel because they never accounted for a distributor in their sales equations. They assumed they would sell directly to the retailer.

Let's look at an example describing this problem. If you sell to the consumer for $1, you sell your product to the store or retailer for $0.60 if they make a 40% gross margin. If you add a distributor to the equation, you'll pay them a 20% to 30% gross margin. Assuming you give them a 30% gross margin out of $0.60, your sales price is $0.42, and you're selling in much lower quantities to distributors, thus increasing your shipping costs. Adding this distributor can hit your profit, and you probably can't reach your profit margins with this price. A minimum gross margin for this type of product is 50% for you, and if you can't produce this product for $0.21, you're out of the convenience store market. Let's look at the numbers once again:

Supermarket Sales Table:

Supermarket Sales	
Consumer Price	$1.00
Price to Store	$0.60
Store Gross Margin	40%
Your Production Price	$0.30
Your Gross Margin	50%
Your Gross Profit	$0.30

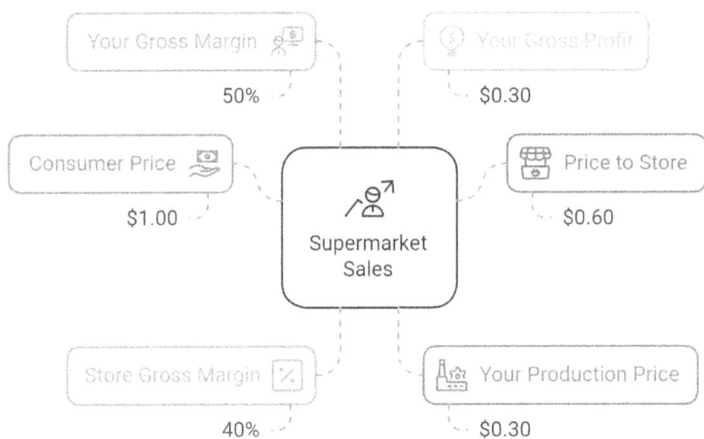

Figure 4 - Supermarket Sales

Convenience Store Sales Table:

Convenience Store Sales	
Consumer Price	$1.00
Price to Store	$0.60
Store Gross Margin	40%
Price to Distributor	$0.42
Distributor Gross Margin	30%
Your Production Price	$0.30
Your Gross Margin	29%
Your Gross Profit	$0.12

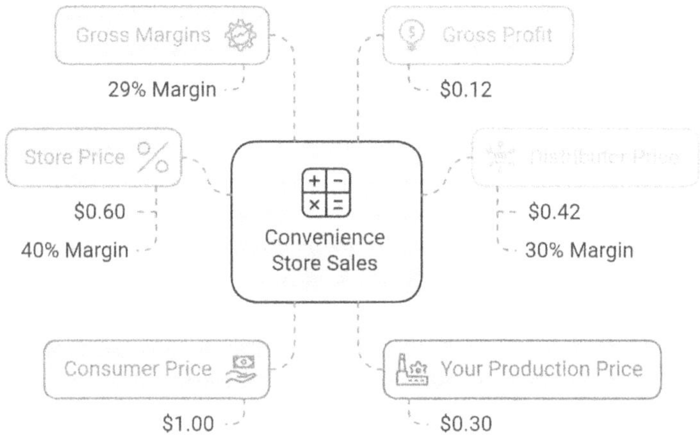

Figure 5 - Convenience Store Sales

You went from a 50% margin to a 29% margin based on your production price in the above example. If you account for the convenience store channel from the start, you can adjust and set your prices higher. How do you fix this from the beginning? Easy: if you always want to make at least 50% gross margin, you must price your product according to the lowest margin you can make; in this case, it's to distributors. You'll earn an additional 20% to 30% gross margin when you sell directly to supermarkets.

What if you had already made the above mistake, as this vitamin company did? Can you fix it? One option can be to partner up with master distributors or even just one master distributor. You offer them one low price, and they handle the rest. They must pay for shipping, promotions, and everything. The trick here is not to compete with them. If you sell to them at $0.37 and then sell to COSTO or Sam's Club for $0.50, it will not work. These superstores will sell the product at the same price your distributor will sell to convenience stores. That can create a mess, and you'll be out of the convenience stores again. Don't turn your product into a commodity. Ensure it remains a brand and track stores sales, including convenience stores. If you don't know how your product sells in convenience stores, you won't be able to support it, market to it, or even run statistical reports.

Use this simple table to calculate your sales prices for these channels:

Now, let's look at your profit for these two channels.

Your Profit Selling in Supermarkets

You Sell To Retailers At:	
Your Cost Is:	
Gross Margin:	
Gross Profit:	

Your Profit Selling at Convenience Stores

You Sell To Distributors At:	
Your Cost Is:	
Gross Margin:	
Gross Profit:	

Figure 6 - Which Sales Channel Should I Choose?

If you don't account for convenience stores, production costs, or even pricing in your business plan, you'll be out of the convenience store market. Even if you start in the natural food market or pharmacy channel, you must see into the future. There's no magic ball included with this book, but there's a formula for predicting prices and channels.

Chapter 3 - What Do Distributors Want?

"Distributors want products with support, not products they have to build into brands."

Our sales manager for The Real Stuff™ hemp cigarettes called one of the largest wholesale distributors in the country and the largest on the East Coast. The distributor has thousands of accounts and sells to hundreds of distributors and wagon jobbers. The buyer liked our product samples and displays and was ready to start working with us. I was pleased that the distributor sent us his marketing requirements to work with our new brand. He had three packages: silver, gold, and platinum. The platinum package was sixty-seven thousand dollars for one year and included space at their booth at NACS (National Association of Convenience Stores). I like this because the barrier of entry to work with this distributor is high, so we already disqualify around ninety percent of all other competitors that don't have the money. Furthermore, I can bring some of my well-funded private label customers into distribution and ensure a high-quality product and category control for all smokable hemp products.

More and more wholesalers, distributors, and retailers ask brands up-front, “How much money are you investing in us?” Ensure you’re funded correctly to go into wholesale distribution and retail channels. If not, focus on other alternative means of sales, such as online sales, direct sales, catalog sales, sales clubs, home sales, and other creative forms of selling. After gaining traction from your sales, raise capital and return to those large mainstream distributors.

Sales Partners and Their Expectations

Let’s jump right here to one of the most critical points of the entire book. We might as well tackle it initially to set expectations and understand the expectations of your potential sales partners. If you’re a manufacturer, including any brand owner or product importer, you are looking for a distributor to “take your product and run with it.” What do I mean? The distributor should take your product, pay for it, open the retail channel, place it in stores, merchandise your product, sample or educate the consumer, and re-stock it when it sells.

If you’re the distributor, you want a brand with millions of advertising dollars and the product already placed in the stores with a proven sales track record. You don't want to go out on the field and put a new product in your stores without knowing it will succeed. If it doesn't succeed, you expect to return the product and get your money back.

Many new manufacturers, and even some veterans, expect the distributor to buy the product from them and sell it. That's not how it works unless you're Hershey's, Coke, or P&G. For all the rest, you'll need to do all the work for the distributor except delivering the product. If you have that as your primary expectation, you'll be ok.

Mike Thomas, one of our sales brokers, was in the office to chat about the price to master distributors to sell some of our products. Master distributors are huge distributors, wholesalers, or cash and carry companies that can buy large quantities. That means they buy six figures monthly and then sell to other regional distributors. Mike wanted me to drop the price to the master distributor or give them even more incentives to buy more products. Negotiating on price is something I often see not only in consumer goods but across sales in general. Mike assumed the master distributors were motivated by price and price only or, looking at it another way, by profit. This could be true if we're selling commodities. Still, in consumer goods, these large distributors want support, advertising dollars, promotions in their cash and carry or stores, and other incentives such as sales contests with their salespeople or a retail chain.

A distributor can list a product and not sell it. They just place it in their catalog and let you go out and sell it. This includes distributors and wholesalers like McLane, Core-

Mark, United Natural Foods (UNFI), KeHE, and Sysco, to name a few of the large ones in the USA. It's true for medium and small retail and food distributors. If you're interested in updated information on the largest wholesalers and distributors, don't forget to go to WolesaleMBA.com and subscribe to our mailing list.

When I had my distribution company, new brands called me regularly. I often met with new importers and manufacturers, introducing new beverages, snacks, novelties, and everything you can imagine. They all wanted help with distribution in the USA and Mexico. "I'll give you exclusivity for Southern California and Mexico," they usually said. Here are some of the fundamental questions I asked; they're the same questions I ask when I screen companies for investors. If you're a manufacturer, have a good answer. If you're a distributor or investor, you should ask manufacturers these types of questions.

Questions Distributors Will Ask Brand Owners:

- ✓ In how many stores do you currently sell your product?
- ✓ How much do you sell per store?
- ✓ What are your total monthly sales?
- ✓ What is your advertising budget for my territory?
- ✓ How will you open new stores?
- ✓ How much does it cost you to open a new store?
- ✓ What is your in-store marketing strategy?

- ✓ Will you give me local chained accounts?

"I'm looking to sell the product to you, and you can figure out what to do," is what I got from most brands. The same goes for my distributor friends. They share dozens of similar stories of how new brands are clueless about how to sell their products. Some brands have a few stores, but make sure you ask the exact number and how they opened those stores. Are they distributing themselves? Did they sell to a distributor? Or did they simply give the product away to those stores to have a few product placements under their belt?

"What do you mean?" my visitor asked. "We expect you to open the stores." "Well, if I need to open stores for you, place and merchandise the product, and collect the money, I might as well create my own brand and sell it to my own customers."

This is how the conversation can go for new manufacturers with both distributors and retailers. The manufacturer is responsible for everything, including selling to the distributor, retailer, and consumer. Yes, it's a lot of work, but that's why they make the big bucks. That's why a company selling a brand has a higher valuation than a retail store or even a distributor.

The Manufacturer is responsible for everything that happens to their brand, including selling to

distributors, opening new retailers, and reaching the consumer.

Get Your Product into Stores

I use the headline "Get Your Product Into Stores" because it's a proven headline that attracts manufacturers and distributors alike; however, that's not really the message I want to communicate. You might think that's your goal, but it's not your goal. Your goal is to obtain consumer reorders. It would be best to think outside the proverbial box, or in this case, "Big Box," as in a big-box retail chain.

After reading the following few pages, you'll have enough information to launch and sell a new product. You must read the entire book, but this shortcut will help you consider your current and future products and sales strategies.

I get hundreds of requests from new and existing entrepreneurs with questions like, "How can I get more distributors?" or "How can I acquire more stores?" You probably don't have a solid business model if you don't know how to get more stores or distributors. It would help if you had a defined business model that you can recite by memory, which you can defend and execute or at least start to implement.

When I get on the phone and ask those entrepreneurs about their business model, how they will open new stores for the distributor, or how much it will cost them to support their distributors, they usually don't know.

Do you know? It doesn't matter because this is why we're here. We will help you build your business model, pivot, and change it according to your goals and how you want to execute those goals.

Manufacturing products without the proper knowledge will become an uphill battle for any executive. This is why we're here; you can discover new ways of doing business, explore product development (starting with the client instead of the product), and see new ways of selling to the consumer and your entire distribution network.

Your Business Model Starts.... HERE

"How can you reach your consumer and make an emotional connection with them? That's the million-dollar question!"

What is a Business Model? Let's give a straightforward definition. Your business model is your business plan but from an execution standpoint.

Let's expand the definition of the Business Model for a Consumer Packaged Goods (CPG) company and a Fast Moving Consumer Goods (FMCG) company. Your business model details how you'll source, produce, sell, and market your products. If you have difficulty with any terminology in the book, you can reference the Glossary at the end of the book.

When speaking with new brand owners, I always advise them to develop their sales and distribution model first, even before securing their production. When you're starting a company, product development seems like an enormous task, followed by production, another considerable endeavor, but it's not. You'll think about development and, to some extent, production, but only for the first six months. After that, you'll think, talk, and dream about sales and distribution for the next several years. This is why developing the sales and distribution part of the business model is much more critical.

How to start your business model

If you haven't already started, this is an excellent time to write your ideas, plans, target consumers, retail channels, and the entire supply chain to get your product into the retailer and then the consumer's hands. Please remember that supermarkets, convenience stores, or online stores are not the only ways to sell your products. Therefore, they are what everyone else wants to do and an easy way to create competitors. Getting and staying in retailers is also time-consuming, so it may not be the best business model. The above requires clarification, so let's dive into the particulars.

SWOT Analysis for Traditional Retail

What is a SWOT Analysis? SWOT is an acronym that stands for Strengths, Weaknesses, Opportunities, and Threats. It's a great way to dive into your business model, identifying the entry barriers, in other words, how easy it is for your competitors, or future competitors, to enter your market. For example, if you develop a multivitamin or a CBD oil, a competitor with $500 can compete with you in price and sell online, on Amazon.com, retailers, websites, etc. You might say, "But my multivitamins are the best," or "My CBD oil is a super-oil, the best in the market, and I want to get a patent on it." This is how most new entrepreneurs approaching the retail and wholesale industry think, but none of these reasons are valid Value or Selling propositions.

Your product, package, flavor, formulation, marketing, influencers, or name are not the main points in your business model. They are not a Unique Value Proposition (UVP), and they are not a Unique Selling Proposition (USP). None of your descriptive lingoes is part of your propositions. If you say you are the best-tasting, best-selling, or best package, you're not communicating your strengths, so you have not started your business model.

We'll discover how easy it is for others to pierce your business model in the SWOT Analysis. Let's take a look at your SWOT retail business model.

Retail Stores Strengths

It takes time to acquire retailers, so your competitors must spend the same time opening stores and the money needed to pay sample products, slotting fees, and posters and develop trust with distributors, retailers, and consumers. On the other hand, selling in online stores, including your store or Amazon.com, is not high in the barrier of entry or the analysis's strength factor because anybody with time can compete with you. They can hire the best Amazon or SEO company to set them up for success if they have a few thousand dollars. Another considerable strength is multiplying your sales across large territories with one customer.

When you sell to a convenience store or mass retail chain, you can simultaneously pick up two hundred or two thousand stores and get paid by a single point of contact. This allows you to scale and be the first to market fast. Please bear in mind that expanding quickly through chains is an expensive proposition. Imagine if each store requires a two hundred dollar investment. If you have two thousand stores, you have an all-in cost of four hundred thousand dollars, and that's just to play with the high rollers. This significant cash commitment is both a weakness and a strength. It's a strength because it further separates you from the majority of competitors that can't pay to play, and it's a weakness because of the capital required for you to play. You need to pay upfront for slotting fees, free product, point-of-sale material, shipping, and production and then wait thirty to sixty days to get some money back, but not all of it. Please note that selling by territory with wholesale distributors might mitigate your expenses if your distributors are willing to pay for the product upfront.

Retail Store Weaknesses

Product owners prefer to sell first to retailers, even more than selling online, but we should note that most end up selling online and not in retail stores.

Let me give you a typical mentoring session with an entrepreneur speaking with me for the first time to drive the point. "I want to get my product into all 7-Elevens in the country," they would tell me. You can substitute 7-Eleven with Whole Foods or Kroger; you get the picture. I seldom get a call that goes, "I want to start my own distribution network of committed brand champions," or "I will sell this product at house parties like Avon does it." I wish more people would call me with incredible, unique ideas on how they'll distribute their products, but they don't. This is why retail sales can be a Weakness in your SWOT Analysis.

Regarding Strengths, I talked about how you might separate yourself from your competitors with a large cash outlay to get thousands of retail stores at once.

Paying for slotting fees is a fast way of pushing your product into store chains. The more cash you have, the more stores you can get. However, you still need money for push-and-pull programs or to make sure consumers buy your product repeatedly so the store doesn't remove your product. Can you imagine getting unlisted from a chain with thousands of stores after paying one million dollars in slotting fees? That would be a terrible day. My product has been pulled from stores before, and it's not fun. I've never been removed from an entire chain, but once my salesperson argued with a district store manager, they kicked me out of 20 Walgreens, a whole district!

Another weakness is that you might not know what's happening at the store level. You're not guaranteed any statistical reports if you're selling through a distributor. Sure, if you have a master DSD distributor or someone with a sophisticated ERP (Enterprise Resource Planning), you might get their reports per store, but this is mostly accounting, not sales information.

You have several options to gather accurate sales data from your accounts. You can do a ride-along, go on location riding with salespeople, and examine the accounts. You can visit accounts on your own, and if you have corporate accounts, you might be able to pull data directly from them. The reality of the entire retail store structure is that you don't know exactly what's going on unless you sell directly to stores using warehouse programs. When you sell to distributors and wholesalers, you lose the ability to track where your product fails. The same happens if you sell to independent salespeople, exporters, or any other channel that you don't own. Once they buy the product from you, it's now in their hands, not yours.

Opportunities

Here is where you need to shine, where you bring your personality, secret sauce, value, and selling propositions. Fill your business model with the opportunities you exploit in the marketplace, including innovation, sales and distribution, and everything you can invent, take advantage of, or disrupt.

What are your opportunities? This has more to do with your brand than with the industry. Sure, you have to comprehend the industry. You need to understand your consumers and the supply chain, but there is no industry standard for opportunities in consumer goods; otherwise, everyone would fill it.

Here, in Opportunities, you can innovate, invent, tap into a niche nobody has identified, or develop a new and improved version of something already in the market. Remember, coming up with an innovation is not the solution. It's the execution of your business model that, in the end, will make you successful.

Let's list some opportunities you might look into and see how you can fill them. Take this time to write your opportunities by consumer, channel, and for a specific target audience.

List of Potential Opportunities by <u>Category</u>:

- Packaging
- Channel
- Country
- Merchandising
- Patents & Intellectual Property
- Innovation
- Ingredients & Taste
- Research and Development

I know it looks like a concise list of potential opportunities. However, each one of these opportunities has the potential to write an entire book. I've worked with companies that took only one element of the list and combined it with the basics (sales and distribution) to dominate the market. For example, when I worked with Fiji Water, I discovered their secret was never the water. It wasn't notably different from any other water, and they never argued that their water had some element different from ordinary hydrogen and oxygen. Their story and package, however, were brilliant.

If you remember, Fiji came out in a square bottle, the first and only square bottle at the time of its launch. Combined with a back label describing their story and image, this square bottle was their secret to success. In other words, the package made Fiji spectacular, but the package was not enough. You still need to execute, and Fiji executed, starting in the natural channel and then going into mass and convenience to be one of the world's most successful bottled water companies.

Let's pause here and look at this beyond Fiji. Let's look at the entire water market. I don't know about you, but I still remember a time when bottled water didn't sell in stores. You got your water from the kitchen faucet or the water delivery person who brought it to your house.

I visited my friend and mentor, Christian Hoffman, in Germany over twenty-five years ago. Walking to his doorstep, I noticed two cases of one-liter flat and sparkling water bottles. What surprised me the most was that they delivered the glass water bottles and picked them up when you were done, recycling the same bottles. My point in this story is that bottled water is not new. It's been part of life in other countries for decades. Although bottled water was sold in the USA, it was nothing close to selling in other countries. Today, thousands of American and international entrepreneurs launch bottled water companies in the USA every week. After reading my book Build Your Beverage Empire, one of my mentoring customers started a water company in the Democratic Republic of Congo.

Let's look at other opportunities you can utilize with your Package.

Packaging Opportunities

1. Intellectual Property - Look at Fiji Water
2. Larger Package - Liter Cola in Mexico and Latin America
3. Smaller Package – Look at the 5-Hour ENERGY shot

Threats

The subject of Threats is of high interest when institutional investors call me to analyze large companies or are exploring a company for a substantial investment, merger, or acquisition. "What are the Threats to this company?" they always ask.

Those investors think entrepreneurs can develop a new brand and compete with the larger company, surprising investors, analysts, and executives. In fact, the opposite is true. Creating a brand that competes in retail stores next to large companies takes a long time and deep pockets. Inventing a new brand is not a significant threat. The threat comes after the wholesale distribution channels are developed.

Threats will be particular to your brand. Please take a moment to analyze what they can be and list them in your business model. For example, a client of mine started a vitamin company called NAH to sell in the natural channel and mass retail. The company was started in 2020 during the COVID-19 epidemic, giving us plenty of opportunities as people were looking for vitamins to boost their immune systems. Still, it also gave us a challenge we didn't anticipate. Due to the political environment in the USA at the time, trade with China affected the importation of vitamins and other raw materials such as bottles, labels, and other items. This political trade war with our leading supplier threatens our business, as we can lose all production capabilities. The co-packer developed new relationships with suppliers from other countries to prevent this from affecting and producing the brand.

At the same time, I imported paper, filters, marketing materials, and other items for our Hemp Cigarette manufacturing company. This was a massive problem for our brand, The Real Stuff™, and our white-label clients. Each of our machines makes thirty million hemp cigarettes per month. They run at total capacity to keep up with demand, which means our customers need the product, as do their distributors, retailers, and consumers. An interruption in the supply chain can prove catastrophic for the brand and its relationship with consumers.

What are other threats that can place your brands in jeopardy? Start with a shortlist, take them as a start, and run with them, writing down what you think is a threat to your business and supply chain.

List of Threats:

- Weather
- Tariffs & Taxes
- Your Supply Chain
- Politics
- International Relations
- Competition
- Private Label from Large Retailers
- Limited Cash Flow
- Poor Credit
- Manufacturing Interruptions

- Raw Material Shortages
- Banking and Credit Card Processing

As you might guess, all the things I listed in this shortlist of threats have happened to me, my partners, or my mentoring clients. Let's take the Banking and Credit Card Processing point. Banking can be a challenge when working in the cannabis, CBD, CBG, or Hemp industries. Five of my customers lost their credit card processing capability when their merchant processor decided not to process any CBD product sales. These customers made most of their money from online stores or physical locations, selling at kiosks inside malls.

SWOT Analysis Conclusion

Remember that a SWOT Analysis can be generic or specific and filled with incredible insight into your product, supply chain, and future opportunities. When developing your SWOT Analysis, don't see it as a task investors or the corporate brass want you to do. Use this opportunity to discover new opportunities in the channel, sales, or products and the existing or future threats you see that can interrupt business operations. Having a well-thought-out SWOT Analysis can make or break your company, and you should plan countermeasures to every single threat you list in your plan.

Retaking the COVID pandemic as an example, did you know the All-England Lawn Tennis Club, the most important and popular tennis tournament, had secured pandemic insurance for the past 17 years? They identified a pandemic as a possible threat by researching and adopting countermeasures like insurance. Most other companies, including professional Soccer Leagues, American Football, Basketball, Major League Baseball, and other sports, lost 8.1 billion dollars in revenue attributed to ticket sales, TV rights, and sports tourism (according to Statista.com). Wimbledon's pandemic insurance paid them 141 million dollars, according to a USA Today article published in April 2020. Why didn't the other sports leagues have pandemic insurance? Maybe they didn't do a proper SWOT Analysis!

Chapter 4 - Develop a Unique Product

"Start with the consumer, then move your idea through the supply chain. This is how you develop a product."

Product Development

I use a formula for every project I start, and it looks something like this:

- ✓ Find the perfect consumer = Avatar
- ✓ Identify who they are. What do they need and want? = Pricing and Positioning
- ✓ Find out where they hang out = Marketing Channel
- ✓ Where do they buy? = Retail Chanel
- ✓ What's vital for you and them? = Unique Value Proposition (UVP)
- ✓ How you communicate the UVP to the marketplace = Unique Selling Proposition (USP)
- ✓ How much money do you need to open accounts? = Cost of Accounts
- ✓ How much do you need to keep or grow accounts? = Marketing Budget

- ✓ How much money will you make from your accounts? = Lifetime Value of Accounts

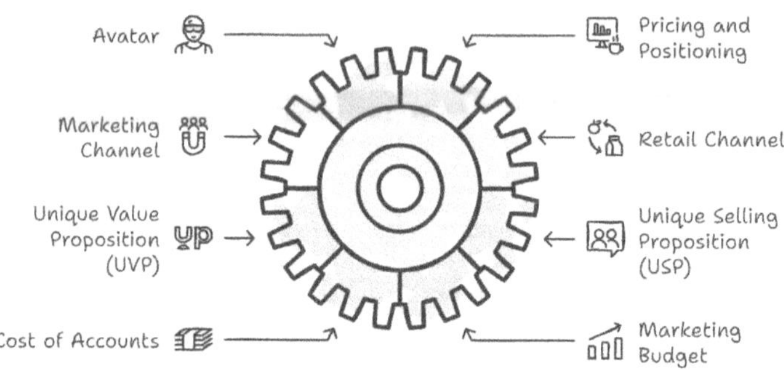

Figure 7 - Comprehensive Project Strategy

Currently, I'm developing several portfolios of products, including one with Snoop Dogg, called Dogg Pounds, spelled Dogg lbs, and another under Lucky To Be. Snoop Dogg products include gummies, hemp blunt smoking paper, hemp tubes for smoking, regular smoking paper, chocolates, candy, and vapes. For Lucky To Be, I'm starting with a beauty line and following up with a nutritional supplement line. I'll go over these brands and the individual products in more detail, and after, I'll give you the formula I use for these products and over one thousand others that I've developed.

Snoop Dogg is not the first celebrity I work with, but he's probably the best right now. A lot of this is timing. I'm working with Snoop after he appeared in Sketchers and

Corona commercials. He's on tour and bought Death Row Records last year. This timing catapulted Snoop's popularity, and we see this in the way wholesale distributors treat us. When we approached the largest distributors in the USA with the possibility of selling Snoop's products, they all said yes. Mind you, this was without any actual product, photos, or sell sheets. We just asked, and not only did they all say yes, but one of them offered one million dollars to be the master distributor. I've never seen this before with any product or person

I work with Tiffany Chin, CEO of Snoop's and Death Row cannabis and hemp line. She's part of the reason working with Snoop is amazing: she's terrific. Tiffany gets things done and done right, fast. This might sound like a no-brainer; everyone wants to get things done, right? Wrong! Developing products can be a long, slow process, especially if you don't have an agile team to go through the product development formula diligently and quickly. I don't usually like to use two adjectives, but diligently and quickly are very important when applying the formula. You need to go through every single step, research, create great artwork, and get the right wholesale distribution partners. You also need to do all these things very fast. We have orders for millions of dollars of Dogg lbs products, and I'm not even done with the artwork. However, by the time you get this book, you'll be able to see the products in stores and online. Tiffany helps us with whatever we need from Snoop and makes decisions quickly, sometimes while we're in the meeting. This is a first for me. On our end, I have Sandro Piancone, Brent Albin, Sergio Oliveros, Louis

Pelliccia, Gloria Olson, and an entire team of artists, graphic designers, R&D, manufacturing, special projects, project managers, and a production team in San Diego and Tijuana over three of our factories.

Working with Snoop Dogg

"We have the pre-orders already, so we need to develop the product fast," said Sandro.

At this point, we had nothing, not a photo of Snoop, no branding direction, only a signed agreement with Snoop Dogg to create a joint venture and purchase orders for gummies from master distributors. Usually, the hard part was selling the product, but for this project, the hard part was creating the brand and manufacturing it.

"I need more time," I said. "We don't even have a clear concept for the brand yet."

Sandro is the captain of the ship. He makes the ship go. However, I'm the creative one, and I've created a bunch of brands at a fast pace. And I wanted to take the time with this one because I knew it could be a national brand, taking over the market, not only with gummies, but with all of the portfolio of smoking paper, vapes, chocolate, and all of the upcoming products.

"Just use the picture from the wine," everyone told me, and we did at first until we discovered Snoop didn't own the copyright to the photo. We discovered this just in time; otherwise, a lawsuit would have been inevitable.

What do you do to spark the creative juices? Do you go to a graphic designer? How about an art director? Well, I have my own creative process. Let me share it with you today, and maybe you can use a few of the strategies.

First, everyone is creative; this is embedded in your DNA; you don't have to be a lifetime artist or study art to be creative. If you need more convincing, I recommend you start reading books on creativity. You also need to practice creativity; you can do this in your head, imagining products or stories. You can also use your hands to be creative; I started painting and sculpting only a few years ago, and my neurologist prescribed it to help with traumatic brain injuries I suffered after a terrible automobile collision that almost killed me, one I'm still recovering from. I paint all kinds of things, not just canvas; I paint recycled coffee containers and use them as gift boxes; I paint canvas shoes that I buy on eBay for twelve dollars and wear them for a year; I design my dress and tennis shoes. For example, Nike and Adidas allow you to customize your shoes, even with logos. I create my own T-shirts and polo shirts for work and leisure. I also use wire to sculpt science fiction and fantasy characters, allowing me to use my imagination, creativity, and hand-eye coordination.

Do you want to be more creative? Read fantasy and science fiction books, and watch movies and TV series; start with the classics or the most popular first, as they're more mainstream. To unlock creativity, you need to rewire your brain, enhance synaptic connections, and harness that neural plasticity to fuel innovation. The complex movement also stimulates synapsis, so I recommend difficult exercises. I used to practice and teach Kung Fu and Tai Chi, but they are challenging to master and teach, and they are a forced way of meditating without thinking you're meditating. Yes, meditation is key for creativity as well. I practice mindfulness meditation with other types; I discovered meditation thirty years ago when it was not popular in the USA or Mexico.

When imagining a product, start with the perfect consumer or Avatar and think backward. For our Dogg lbs project, I imagined our product would be next to the cash register in a liquor store and 7-Eleven. Someone waiting in line to pay for their beer or other beverage spots the impressive point-of-sale packaging and asks, "What is that?" As they move forward in the queue, they grab and feel the soft touch package with an image of Snoop Dogg artistically rendered into both the product and the point of sale. "I'll take these," the young man says to the clerk.

For Dogg lbs, I did everything that I just mentioned. I meditated, practiced visualization, and tried divine inspiration, you name it. One thing has been a game changer for my consumer goods conceptualization: Artificial Intelligence, or AI.

Before AI, I would do all my creative exercises, record an audio or video of my idea and concept, maybe even doddle it, and send it to an artist or graphic designer. From there, the designer would send me a few ideas, trying to align them to make a vision of my audio description. It worked because my designers know me well, and they understand my prompts. However, I didn't always get what I wanted the first time, so I would have to go through corrections and changes ten to twenty times before we even got to a concept I wanted. Once the idea was to standards, we would go through hundreds of changes. We did this for packaging, logos, images, products, swag, vending machine wraps, and everything else in our portfolio.

Now, I start with AI, writing my prompt just like I would dictate it to my designer. The difference is that I can make changes on the spot, and in a day, I can create half a dozen art concepts for products, book covers, master cases, displays, you name it.

AI is already changing product development, and I'm heavily invested in AI. I developed a consumer goods creation and testing methodology that will rapidly test products on social media using hundreds of thousands of images and videos.

Most logos I've created recently have been created or idealized with AI. For example, I started with AI when I wanted to develop a beauty and wellness brand called Lucky to Be. I'll expand on this story in the next chapter.

For Snoop, I had what I thought was a great idea; I would create a tribute to his music album Doggystyle. I went to AI and told it to make a brick wall on a barrio with Snoop Dogg painted with blue, purple, white, black, and gold colors. After two dozen corrections, I thought I had a masterpiece; it was fantastic, with an actual graffiti-style Snoop Dogg image that I wanted to print and hang in my office. However, Snoop and Tiffany didn't like it, so I had to start from scratch.

Tiffany called to tell me Snoop didn't want AI in the packaging, which broke my heart. I had been fifty hours into creating the AI Snoop concept by then. So, back to the drawing board, or in my case, meditation. Tifanny sent me the paisley Snoop liked and his signature on the font used in Dogg lbs, so I started imagining a product with the signature. However, I still wanted to use Snoop's photo; I think it's a double whammy. Snoop gets publicity for himself, and in other packaging, for his music or his music company, Death Row Records.

When I started working with Snoop Dogg, we had already signed a joint venture with Rick Ross, Hemp Hop Smokables, and Cheech and Chong, Cheech and Chong Smokables. These are companies that Hempacco created, where Hempacco owned fifty percent of the market share, and our partners owned the other fifty percent. To refresh your memory, Hempacco is a company Sandro and I created to Disrupt the $1 Trillion tobacco industry, now publicly traded on Nasdaq under the ticker symbol HPCO. I've wanted to work with Snoop Dogg long before we even thought about creating our first hemp product: The Real Stuff Smokables. As you can imagine, Snoop's team didn't return our calls, as Snoop gets pitched every day by many different companies and entrepreneurs. One of the strategies I use to stay on top of my marketing is clippings; you don't need a fancy, expensive service; you can start with Google Alerts. Just type Google Alerts on your search browser to find it. You then give it a keyword, name, or company, and you'll get an email every time Google finds a new mention.

One of my keywords is hemp cigarettes, and I got an alert that Snoop Dogg registered a trademark to use hemp cigarettes in the metaverse. This was my sign, my chance, so I called Brent, our Business Development VP, and told him to get Snoop's business manager to San Diego. I asked him not to call his agent or lawyer but to get someone who could help develop the products. It wasn't easy, but Brent found Tiffany and got her to visit us in San Diego. I wanted to do smoking paper with Snoop, maybe a vape, and by the time he finished a tour of one of our factories, she told us we could do an entire portfolio of products for Snoop and Death Row records. We decided to start with gummies, chocolates, smoking paper, hemp smoking tubes with a glass tip, some candy products, and vapes, all with hemp-based cannabinoids, including CBD, CBN, HHC, and others. We also worked on special projects, such as smoking paper for his re-release of the Doggie Style Album.

The name of the brand would be Dogg lbs. I needed to create products, and I took out my product development formula to start working on our new portfolio of products.

Snoop Dogg's Product Development

The new Dogg lbs product will be sold in convenience stores, including smoke shops, gas stations, franchised C-stores, liquor stores, truck stops, and some supermarkets, not to mention online stores. This, plus feedback from our brokers and distributors, Snoop and Tiffany, allowed me to get the perfect Avatar or consumer. I already had the type of distribution we wanted, the typical convenience store wholesale distribution, consisting of:

- Master Distributors or Consolidators
- Large Distributors
- Cash and Carry
- Smaller Distributors
- Wagon Jobbers
- Chains

Hempacco will sell to the Master Distributors and Large Distributors, and they, in turn, would sell to the other distributors and independent franchisee owners. Hempacco would also sell directly to chains, such as 7-Eleven, Circle K, and other smaller and regional chains. In this case, we already had the distribution lined up, even before we had our first product.

The team and I tackled multiple aspects at once. My art team focused on designing the label's look and feel, creating a custom gummy mold concept, selecting the perfect image of Snoop, and sourcing raw materials like bags, stickers, test tubes for the hemp tubes, and more. We also worked on the flavors for all the products with our

R&D team and the papers in our Tijuana factory, where we manufacture hemp, rose petals, and other smoking paper for us and for RAW, the leader in the smoking paper industry worldwide.

Our first challenge was with the artwork. We worked on several concepts, and Snoop linked them to our second round of artwork. However, Snoop decided not to use the selected photograph, and nobody had another usable photograph, as crazy as that may sound. We decided to create portraits from scratch with the help of Gustavo Mayoral. Gustavo and I have been friends since we were fourteen, and our friendship continues to this day. Gustavo is an award-winning artist known for his unique talent of transforming portraits by painting over them with custom brushes he designed in Photoshop. His specialties include portrait painting and product photography—a skill I asked him to develop to support all our brands at Hempacco and GGII.

We presented a new batch of photos, and after two weeks of back-and-forth, Snoop finally selected one. I took my time perfecting the image, as we had decided to incorporate Virtual Reality or Augmented Reality into the label. This meant that Snoop's label would actually come to life—talking, moving his lips, and changing facial expressions.

Now that we had the label concept and an image of Snoop, the team provided the specifications for flavors, nutritional supplements, and die lines for various products, retail displays, and even master cases. We also brainstormed ideas for custom gummy molds. My initial idea was a bone-shaped gummy, but it looked inappropriate, so I returned to the drawing board. This time, I came up with a small doghouse design inspired by Snoop's Doggystyle album cover—it was an instant hit. We ordered the molds from China and finalized the label design using Snoop's favorite colors: gold, purple, and blue.

With the elements, colors, and Snoop's image finalized, it was time to bring everything together and design gummy bags in five- and twenty-count sizes and a vape, vape box, and all the other packaging. This phase was much smoother since all the elements had already been pre-approved. However, time was ticking. We had pre-orders to fulfill, but I was determined to get it right—this was a major project with the potential for significant sales.

Here's an out-of-the-box tip I use for all artwork, packaging, and final products—a mental exercise to visualize success. I close my eyes and, using my mind's eye, imagine customers enjoying the product. I picture them picking it up from a store shelf or counter or even browsing and purchasing it online. I focus on how the product will be merchandised, envisioning its placement in a convenience store or its presentation on a website.

This process not only helps refine the product but also engages your brain in figuring out how to bring that vision to life. Once you can clearly see the product on the shelf, take it a step further: imagine holding it in your hands as a finished product. How does it smell? How does it feel to the touch? What sounds does it make when you scratch or handle it?

Finally, think about the outcome of your efforts. Will it translate into strong sales, an IPO, a life-changing innovation, or a product that helps people? This exercise can sharpen your creative vision and guide your project to success.

We've spent the past month developing and refining Snoop's product and packaging, creating over one hundred unique images and ideas. These include concept designs, photos of Snoop, GIFs of him talking and moving within the packaging, and much more. If you'd like to see a video showcasing all the images, packaging designs, and even updates on the product in stores, visit **WholesaleMBA.com** and leave your email. I promise only to send valuable information for your product development and sales efforts.

Product Development Formula

Where do I start? I start with the consumer, the Avatar, and I move back from there, identifying who they are, their motivations, income, disposable income, and geographical information like where they live and shop. I like to call all of this geographic and psychographic information. The most important thing is to know your end customers, discover how to connect emotionally with them, and establish a trusting relationship with a positive customer experience. Together, these two can launch your brand, even if you lack wholesale distribution. Many brands have started and reached national success by selling on their website, Amazon.com, or through infomercials.

When researching your Avatar, or ideal consumer, remember this crucial rule: you are not necessarily your customer—and neither are your friends or family. So when sharing information or conducting your research, make sure you test it on your Avatar. If you plan to sell in convenience stores, you need males from sixteen to thirty-four. When I show my hemp cigarettes to people who don't smoke, and they don't know anyone who smokes cigarettes, pipes, hemp, or cigars, and they're not involved in retail or wholesale distribution, they tell me: "I don't think this is going to work, I would never buy this." I ask, "When was the last time you smoked?" and they respond, "I've never smoked." I then ask, "When was the last time you shopped at a smoke shop, convenience, or liquor store?" They tell me they don't remember or never.

Since my product is in most of these stores around the country, they've never seen my product. In other words, they're not my target market, so they don't understand why my product is successful.

Another question I often get is, "Why would anyone smoke hemp?" Again, the question comes from people who are not my Avatar. Now, I take some time to educate my non-consumers and tell them, "Maybe they want to quit smoking tobacco, or they smoke pot and like hemp, or they want CBD instead of nicotine." The tobacco industry sells nine hundred billion dollars per year. Why would anyone smoke nicotine-filled tobacco? Well, I'm not sure, but a lot of people smoke.

The list of things to do for product development is relatively short, but it contains the essential information you need to (almost) guarantee success. I've never seen a brand that goes out of business when completing this exercise and executing the results. If you have the information and don't perform, that's on you, not the procedures!

"Implement whatever we decided in the meeting, and implementation is a piece of cake when I know the outcome."

I use the same process with my brands and my customers' brands on a Mastermind Day. This is where I close my conference room door in San Diego, California, step up to the whiteboard, and review all the points on the list. It usually takes around six hours to complete if we have all the research, information on the cost of goods sold, pricing, and some idea of the distribution process and target consumer or Avatar. It's an intense six hours, and we all feel drained afterward because we have to concentrate and use our neurons to decide and plan every detail. This time is worth a lot because I usually have to implement whatever we decide in the meeting, and implementation is a piece of cake when I know what the outcome needs to be.

The list alone is enough to fill the pages of this book. I have an entire course just dedicated to this concept for Fast Moving Consumer Goods (FMCG) and a recorded marketing workshop on the whole process of developing your Avatar, USP, UVP, cost of customer acquisition, lifetime value, and all that jazz. Let's just say I consider it extremely important. It doesn't matter if you're starting or already have the product. Use this list to ensure your commitment to the customer experience and develop an emotional connection with the consumer.

My Top 3 Sales Research Hacks

How can you conduct some lightning-fast sales research? Let me give you my top three hacks!

My top 3 Sales Research Hacks are:

1. Google.com search tool.
2. Amazon.com sales rank
3. Facebook audiences or advertising

Figure 8 - Sales Research Hacks

I have a fourth bonus, LinkedIn.com, where I conduct research and communicate with investors, wholesalers, and retailers. LinkedIn.com is not a hack because it takes time, but the other three are lightning-fast. In the next hour, you could have excellent sales information on competitors, categories, and the potential for a product in online sales. You can then look at month-to-month trends and see what products are popular.

Whenever I have an idea for a product, I go to Amazon.com, Google Search Tool, and the Facebook Advertising Platform. I use LinkedIn.com for anything trade-related or to interact with wholesale distributors, retailers, or investors. If you're ever wondering what I'm working on, just go to my LinkedIn profile, and you'll probably find my new projects.

These platforms have incredible and free tools to search for your Avatar, understand how they buy what they like, and even run some small tests with a few advertising dollars. The first thing I usually do is go to the Google Search Tool. If you have a Gmail account, you can open a Google Advertising account and access the tool in one or two clicks. Once inside, conduct research volume density queries or times people look for a product or category.

For example, if your product is a Protein Cookie, you would go to the tool and type protein cookie to get all the searches and the number of times people searched for this term. Not only that, but Google will also tell you all other related queries that might help you. For example, you might want to know more about searches like Protein Diet, Protein Bar, Protein Cookie Recipe, Best Protein Products, and other keywords. This is important because I can gauge demand for a product or category in five minutes. Google can also inform you who conducts the searches and where they live. Yes, Google can provide you with data on the age, sex, and other information about people conducting investigations. You can also do searches by city, state, or country. This is true for many other countries as well. It works wonders for me because I can advertise online and send customers to a convenience store with my product with a message like "Buy Now or go to XYZ convenience store around your corner."

Amazon.com is an excellent place to test item sales on their platform. You can determine what any given product sells monthly in units and dollars. Again, this is a great way to acquire quick sales information without paying for scanned data or calling distributors or retailers. In ten minutes, you can see what the top sellers in your category are doing on Amazon. You can do this by looking at the category and sub-category of the products, getting their rank, and then looking online for an Amazon sales rank tool. You can use free tools for a few searches before Amazon requires you to pay for them.

With Facebook, you'll need to set up an advertising account and leverage its audience research tools. These free tools provide valuable insights into Facebook's members as well as Instagram users through Meta's platform. This resource is incredibly powerful—it allows you to create a detailed avatar or audience profile.

If you're advertising, you can use this tool to identify and target your ideal consumers directly, whether through drop shipping or directing them to a retailer. Beyond advertising, the tool is also excellent for conducting market research. Your goal here is to gather data on how many potential customers exist in your niche, where they live, their income levels, and the best ways to reach them. This data is essential for understanding your market and refining your strategy.

Remember, after doing all this research, you could go back to each platform and write your sales copy according to the market search for your products. You can also advertise to your Avatar on Amazon, Google, and Facebook/Instagram. After all, you already did your research.

Top Mistakes in FMCG Sales Research

Imagine you have an idea for a wonderful product. It can be a snack, beverage, nutraceutical, or fashion accessory. You can place your idea here. I'll pick on the idea of an energy drink because I've developed several, and I keep getting calls from entrepreneurs wanting to do energy drinks. Let's say Joe Santos intends to start a twelve-ounce healthy energy drink in a skinny can.

Joe starts researching online for energy drinks. He googles "how to start an energy drink" and finds a formulator, where he might end up paying twenty thousand dollars for the formula because Joe thinks this is the most critical part of developing a product. Joe says he'll spend only ten thousand dollars without realizing he'll pay double the amount. And maybe he can't use his formula because he didn't check with the bottler first. Next, Joe researches co-packers or bottling companies for his energy drink. He now realizes he'll need to spend another fifty to one hundred thousand dollars to start. Like a good entrepreneur, Joe looks for a co-packer who can produce samples and spends another ten thousand dollars on samples.

At this time, Joe is pleased because he can see and touch the product, and it's real. It's quite an accomplishment. Joe is lucky because he only spent around fifty thousand dollars and months of his time. The average entrepreneur spends two hundred fifty thousand dollars and two years before having a product in distribution.

Joe is ready to sell. He decided to sell his product at Whole Foods because it is healthy and at 7-Eleven because they are a recognized chain. When Joe goes to Whole Foods, a manager tells him they can't take his drink because it contains an ingredient they don't accept. "Didn't you ask about our requirements?" the manager inquired. Let's reformulate this drink, but first, let's go to 7-Eleven. "We don't take Energy Drinks," says the store manager. What?

Joe doesn't give up. He goes to a local beverage distributor and tries to sell his product to them. After all, they might be able to open some stores. "We don't take Energy Drinks," says the distributor, and so does the next one and the next one after him. Joe calls twenty distributors, and they all say the same thing. One friendly distributor takes Joe under his wing and shows him the ropes, "If you have a product, excluding energy drinks, you'll need to open three hundred stores before we take it over," says the distributor.

Now, Joe thinks the beverage industry sucks, and his idea of starting an energy drink was a waste of his time and money. By now, Joe has spent one hundred thousand dollars. He paid for reformulation, trade shows, travel to see distributors, and marketing on his Instagram.

Don't be like Joe! Start your product development at the end, and work your way to the start of the product.

What Are Your Barriers to Entry?

"Your barrier to entry is the time, money, or skill needed to copy your business model."

Developing barriers to entry keeps competitors at bay. You can develop many different barriers to entry that will make your products and companies more valuable when you seek investment or decide to sell your company. Barriers to entry will also make you money in the short run, as competitors will scramble to compete with you but hopefully be late to the game because you're constantly evolving your barriers.

Like most essential points in the book, let's go over the barriers to entry, what they are and are not, and the mistakes and wins I've seen. This way, you can strive for a better product while learning and avoiding mistakes other entrepreneurs or I have made.

Your idea, label, or secret sauce are not your top barriers to entry. It's challenging for new entrepreneurs to list or accept entry barriers, or the lack of because they're in love with their products and think they're unique.

Imagine you're in a Wholesale MBA course or mastermind with other executives like yourself and me. You're excited to network and learn from everyone there. This is where "Hot Seats" are an excellent tool. I like to do Hot Seats in many live events, where I put an executive on the spot, in front of the room, facing the audience. It can be ten or a hundred people. If it's an online event, it's typically about one hundred people. During the Hot Seat, I ask the executives questions about their product or company to see their problems or weaknesses. No, this is not a shaming operation; on the contrary, it's a building and learning experience. The audience, fellow consumer good executives, and entrepreneurs help and contribute with their comments, inquiries, and ideas.

Being part of a Hot Seat is advantageous because you get insight and help from the entire community. When veteran Brand Owners are on the Hot Seat, they explain that sales and distribution are the entry barriers into their business. Even executives at Fortune 500 companies like P&G, Coca-Cola, or Kellogg's confirm distribution is the game's name. On the other hand, when first-time brand owners sit in the Hot Seat, they say their Flavor, Package, or Secret Sauce is their barrier, only to be dismantled by the audience of veteran brand owners. In this case, my job as the mentor is uncomplicated. I stay quiet and let the audience lecture the newcomer on what they think about their barrier to entry.

Let me give you some examples of mistakes I've seen recently in CBD Hemp, Beverages, Taste, Electronics, and

Vitamins, to name a few. Many entrepreneurs and executives mistake barriers to entry with the time it took them to develop their product, the extensive taste testing, or the changes they made to their logo or package, none of which are barriers to entry. These are only the standard part of doing business. Some companies can develop products in a week, and others take a year to create the same product.

I developed over one thousand products and multiple retail programs in only two years when I owned the distribution and consumer goods companies (Bargain Baskets and DSD Merchandising.) How did I do it? I did it fast!

Doing things fast is not just a goal. It should be your obsession because it's not how many products you start; it's how many you finish, sell, and distribute. Waiting for a product to be perfect is not in the consumer goods world. After all, you can always make it better. I don't care if you're a snack company like PepsiCo, a car company like Tesla, or an electronics company like Dyson, where executives are obsessed with perfection. Their product is shipped before it's perfect every time. Even this book can be better. I always publish my books, knowing they're not perfect. They can always be better, adding more trends, examples, and statistics, but I would never publish a single book if I waited.

I was always under pressure when I had to develop one thousand products, like my graphic designer. We second-guessed our selections, packaging, pricing, and point-of-sale material. Our programs had fifty items in every program. For example, we had a tool program with fifty different and unique products, all with the same SKU, and our metal and cardboard displays held up to two hundred products that we also had to design and ship. How did we do it? We made fast decisions, created the programs, quickly developed each of the fifty packages, and sent the purchase order to China for twenty monthly containers. Talk about pressure! Our corrugated displays were printed and produced in Mexico, so we also had to design them, usually table displays in shipper boxes that we sent to Walgreens and other large companies.

Let's start with making claims about your products. Making claims is always a difficult conversation to have with any supplement company brand owner. These could be beverages, nutritional supplements, or healthy snacks such as protein or fruit bars. Their argument sounds logical as they want their vitamin C product label to read "you won't get sick" or "promotes a healthy immune system." The lawyers will strike that before making any other changes. You can't make any claims hinting at anything that addresses a medical condition, such as a cold, cancer, pain, or something similar.

My partner and I own a hemp cigarette manufacturing company called Hempacco Packaging, Inc. As part of this company, we also own our hemp cigarette brand, which I created from scratch and nurtured into the number-one-selling product in the marketplace.

Like any entrepreneur turned brand owner, I love my brand and think it's the best. However, we also sell White Label manufacturing services to other entrepreneurs. In other words, I'm also responsible for producing my competitors' hemp cigarette brands. I've created many brands, including hemp, CBD, CBG, beverages, novelties, food, etc. I know our selling proposition and how to market and stay ahead of the competition. At the same time, I encourage other entrepreneurs to sell to their strengths. In other words, having vitamins, minerals, or an incredible formula is not a barrier to entry.

I see this all the time in hemp-related products. Hemp is not a new ingredient; it's not even a new trend. I've been developing hemp products for years, even before the Hemp Bill passed in 2019. I've seen an explosion of CBD, CBG, CBN, and other Hemp-related products that include tinctures, creams, oils, pills, beverages, and many other consumer goods.

Here is the CBD scenario: I get a call from an entrepreneur who tells me he has the absolute best CBD in the market. I hear them describe something "special" about their farm, hemp, oil, or distilling process dozens of times. Let's flip the narrative for a second. I've never gotten a call where the entrepreneur says, "I have the same CBD oil as everyone else, but I have twenty thousand points of sale around the country." Now, that's something I want to hear; that's a real barrier to entry. The sad news for CBD entrepreneurs is that they can compete with anyone with a few dollars. With a few dollars, you can order some tinctures with your label. One of my clients even bottled his product at his kitchen table. Let's take this example and run it through the distribution network.

You want to get your product into retail stores. You call a distributor and tell him, "I have the best CBD product." He responds that he gets similar calls too often. Next, you call retailers directly and tell them you have the best CBD oil, and they tell you they already sell CBD oil with the same claim. Then, you inform consumers that you have the best CBD product on the market, and they still don't buy your product or even recognize the name. The question to consider is how else your CBD company can differentiate itself. You can't claim CBD has anti-inflammatory properties or helps with pain; those are all medical claims. You get the idea.

Investment can be a barrier and so can complicated production. However, the most significant barrier I want to zero in on is sales and distribution. I help all my clients, and even in my projects, I try to use the very best ingredients, formula, packaging, and everything around the products I create or market. Still, without a distribution network, these are worthless.

When I created The Real Stuff™ hemp cigarettes, the only competitor used low-quality hemp in their cigarette or no hemp at all. This fact inspired our name, as we make it with "the real stuff." It wasn't easy to source all the necessary materials to get the product exactly how I wanted. It took me two years of learning, observing, tweaking, and testing to finish the first product samples. I also developed line extensions with flavored and scented hemp cigarettes in menthol, mango, whisky, pineapple, and pina colada. After two years of work, establishing a supply chain, and investing one and a half million dollars in equipment to produce the product, we ended up with a dozen processing, manufacturing, flavoring, and merchandiser patents to display the product on convenience store shelves. Despite all of this, I can still tell you that there is no barrier to entry as strong as my distribution network. Why? I think it's simple, so feel free to use this test on your products and other products you find in the marketplace. Ask yourself this question: How much is the brand worth with and without distribution? Can another brand without all the patents and Research & Development sell in convenience stores? The answer is yes. With this premise, I would argue that wholesale distribution is the most significant barrier to entry, not intellectual property or equipment.

Use the same formula for your product, list all the actual and fictitious entry barriers, and start recording how long it would take somebody else to compete and how much money they would need.

Let's go back to our CBD and Hemp Cigarette examples. The CBD example has the lowest barriers; you only need $20 and a few days to create a website to compete. Or you can sell it door to door or at your local farmers' market, and you're in business. Now, let's look at Hemp Cigarettes. First, let me clarify one technicality: these are not pre-rolled smokables; in other words, they are not made on a kitchen table. These are machine-made and packed, so speed and scalability are built into the business model and entry barriers. So, how much do you need to compete in the hemp cigarette industry? You need around fifty thousand dollars for production alone. You can still sell these at your farmers' market, but you'll need fifty thousand to start.

Now you have two barriers in cost: one is around twenty dollars, or let's say that with inventory and some sell sheets, you need five hundred dollars, that's the CBD tinctures, and we have fifty thousand dollars with the hemp cigarettes. The wholesale distribution part, the sales, support, shipping, and account management are the same for both, so in this case, I would rather be in Hemp Cigarettes, as I will have much less competition.

I am biased towards the barriers to entry that have to do with sales, marketing, and wholesale distribution. Case in point: This book is about wholesale distribution, not research and development. Research and development are barriers to entry, as are your manufacturing process, patents, time to market, and even your supply chain. After all, if you're the only company that can purchase or that produces the main ingredient, nobody else can compete based on that main ingredient. On the other hand, if the ingredient is a commodity, that would not be a barrier.

When you list all of the barriers to entry you want or have, don't forget to include wholesale distribution or your sales model.

We have already established that a substantial and valuable barrier to entry lies in your sales channels. In my case, they are wholesale distributors. Another minor barrier to entry in the Hemp Cigarette business is the minimum investment versus what it takes to start a CBD tincture. In our pursuit of more barriers, my partner Sandro and I decided to establish a research and development department, focusing our efforts on **Disrupting Tobacco™** and directly competing with the tobacco cigarette industry.

To go head-to-head against big tobacco, we need lots of money, a solid wholesale distribution plan, and consumer education and marketing. To get into wholesale distribution fast, we partnered with the most prominent master distributor in the country, giving them a percentage of the company; in other words, we paid to play! We covered distribution, as they already encompass eighty percent of the accounts we want to be in. The other twenty percent will be covered by our sales brokers selling into supermarkets, pharmacies, and other large mass retail accounts and convenience stores in rural areas our partner doesn't reach.

Having wholesale distribution does not guarantee success; it allows us to sell to other large distributors, but we still need to do the work. We need to train our partner's salespeople on how to sell our product. We must develop a new business plan and model to support each distributor. I'm currently writing this master plan. It's around thirty pages long and details what we'll do for our distributors, including sales contests, spiffs, training, sampling, samples, free fills, etc. We also need money, lots of money. To start, we're spending two million dollars and have already raised enough to have our valuation at twenty million at the time of this writing, but it will double in less than six months.

My Top 3 Types of Intellectual Property

Yes, we still need more money. For this, we're developing new ways of raising our valuation and getting an advantage over our competitors. My strategy is intellectual capital, which produces tangible and non-tangible assets. Let me list them here and explain what they do for us and what they can do for you. The first Intellectual Assets are easy, and they come with trademarks of logos, images, and words, such as "Disrupting Tobacco™, where the asset can be intangible because it can be worth a lot to an institutional investor but not to the end consumer or even the retailer and distributor.

The second type of intellectual property is in manufacturing, including pre-manufacturing processes, the actual manufacturing, and hard assets, such as equipment we made and patented. We filed several patent applications, including the method to blend CBD and CBG hemp flower to run through the cigarette machines. A second patent was for the unique ways we flavor the hemp cigarettes. A third patent was for the machinery we designed, which manufactures our Solito™ single hemp cigarette stick.

The third type of intellectual process has everything to do with the customer's experience. Our patents are in several merchandisers we developed to fit our Solito™ singles and our twenty packs right on the counter using our design of corrugated displays. As I mentioned in the former paragraph, our Solito™ cigarette is also patented, not only the name and trade dress but also the manufacturing of the stick. The customer experience starts when they see your online post, television commercial, or any other type of advertising. It follows the customer into the store, where you might have posters, stickers, and other points of sale material. Finally, at the point of purchase, the customer sees the product on the shelf, rack, or counter and pays for it. In our case, we patented our point of purchase experience that starts with the product on the counter with large, clear, prevalent signage, in this case, Hemp Smokables. We're purposefully not just writing the name brand on the package. As a new company, our brand is not well known, and this would confuse the consumers, or they would glance over our product name without knowing what it is. The product itself is too small to act as the only point of sale message to the consumer, the 20-packs are small, and the Solito™ is diminutive. This is why our signage and displays are descriptive and critical.

You would think that our Intellectual Property stops with the point-of-sale material, but it doesn't. We're taking the extra step to patent the experience of opening and smelling our product in the original, mango, mint, and other flavors. We're not just creating intellectual property and barriers to entry; my partner and I are also developing a Fast-Moving Consumer Goods brand.

Sell to Your Strengths!

"If you have an existing distribution channel, don't start a new one."

What do I mean by this quote? Imagine you have an online store where you sell sunglasses, and you want to start a brand of headphones that you want to sell in retail electronic stores. This is a good plan; however, you should start by selling the headphones to existing online customers and subscribers. If you have an online store or presence, your number one priority should be collecting their emails. I know you want to sell, but selling directly to a cold lead who just visited your store is not as likely as selling to someone who visited your store, left their email, and received excellent content via email. So, in this example, you would start an introduction to your new headphones brand with emails, maybe telling your subscribers why you started the brand, why you think they will love it, and how they can buy them even before they're available for retail sales.

Always Sell to Your Strengths. If you are an internet marketing wizard and can bring tons of traffic, start selling on your website. If you have a million followers on social media, start introducing them to your new product. If you're a distributor with one thousand accounts, sell to your existing stores before going elsewhere. If you're an incredible salesperson, you can choose to sell to wholesalers and distributors, open stores one by one on a route, or accompany a distributor and train them on your product. If you're not good at anything I listed, you could consider being great at leadership and hiring the best people in the mentioned areas. However, you'll need money to hire your team; therefore, you should also be great at raising capital to pay for your team.

Selling to your strengths also means concentrating your energy on what moves the needle and not wasting your time solving minimum wage problems. In my first business, I was guilty of making this mistake repeatedly. I was the webmaster, the online marketing specialist, and the buyer, and my company didn't grow the way I wanted. I call this "a minimum wage solution" because you can probably pay someone minimum wage to do the work. I have partners and suppliers in Mexico who help me with this work in marketing and web mastering. You can probably hire someone exceptional in this area from Mexico, India, or the Philippines.

Before starting my workday, I always ask myself: Why am I doing this? Ask yourself this question before you look at your phone in the morning, answer an email, get on a phone call, or enter a meeting. Don't just do the work because it's on your schedule; ask yourself why you're doing it and if it will move the needle or make you happy.

I'm not good at many things and capable at some things; however, I'm good at a few things, and marketing is one of them. More importantly, I have specific marketing skills that nobody in our company has, so I always ask myself if I'm doing something that nobody else can do. If the answer is no, I don't do it, and I focus on what I can do well and move the needle to grow our sales and company value. Writing is a good example. I like writing books, which bring me pleasure and business, but I also write sales copy. I write our brochures and corporate communications information. I do this because I'm good at writing sales copy, and I'm the brand manager of our consumer goods, so I carry the vision on my sleeve.

The company's sales and operations are left to my partner and co-founder of The Real Stuff™ hemp smokables. He's excellent at both and has scaled companies from zero to two hundred million dollars using his wit and leadership. Although Sandro is on top of sales, I'm often tempted to call on accounts, follow up, or close a deal. Closing the deal would move the needle, but I ask myself, "Can Sandro do this?" the answer is always yes, so I don't do it and focus instead on my strengths. Delegating is how we're scaling the company to be the largest in the country and soon the world.

Thinking Outside of the Traditional Retail Model = Grow Your Barriers to Entry.

You can use different barriers to entry to keep competitors chasing you instead of looking at what they're doing and wondering why nobody in your company thought of that. There are many ways to sell and market your product; start listing all the ways you can sell your product, especially those that take time, relationships, or imagination. Each separates the gap between you and all existing and new entrants into your vertical.

Think and write down all the different ways people can use your product, and then list all the different ways you can reach your consumer, maybe magazine articles, radio interviews, or even road shows. Don't write down social media, as that's not specific enough. Precisely write the social media platform and what type of advertising, promotion, outreach, contests, or videos you'll use. Now, make a list of all the different ways you could get your product into the hands of consumers. Would you go to universities? Or maybe organize home parties as Tupperware did? If you need help, get marketing experts to contribute to your strategy.

How about multi-level marketing or direct sales? Think about it, speak with everyone you trust in and out of your company, and write everything down. Don't leave something out because you think it's outrageous or different; that's precisely what you want, outrageous and different. The more it departs from convention, the better for this exercise. The harder it is for others to copy your ideas, the more you should explore them. Include your know-how or connections in these ideas. Maybe you know the owner of a hotel chain, a professional athlete, or a celebrity doctor on primetime television. Write it all down.

Write down why your product is different. We call this your USP and UVP – Unique Sales Proposition and Unique Value Proposition. What is the difference between your product and other products you don't have? Your flavor, package, and presentation alone don't make it unique. Sorry! I say that because I've gotten at least 30 calls in the past decade saying, "I want to launch an energy drink, and it will sell because it looks and tastes better than Red Bull." Sorry, but this is not a good enough reason to launch that energy drink.

Once you develop your uniqueness, test it with friends and other businesspeople – preferably distributors. Ask them if that makes your product unique. If it doesn't, go back to the drawing board.

Now, you have a few ideas on the uniqueness of your product and how to place it in the hands of consumers. At the same time, you identify your perfect consumer and how to sell to them, including where and how.

If all you have on your notes is "reach the consumer in a supermarket and convenience store," you're not trying hard enough. You need to find all possible selling methods, not just the one that hits you in the head. Take the top two or three ideas for selling your product and list them along with strengths and weaknesses.

Is Your Idea Sustainable?

The first (much more to come) test of your idea, let's call it your business model, is to discover if it's a sustainable idea. What is that? Can you operate under this single model and grow exponentially using this model? If one of your ideas is to use your friend who manages a small regional hotel chain to get your product in the minibar, that's not a sustainable model. Relying on any sales connection is usually not a good business model. It will work to open the door, but don't think for a moment that it will substitute your long-term success model: create emotional connections with your consumers and get them to buy repeatedly in the store.

Let's explore the connection myth. You know someone who manages five hundred convenience stores and asks, "Can you buy my product for your five hundred stores?" This could apply to large chains and other accounts as well. The first consideration is: Will your product sell? If your product sells, placing your product is not a problem. If that's the case, you don't need a connection in the store. You just tell them, "It's a guaranteed sale." That means you don't get paid if it doesn't sell, or they can return the product. Imagine that you produce enough products for five hundred stores, maybe spend $50,000 in production costs, and they send all the products back after thirty days. That wouldn't be good.

Let's look at the numbers for this example:

- Number of Stores = 500
- Sale Per Store = $200
- Total Sale = $100,000
- Your Cost = $50,000

Figure 9 - Financial Overview of Store Operations

Let's see the other side of the conversation. You call your contact at this chain and ask, "Can you buy the product for your five hundred stores, and if it doesn't sell, you eat the loss? That way, I get my money no matter what, and you're stuck with a bad product." That conversation will not end well. This is what many new manufacturers don't understand. <u>Your product doesn't sell until the consumer pays for it.</u>

Yes, someone can introduce a connection, but you must sell the product to the consumer to succeed in that account. If you don't have a plan, money, and execution, it will not happen. On the other hand, you don't need a connection if you have all of those. You just pick up the phone, you call any buyer from any company, and they will take your call. I have never had a buyer NOT call me back in any company for any product, including national retailers and distributors; I always get a callback! Now, on the other hand. I don't even call them if I know I have a product that will not fit into their portfolio. It would be a waste of time for both.

If your business model gets more and more consumers to buy repeatedly over a long period, that's your perfect business model.

Can somebody copy your idea?

This is a good test not only for your business model but also for your product. How difficult is it to copy your product or your company? How long would someone take to duplicate it?

Being first to market usually gives you a competitive advantage. Think of all the new products that invented a category, from the George Foreman Grill to the 5-Hour ENERGY shot. Those two are great examples because they both created a product and a category. George Foreman did it with infomercials and later with national retail sales, and 5-Hour ENERGY did it by getting away from energy drinks and selling their product, not in the refrigerator, not even on the shelves, but on the counter. These are good examples of first-to-market products that dominate their industry; the number two competitors are so far behind in sales that it's even hard to call them competitors. Yes, you could copy their idea, and hundreds have tried, but it's too late; you can't compete.

What are the results? 5-Hour ENERGY sells more than one billion dollars, according to Forbes magazine. The George Foreman Grill sold over one hundred million units, according to a February 2009 article in Success Magazine. The article reported Foreman signed a deal in 1999 for the rights of the product for $137.5 million, proving that infomercials combined with traditional retail channels are an excellent sales combination. With all that said, both the shot and the grill are straightforward to reproduce. Their barrier to entry was to be the first to market and channel.

Besides inventing a new product or category, do you have something that prevents competitors or future competitors from duplicating what you're doing? We call this The Barrier to Entry.

What is your barrier of entry? Maybe it's so expensive to enter your industry that someone would need millions of dollars and years to copy and produce your product. Perhaps you have a patent over the process you use for production, or your product itself is under patent. I mentored a company with a wireless encrypted and patented flashlight years ago. Applications for such a product are in the military and law enforcement. They mount the flashlight to long weapons, turning it on and off with the flick of a handle switch. It was a great idea and a good patent; however, selling to the military and competing with well-established, prominent vendors was not easy. The sales process, or entering a specific industry, could also be a barrier.

Having a high barrier to entry makes for a phenomenal business model. Try to have natural barriers; these naturally exist in the marketplace and are not artificially inserted by the government in taxes, tariffs, or special permits given by one administration. Natural barriers include patents, trademarks, business processes, unique production methods, and other trade secrets. A particular distribution method can also be part of your barrier to entry if nobody else can mimic it.

If you rely on the government or other artificial barriers, you might quickly find yourself out of business if the law changes or a new administration comes to power. I see this every six years in Mexico with the change in government. Companies with "connections" to government officials are out of business as the new government brings their friends and connections. This is a good example of an artificial barrier.

Artificial barriers can happen in a retail environment. Your friend knows the buyer for a large retail chain, and they buy your product. If that buyer is out, unless your product sells strongly on its own, it will be out of the store in no time. Also, if your product doesn't sell as well as it should, the buyer will kick it out. They will not risk their job or bonus for a favor. If your product sells well, you don't need that connection initially. You can get your product into that chain based on the product's merits.

Be the Distributor

I started as a wholesale distributor in my business. I also developed hundreds of products but never developed a brand. There is a significant distinction: I sold products but never built brand value. I was just a distributor. When my partner Sandro and I grew a company to one hundred million dollars in sales, we had products and distribution, including a Miller Beer distributorship. Now, we have brand value and control our distribution to large accounts, including food service, convenience, and supermarkets, and we use distributors for smaller accounts. My point is you can be both; just because you're a brand owner doesn't mean you can't be the distributor, and if you're a distributor, you can have equity in brands or start your own. Vitaminwater famously gave equity to its distributors, and when it sold to Coca-Cola, distributors made much more money from their equity than from distributing the beverage.

Most of my knowledge came from being a distributor. I already knew internet marketing, branding, and influence, but I didn't know much about channels, retailing, wholesaling, or merchandising to succeed in the industry. I learned everything hands-on in my business and with the help of my wholesale mentor, Marshall Shields (RIP.)

Distribution can open the door to a wealth of knowledge about your product and your consumers, and yes, it has pros and cons like everything else. One of the most considerable drawbacks to being a distributor is that your single product is insufficient to make money from a store visit if you're starting from scratch.

If you're selling "Hangy," a hangover remedy, in convenience stores, you'll sell anywhere from twenty-five to one hundred dollars for a large product displayed in pill or powder. This is for your initial sale. You might continuously sell an average of twenty-five dollars per store visit.

Imagine now you have your route of stores. They all carry your product, so you just need to refill it with fifty-dollar orders. If you visit ten accounts, you'll sell two hundred and fifty dollars; that's great, but what if you need to pay the driver, insurance, gas, and the product? You're down to maybe a twenty-five-dollar profit per route, not much. This is why distributors don't carry one but many brands. I did the same thing; I only moved my brands initially, but I quickly discovered I could double the delivery if I carried other products, so I started carrying hundreds of new products.

Do the math, come up with the minimums you need to sell to make money and scale, and then you can decide if you want to start your distribution. Don't forget to add your fixed operating costs, such as rent, vehicles, insurance, salary, gas, and anything else you'll need.

If you're already a distributor, adding your brand is a no-brainer. Suppose you don't have time to do this; partner up with entrepreneurs who have already invested in a brand and ask for equity. Finding brand owners is the easiest thing; you only need to search any social media network and search for the type of brand you would like to distribute. These brands could be CBD, hemp, drinks, vitamins, snacks, electronics, pet supplies, toys, etc. You'll find hundreds of them. I'm very particular about LinkedIn, as it's a business-to-business social platform, and the brands you'll find there will be better organized and professional.

If you have a brand, make sure you're on LinkedIn. By the way, I have a LinkedIn group you can join. At the time of this writing, it has forty-five thousand members and is called the FMCG and Beverage Business Group. Use it to network, find distributors or brands, or collaborate with like-minded entrepreneurs and executives.

As you can tell, this book is not just about selling to distributors; it's also about being the distributor or at least understanding how they work, think, and what motivates them. Many of you are already distributors or would like to become distributors. Maybe you want to start small, selling your brand or representing other brands selling to retail stores. Or just maybe you want to start big, buying a fleet of trucks and going all out from the start.

As you read this book, you'll see you have many options as a wholesale distributor. You can choose your business by distribution channel, product, price, or niche, such as a luxury niche for jewelry or expensive art. Traditional wholesale distributors must remember some crucial things: you must know your margins, stops, and sales per stop. That's it!

There's a bit more to it, but those three are very important. Yes, the product you sell is essential. Still, unless it's your product, you have no control over the store's marketing or sales, so you have to concentrate on the things you do control, such as how you manage your route, including when you visit stores, what you sell in those stores, and how you open new stores.

If you're a traditional distributor, you'll deliver the product to stores using your trucks and probably service those retailers – that makes you a DSD or direct store delivery distributor.

Chapter 5 - Jump into the Most Profitable Industry of All Time

---

"I discovered that Wholesale Distribution was one of the easiest and most profitable businesses to be in!"

I didn't know this was a profitable business when I started. I only knew I could get in quickly and experiment in the wonderful world of entrepreneurship. My desire to leave the corporate world and substitute it with owning my own business was more to gain time than money. I was motivated by working at my pace, when and where I wanted, without knowing anything substantial about wholesale distribution. My education in this matter would be the same way I learned to swim when I was four. The instructor took my hand and foot and tossed me in the middle of the pool. As I made my way back to the edge, with what I remember being the dog paddle strokes, the swimming instructor pulled me out and said, "You see, you can swim," and tossed me back again. I cried and screamed; my uncle told me he could hear my profanities from the parking lot, but you know what? I learned to swim that day.

I don't want this experience for you, so I am offering some floaties or training wheels. I have much knowledge and experience packed into these pages, plus videos and other information you can absorb quickly. Maybe you're a corner office FMCG executive, account manager, inexperienced entrepreneur, or one jumping in with tons of experience. We have something, a lot of something, for everyone.

You might have several interests in the world of wholesale distribution; let's list some examples of what you can do:

1. Start a wholesale distribution business
2. Sell your brands to distributors and retailers
3. Sell directly to consumers
4. Be an importer or exporter
5. Invest in consumer goods companies

You can have many more reasons to get into wholesale distribution. It doesn't matter if you have products or want to sell products. Knowing your supply chain, partners, and how they work is essential. This is why elevating your wholesale and distribution IQ is vital. Creating or extending your business model without knowing your channel is hard. If you separate from the rest and know how to sell your products, you can outmaneuver and outthink your competitors.

Many of you are looking for investors or will eventually need investors to grow your distribution or market share. I've seen entrepreneurs crumble in front of investors when they ask for channel specifics, like the type of distributors they need or how many accounts they can get with specific distributors. One New York investor invited his analyst and me to a potential investment meeting. It was a new beverage brand with some seed capital and samples ready to go. The beverage company was in the functional beverage niche, planning to sell into the Natural Channel before selling anywhere else.

After the investor and analyst finished asking all of their questions, they asked if I had any questions. For starters, I saw several red flags in their presentation. They wanted to capture 1% of the market. Why is this a problem? Because it's common to say when you have no idea how much you can sell and when. I asked, "How many stores do you need to sell that amount?" It seems like an easy question, but they couldn't answer it. The investor told him to do more research, but he lost complete confidence in the management team presenting the pitch.

My follow-up questions are:

1. How many cases do you need to sell per store per month?
2. How many customers do you need on that channel?
3. How many distributors do you need?
4. How will you open an account?
5. How will you support the accounts?

6. And my favorite question, one that I ask myself, my customers, and every brand company, is, "How much does it cost to open each store and keep it?"

A Series of Wholesale Coincidences

Most people who contact me, and I suspect that read this book, have started a brand. The brand is probably an FMCG or Fast Moving Consumer Good, such as something you find at a supermarket, natural food store, pharmacy, or convenience store. It can also be a durable or semi-durable good, such as electronics, pet supplies, tools, or other things that are not FMCG but not a long-term classic good, such as a refrigerator.

That wasn't the case with me. I didn't go into the wholesale distribution business as a brand owner, and I didn't do it to start a consumer good; I went in as a distributor. Looking back, this was my first mistake. It would have been incredible to build a brand and place it nationwide in mass retail and all the independent store distribution I had, but it wasn't my time, and I exited the business by selling it.

I had several run-ins with wholesale distribution over the past thirty years. The first one was when I was in high school and needed money to pay my way into a basketball travel team. My first business was imaginative, simple, and not very good. I visited a local coffee roaster, purchased some coffee, and stood at the corner of a busy street selling it. I made enough money to pay for one pair of tennis shoes. After that business failure, I went into the beverage industry, purchasing a few soda cans and ice and selling them at the Tijuana-San Diego border in the summertime without a permit. I sold a few coolers before the other experienced vendors kicked me out. Next, I ventured into a TV Guide-type magazine with my mother, selling advertising in our small ten-page magazine to local stores. I did this for four years!

After college, my first significant introduction to business was working in software for the food processing industry. There, I learned the inner workings of manufacturing and wholesale distribution; however, I didn’t learn how to buy, sell, or distribute, and it was all from a high-level best practices point of view. I learned the ins and outs of operations when working with large manufacturers. The executive world's fundamentals and best practices carried into my future entrepreneurship ventures.

After graduating from college, I couldn’t find a decent job. In my head, it was simple: you study, get your degree, interview for a job, and convince them you’re prepared and willing to work hard. Everyone will want to hire you, right? Wrong! I was stunned and sad when I couldn’t find work after finishing college. It was shocking, and I wondered if I would ever find a job. I was applying to every job I could see that required a bachelor's degree, and I couldn’t land an interview.

I worked part-time at the Berlitz language school in San Diego without any real prospects, where I taught Spanish, my mother language, and Business English courses. Here, I would like to share another belief that could, or should, be transferred to your business. The idea is that opportunity hides behind hard work, and sometimes it wears a disguise. In my case, I taught executives from all over the world, including Vice Presidents and CEOs of Fortune 500 companies. I remember teaching the CEO of Deloitte & Touche, his wife, a South Korean stock market team, and many others. Among my students was a six-feet-four German businessman named Christian Hoffman. I didn't know it then, but he would be one of my best friends and a mentor who changed my life by employing me and allowing me to be a CEO in two years.

Christian seemed a happy-go-lucky young executive who came to San Diego to improve his English and later opened the American market to ERP software for the food industry. We became good friends very quickly, and a few months later, I was living and working in Germany as a software consultant. I quickly learned the best practices you need in the wholesale industry to operate and scale behind the scenes. I didn't learn merchandising or FMCG branding, but I understood what happens in the companies that manufacture, warehouse, and sell those products. I started as a business consultant with Christian, learning everything I could about different companies and their methodologies, the same methods I later used to have the upper hand on the competition when I was a distributor and now a brand owner.

That was not my last executive gig. I made it to the CEO of US operations with the ERP company. I was later hired by a San Diego project management software company as their Vice President of Business Development. I was twenty-nine and continued learning the methodologies you need to operate large companies as I worked on projects with Chevron, the World Health Organization, FCB, Schlumberger, and other large companies.

The opportunities I received as a young man were invaluable. I met my executive-level goals at the age of twenty-eight. I went from living in Tijuana with no running water or electricity to being CEO and retiring my mother and grandmother. It was time to pursue my entrepreneurial dreams, but what to do next? Maybe software, since all of my experience so far was with software?

My "real" jump into the great wholesale and consumer goods world came after I left the software industry. I did not plan to go directly into wholesale sales and distribution. I wanted to go into business, any profitable business. Growing up in Tijuana, Mexico, I learned nothing about being an entrepreneur. I didn't learn anything at home either. My mother was a scholar and a professor of philosophy and literature and later became dean of education at a technical university in Tijuana. I didn't share my dreams of entrepreneurship with anyone, not even my family and friends, as the feedback I usually got was not constructive; it was more like, "You're crazy." My mother and wife have always been believers, though. They've always supported my crazy ideas, from writing books to starting businesses to all the projects I've been involved in along the way. Even though money was scarce growing up, my mother instilled a belief system that centers on taking responsibility for your actions, successes, and failures. This attitude has allowed me to make bold decisions in my life. After all, when you think you can't fail, you're bound to succeed once in a while.

It's crucial for this book, your company, and your products to know that your dreams and goals are possible; it's just a matter of knowledge and application. You're likely to succeed if you don't skip these two essential points. Please know that I'm your fan, your cheerleader. I want to be your customer and wish you nothing but your most giant dreams to come true. I'm here to help, cheer, and advise if I can be of value. If you need help or positive reinforcement, please contact me on my social media or website. I check my LinkedIn InMail weekly; that's always the best way to hit me up.

I decided to buy an existing business in my entrepreneurial dreams because I didn't know any better. I had some savings and thought it would be great to hit the ground running with sales and customers instead of developing them from scratch. So, I searched for about two years and educated myself on the finer points of buying a small business. I spoke with several business brokers in town, reviewed the newspaper's "businesses for sale" section, and went online to view, read, print, and analyze businesses to see their cash flow, worth, sales, etc. After I felt prepared, I dove in and started making offers.

I met with business brokers in town and visited businesses for sale, from daycares and vending routes to laundry mats. I explored cleaning pools, landscaping, consulting companies, restaurants, coffee shops, and anything else available!

How I Bought a Business through the Classifieds

Finally, I read a classified article in the San Diego newspaper about buying a wholesale distribution business. After a few minutes on the phone with the owner, I knew I had found my company. It was a thirty-year-old business with many customers, sales, profitability, and an existing inventory of products. What did I know about wholesale distribution? Nothing! However, after looking for a business to buy for so long and analyzing the financials and business models of every business for sale in San Diego, I thought I could spot a good deal, and this seemed like one.

Before becoming a full-time entrepreneur, my last job was as Vice President of business development for a software company. My job was mainly to sell software for a range of three hundred thousand to three million dollars. The time it took to close a software sale was very long. It took years from when a salesperson started talking to a potential customer to when they finally purchased the software. I was used to the long sales cycles. Not all of them took years; some took a few months to close. The bottom line is that it took a very long time. This changed with wholesale distribution, which was one of the things I liked the most. I quickly learned that selling in this industry was easy.

At the time, I would explore businesses on sale by going online and scanning the classifieds in the San Diego Union-Tribune. This must sound odd to you in a world of Craigslist, Facebook, Linked In, and Google, so look at these two points; this was over twenty years ago, and I thought I would find a gem and get a deal in the classifieds.

Indeed, I did find a gem. Most of the companies I called were way above my budget. Most companies I liked asked for one hundred to two hundred thousand dollars, not anywhere in my wheelhouse.

I answered the newspaper classified for a distribution business with accounts, so I called and had a terse conversation without talking about the price. The next day, I visited the company in San Diego. I walked in and met the owner, Marshall Shields. He seemed old and tired, but I later learned he looked like that, but he was full of energy and passion. Marshall should have sold the company for more than the thirty thousand dollars he asked for, and I quickly learned why.

Before we jump into the company, I want to tell you about Marshall. He looked old and tired, spoke slowly and whisperingly, and walked at turtle speed for such a tall man with long limbs. His office was messy, with stacked papers and folders six feet high everywhere you looked. I noticed no computers in the entire building; all of his inventory, sales, procurement, and route management were made by hand, so the piles of paper were starting to make sense.

Marshall gave me a tour of his two thousand-square-foot office, and then we went out to the warehouse. Oh my, this guy was a hoarder. He had newspapers, magazines, and papers stacked to the ceiling. Merchandising racks were everywhere, and old merchandise, primarily tools, was in pallets, boxes, and on the floor. It was challenging to walk around the warehouse because of the clutter and fear for my life.

Marshall pointed to a spot on the warehouse next to a wall, "Your office will be there," he said. "Office?" I asked. "Yes, you should stay here so I can teach you what to do," he said. "Well, alright," I said, shrugging. Marshall then introduced me to his only route salesperson, Steve Anderson, a very chipper gentleman with only a crown of white hair adorning his head. I liked Steve from the moment I met him.

Marshall explained how the deal would go down. He operated a San Diego distribution business for twenty years and had around five hundred convenience stores carrying his products. What were his products? Marshall created programs, not individual products; his best-selling program was tools. He had two-story, white wire metal racks in two sizes; one size could fit two hundred tools and the smaller fit one hundred tools. The baskets were four feet tall, and a red ribbon and sign read, "Bargain Baskets, any item $1.98."

Marshall was a Rack Jobber, and the work was two-fold: one, place the basket in the store, and two, keep going to the store to refill it. Rack Jobbing is a business model part of DSD or Direct Store Delivery. Rack jobbers include potato chip distributors like Frito Lay and Barcel, bread distributors such as McKee Foods, and Grupo Bimbo, the largest bread company in the world. Some of the bread and potato chip distributors are independent owners, and they can grow their own businesses in their given territory. I've visited a few Barcel distribution centers in the USA. Grupo Bimbo owns them; my cousin and former business colleague, Eduardo Enciso, now works for them.

Why was Marshall selling the business for a fraction of its worth? Because he wanted to be my leading supplier and still make money from importing and warehousing tools. I spent a couple of days doing store visits with Marshall. The sales rep had not serviced many of the stores, some baskets were empty, and the liquor and convenience stores' owners weren't happy. I didn't mind it much, as I knew we could fix this with good customer service and by visiting the accounts repeatedly, maybe even with new products. I was considering buying this business as other significant and expensive life events were happening. My wife, Gloria, and I married, bought a house in San Diego, and handed Mr. Marshall Shields the remainder of our life savings.

Marshall's salesperson, Steve Anderson, stayed to work with me. My wife eventually left her job and came to work in the business, as did my mother. I also called in my cousin Eduardo Enciso, the now big shot at Barcel, to help me with the route. For nearly fifteen years, Eduardo and I worked on many beverage, food, snack, beer, and vitamin projects and companies. Eduardo is an excellent rapport builder, making him an extraordinary salesperson. He got his experience in San Diego, calling on independent owners that turned out to be the toughest in the country. If you survive in San Diego, you're automatically a start everywhere else.

Eduardo and Steve did the routes and sales, Gloria managed the payroll and accounting, my mother helped in the warehouse, and I did procurement, warehousing, and learning. Because my office was next to Marshall's, we became good friends, and he taught me thirty years' worth of sales, merchandising, and distribution in six months. Marshall owned Bargain Baskets and was involved in massive merchandising projects that totaled one hundred million dollars in yearly sales, so the man knew what he was doing. Marshall was a serial entrepreneur, and he had several businesses and investments. Besides learning the wholesale distribution trade from him, I also learned something important, "Ship it." What does "Ship it" mean? It means you must get it out there, even if it's imperfect. Until now, I was a corner office executive; sure, I made sales, but I did it in a custom-made suit and was a perfectionist. This quickly changed when I realized that sometimes "just good" is good enough. Getting products out first is essential, and getting products out fast is equally important, instead of dwelling over artwork details. I sold it, and I fixed it as I went along. This is a lesson I've applied when writing books, developing my brands, mentoring CEOs, and now I give it to you.

"Just good is good enough.

Ship it and fix it as you go."

I've developed a few hemp cigarette packages in my current project, as well as plenty of artwork for posters, stickers, sales sheets, pole signs, and even a couple of patented displays. Let me tell you something: I've never been happy with the results, but I always ship early. Our main product, The Real Stuff™ hemp cigarettes, had grammatical errors on the package! Oh my! It took us four sets of production runs to meet my specifications. For example, the designer changed my font to a manuscript font in one printing. I had instructed the designer to print it with Hemp Rules™, one of our trademarks, and a product identifier on the counter. The designer printed it using an illegible manuscript font, and I couldn't read it one foot away. Imagine if it's four or five feet away from the counter. This is a rookie mistake. By the way, that's an effortless way to determine if you have good packaging. Can you tell what it is from a few feet away? A recurring mistake in new brands is focusing on the name and logo without telling consumers what's inside. For example, in our error, the only thing you could see on the package was

"The Real Stuff™." If you see a few boxes on the counter, you'll think they are tobacco cigarettes, but if I add the word Hemp in a large font, embossed in gold or silver, you'll at least know they're hemp cigarettes. If I place them on a large display that reads "Hemp Smokables," well, now we're talking.

I also learned this trick from Marshall; he was the expert on impulse-buying items, off-the-shelf programs, and signage. He would get so mad when he saw a Bargain Basket without the bright red sign and pricing, "Do you like losing money?" he would ask me. The whole Bargain Basket team worked hard to get back into all the accounts the company had lost. I also introduced more products from other suppliers and developed different programs and merchandisers, like electronic spinner racks filled with gadgets, pet supplies, and car accessories. My goal was to increase the sales per stop. If the tool program sold an average of $100 per stop, I wanted to expand it to $200 per stop, but I could not do it with my tools in the basket. The baskets couldn't fit anything else, so I had to develop new products and programs and buy and test new items.

The Secret of My Failure

Here is the secret to my success later in the industry and my failure in my Bargain Baskets venture. The failure was simple; I didn't create a brand. As we'll see throughout this book, real money combines brand and distribution. I already did the hard part, distribution, and it never occurred to me to start a brand. What brand? I carried all those products and knew how to sell any brand; you name it: tools, electronics, clothing, snacks, beverages, and vitamins. It's not that I failed at the business; it's hard to fail in wholesale distribution if you just work hard. I could not identify that I had the golden goose and could start a brand or partner using equity with other existing brands. This was not even a small failure with my company. It was a much larger one, for I took my little company to the national stage in the next quarter.

"It's hard to fail in wholesale distribution if you work hard."

The early days of working with Marshall were enlightening. I also had to wear many hats: be the warehouse manager, wash and load the trucks, learn accounting and QuickBooks, and product development, marketing, sales, and distribution. What I brought to the table was the structure and best practices from the software world. I could see the flaws in distribution and procurement, and I could turn around and develop a solution and documentation in twenty-four hours.

The first thing I did was introduce new programs. The largest of them was a counter or checkout program. This program had many novelties, toys, lighters, vitamins, and other items sold on the counter. I did this for three reasons:

1. Counter items take up minimal space in my warehouse and the truck but make the same money as my large bulky tool displays.

2. They didn't require extensive merchandising. My racks and baskets needed cleaning and servicing, which took up to thirty minutes per stop.

3. My sales guys would walk in with a small wire basket measuring two by one foot, an easy-to-sell strategy. This small basket was filled with trinkets and flashy things. The salesperson would place it on the counter and service the rack, and when he was back, the store owner had picked around one hundred dollars' worth of products; it was an effortless sale.

I quickly doubled my company's sales, and Marshall observed it all. After a few months, he came to me and said, "Let's take this thing nationally," to which I said, "Sign me up." Marshall had the capital to invest in inventory, warehouses, employees, trade shows, travel, and other expenses, and so we did; we created a new company, DSD Merchandising, and took the show on the road.

Some of my other family members joined the team, and my cousin, Paula Ortega, helped Gloria in accounting. My cousin, Ybon Rambeau, assisted my mother in the warehouse. Victor Enciso started as a graphic designer but became the project manager for the one thousand consumer packaged goods he and I developed in only two years.

The company took off quickly, and we got into chain accounts in supermarkets, convenience stores, and pharmacies like Walgreens, Kroger, 7-Eleven, and Circle K. I developed a shipping room where we could send products directly to the stores, even if we lacked local distribution. We worked with sales brokers, distributors, wholesalers, and other sales partners. We also sold through warehouse programs, where we shipped to the store's central distribution center and developed custom programs for Target, Rite-Aid, and 7-Eleven.

That year, we attended several trade shows and met the largest wholesalers and distributors in the entire country and the chain's category buyers. And yes, Marshall knew them all. He also knew the largest importers and manufacturers of novelties, and I quickly learned how to build ad-hock products and programs I could turn around and sell tomorrow. This was great because I didn't wait three months for our containers to arrive from China and didn't have to spend a hundred thousand dollars for an order. Because they knew our volume, they would sell us at great prices for a month's worth of product. This way, we didn't invest in inventory or warehousing rent. For example, I bought watches for $1.25 and sold them to the store for $4.99 wholesale and $3.00 in bulk to other resellers and drop shippers. I did the same with lighters, toys, pens, electronics, hats, shirts, and belts and created new programs such as winter, summer, hats, and a complete portfolio of programs and products. I could build fast without the burden of extended inventory cycles. This is important as cash flow is a problem when selling consumer goods.

For example, if we ordered from China, we pre-paid the inventory and waited three months to get it, so we were out one hundred thousand dollars for a month. Then, we need to inventory the products and slowly sell them over the next six months, giving our clients thirty days credit from the moment we ship, so we don't see a complete turn for six months to a year. Before getting paid in full for the entire container, we spend another hundred thousand dollars to bring another container. Imagine if you import twenty containers per month; it's tough on your cash flow. This happens to beverage companies, snacks, novelty, and every FMCG, especially durable goods brands selling in stores with longer sales cycles.

When Distributors Fail You

"Distributors failed me, or did I fail them?"

Expanding distribution was one of the things I needed to do fast, and I'm not talking pallet dropping; I'm talking about Rack Jobbing and full-service DSD distribution. My logic was simple. My distributors could quickly sell one thousand dollars per day each, so why were my large national distributors with thousands of stores not even selling one thousand dollars per month?

According to my calculations, I wanted only one hundred dollars per store per month in sales. If a distributor had 1,000 accounts, well, I did the elementary math of:

1,000 accounts x $100 = $100,000

Even if a distributor only sold into one hundred accounts, I could expect to make $10,000 from that distributor. I had more than one hundred distributors. I had the largest distributors in the country, so if only a few performed poorly and only sold into a minimal number of stores, I could expect to make a few million dollars per month. Close the book; we're done, right?

Not so fast! Some of the distributors made an initial order and never ordered again. Others gave me a few orders for the first five or six months and then disappeared from the face of the wholesale planet. I called them, followed up, sent point-of-sale material, and tried to organize contests and other spiffs, and nothing happened. What was going on? Was it me? The short answer was yes, it's always me or you, not the distributor.

Distributors had another point of view on this transaction, "you failed me," they said or wanted to say. They're more well-mannered than that and let their purchase orders do all the talking. In other words, no more purchase orders.

The only thing I knew about wholesale distribution was what I learned with my own business, and I could sell a whole lot of any given product. I only needed to give my sales team a special commission or a contest and print a new sales sheet. I didn't expect the same contribution level from my distributors, but I expected something, so I was disappointed when I got nothing.

This distributor experience gave me a wonderful lesson, the one I'm passing on to you: distributors don't want to build your brand. I learned distributors are not in the business of creating a brand that needs building. They want a pre-built brand they can just deliver and make money. This is why you'll see me refer to distributors as pallet droppers or mailmen or mailwomen: just like the post, they don't sell; they just deliver. Now, if I opened a chain for them, let's say Walgreens, they would be happy to offer my programs in their territory.

My solution to this was not to go and open accounts for them. I was disappointed at the rejection when they didn't even try to sell my programs. Instead, I solved this problem by taking it into my own hands, my marketing hands. I didn't have the budget to open accounts for all my distributors, which requires boots on the ground, training, and cash. Instead, I used my marketing wit and fractured writing skills to get an entire army of distributors working exclusively for me. Want to know how? I'll give you the whole formula right here.

Building a Private Army of Distributors

After failing at my first attempt at establishing a national network of distributors, I decided to start my own. My strategy was to attract and train new distributors or entrepreneurs who wanted to be distributors for this task. In other words, I would start from scratch and make a brand new channel of small rack jobbers that only sold my products.

I know it doesn't sound effortless. Still, when you don't know that, it's pretty easy. Remember, my expertise was in marketing, as I was only starting to gain experience in wholesale distribution. Armed with my marketing ego, I ran the same campaign that I did during my software years, a recruiting business campaign based on sharing knowledge, and I did it with the help of Google. The result was a national network of motivated distributors loyal to our company.

In my software years, part of my job was sales, marketing, and business development, or, as I like to say, getting money into the company. I ran direct response advertising campaigns by mail and email to do this. I pointed my potential customers to a landing page with vital industry information, such as a production whitepaper, industry trends, etc.

This is called a funnel in today's marketing jargon, and my funnels go back more than twenty years. And you'll be pleasantly surprised to know they still work to this day. I'm running a replica of my old funnels right now, directing traffic to a Hemp Cigarette Whitepaper, which has been a fully funded, vertically integrated company with thousands of leads, distribution, and weekly offers for acquisition. What I want to say is that it works!

Let me break down my distribution attracting funnel for you. I first wrote an eBook called "How to Make Money as a Wholesale Distributor." I then placed ads on Google, attracting people to a website called DistributionBusiness.com. I still have this funnel. You can subscribe and see how it works. Although the funnel is modernized, the premise remains the same.

People will see my advertisement by Googling "distribution business," "wholesale distribution," or similar keywords. Eventually, I didn't have to pay for advertising, as my site ranked with my conventional online marketing efforts. I ranked number one in twenty of the top keywords at the time.

The visitor would then click on the Google link and go to a sales page with a video explaining how to be a wholesale distributor, and for $47, they would get the eBook. I also set up a squeeze page. A squeeze page is a website that collects emails in exchange for something of value, such as a whitepaper, video, or course.

I had eighty percent of visitors leave their email and sold many eBooks. Once people bought the eBook, I would upsell another $20 for a 2-hour "How to be a distributor" recording. I had many people buying, and I sunk every penny back into advertising because my business wasn't selling eBooks; it was selling merchandise.

Once people purchased my materials, I would invite them to come to San Diego and train with my sales team for free. They only had to pay for their plane ticket and hotel stay. I had plenty of takers, as this is a real, hands-on business opportunity. After people saw how easy it was to sell one thousand dollars per day, they would become my distributors, and the minimum purchase was ten thousand dollars in inventory and racks. I'm happy to report that I had a hand in helping people start their businesses.

I did that; the rest was support, documentation, and other proprietary information I use today. The result was seventeen thousand accounts with great DSD rack jobbing. I even gave my distributors corporate accounts in Walgreens, 7-Eleven, and other chains. Additionally, I had my trucks and employees with routes in San Diego and opened routes in Orange County and Phoenix.

You can apply this information in many ways; here are a few:

1. Distributors want your support. Your distributor will fail if you can't support them with money, incentives, advertising, and accounts.

2. You can open your distribution or take the same approach to train existing or new distributors, assuring you'll make them successful.

3. You can think outside the traditional retail box and open new channels by training people on selling not to stores but offices, construction sites, little league games, or online as an affiliate or by drop shipping.

A couple of months ago, I trained college students in San Diego, including Michael Piancone, my partner's son, to open accounts for our hemp cigarettes. These students quickly opened one hundred accounts following my scripts and directions. They also told me they learned more in the training sessions than in an entire year in business school. I share this with you because that makes me proud. After all, teaching, training, and seeing people succeed make me happy. That includes you and your company. If you applied something from the book or your ideas, let me know; send me a video, and I'll include it in the book's website and learning materials; this way, you can inspire others to succeed, and we can do it together.

Chapter 6 - How to Profit from the Best Business in the World!

"Wholesale Distribution is the most disruptive business of all time."

How will you disrupt the marketplace? Will it be with your products? How about a brand-new way of communicating with consumers? Or maybe, with an innovative way of getting your goods to your customers? From the Silk Road to the Industrial Revolution to Walmart and Amazon.com, you disrupt the marketplace whenever you introduce innovation in processing, manufacturing, specialization, supply chain, ideas, or technology. How will you be disruptive?

The wholesale distribution business is one of history's oldest and most profitable businesses. One of the reasons is scalability. You don't need to always be there to make money; many other businesses are selling your products for you. These businesses could be distributors, retailers, or even the end consumer; they are all your customers. This is a rule of multiplicity. If you're a distributor, you can have one thousand stores selling a product you'll refill, which is how you multiply your business. If you're the brand owner or manufacturer, you have all of them, distributors and retailers, all multiplying your reach.

In a world where Artificial Intelligence is disrupting our educational system, work, financial institutions, programming, and even writing books like this one, we can compare it to the world of Wholesale Distribution as a disruptor. Yes, AI will change the world forever, just as trade changed our hunting and gathering society to an economic system that we still use today. Yes, AI might change commerce in unforeseen ways, but for now, AI is being used within our current financial system; in other words, wholesale distribution and the trade of goods are still the most significant social and economic disruptors in history.

Scalability is terrific, and your product can be in eighty thousand convenience stores in the USA and six hundred thousand in Mexico. You can have national or international distribution without creating a brand portfolio. However, this is not the main reason wholesale distribution became the most disruptive business globally; the cause was scarcity. When this business started hundreds of years ago, it was based on scarcity, meaning having goods you could not get elsewhere. The process of filling this scarcity became what we know now as supply chain or wholesale distribution. Back then, the industry was focused on trade, such as going to another city or country and bringing back goods for sale you could not find in your town. It was also, to some extent, about brands. You could have a particular rug weaver who became famous because of their work and, therefore, more desirable. Or how about a blacksmith with the most durable swords, and the scarcity of these swords made them more valuable?

The modern world of wholesale distribution includes brands, commodities, and everything in the middle. People and businesses buy and sell products; others might be importers or exporters. Foodservice distributors only deliver to places that consume products on-premise, such as restaurants, bars, or hotels.

Wholesale Distribution and what's considered the supply chain are now seen as old school, replaced by just-in-time inventory, next-day or even same-day delivery, and real-time inventory tracking with chips and satellite. However, the supply chain is not the only thing that has changed. How brands communicate and deliver their customer experience has changed, giving real power to small businesses and giving a thunderous voice to consumers.

I ordered coffee online for my Nespresso machine today and expect to get it tomorrow. "What's the big deal?" you ask. It's a huge deal, utterly new to the supply chain and customer expectations. Amazon.com disrupted the market in more ways than free overnight or next-day shipping. Before Amazon Prime, I had to wait a few days, maybe a week, and ask my wife, "Do you need anything from Amazon?" because I wanted to get the minimum order for free shipping. I can order a spoon, and Amazon will deliver it today or tomorrow. That's ridiculous!

I recently visited a vitamin manufacturer. It's a small operation in California that makes and sells vitamins online and on Amazon.com. The owner said, "Amazon is great, and it's not. It delivers my product the next day, but I must do the same on my online store." I explored his business model and discovered that the problem is typical in today's marketplace. Amazon is fantastic for the consumer, just as Walmart was when it first arrived. It gives consumers an outstanding customer experience with software that predicts what you want, pricing, or shipping. I testify to that. As wonderful as it is for the consumer, it creates significant problems for us, the manufacturers, and now retailers.

Like the vitamin manufacturer I visited, most small businesses have a social media presence and an online store. Their customers now expect free shipping and next-day delivery from their store, something the company can't offer. "Maybe we can pick and ship the next day, but then it depends on the postal service," said the owner of the vitamin company. He also needs a minimum order of $40 to offer free shipping to his clients, a few years behind the Amazon customer experience. So what happens here? What can an entrepreneur and a consumer do? Many consumers visit his website, learn about his products, and then go to Amazon for the hassle-free, no-minimum free shipping experience, not to mention the reviews and feedback they can read from other consumers.

What does that mean to you? Amazon is not the first disruptor in the industry. I remember supermarkets had to adjust and implore their technology fifteen years ago to compete with the fully integrated supply chain Walmart introduced. Walmart was responsible for hundreds of independent retailers going out of business. It also pushed big supermarkets to improve their technology and best practices, and others had to close or sell. We see the same with Amazon's push out of brick-and-mortar retail giants, companies like Sears and Robinson May.

The 2020 pandemic also exposed weaknesses at retailers' tip of the supply chain. Many of these never invested in reaching consumers how they would like to be contacted, forcing them to enter stores for their retail experience. What happened? During the pandemic, these brands declared bankruptcy: GNC, Brooks Brothers, Tailored Brands, Century 21, J. Crew, Neiman Marcus, JC Penney, Pier 1 Imports, and others. Why do you think this happened? I would like to hear from you on this. Tell me how you think these companies could have pivoted or adjusted their business model. It was a matter of consumer relationships, online education experience, and online marketing to gain their attention using articles, videos, and other intangibles.

Even brands that didn’t have a way to establish a direct emotional connection with consumers suffered. The pandemic exposed kinks in many new and name brands’ armor, not just retailers and restaurants. What are you doing to shield your business against the next pandemic or pandemic-like crisis? Write down what you're doing with employees, wholesale distributors, and retailers as part of your business model or best practices and how you'll develop connections with the end consumer if you need to sell directly to them.

A pandemic would have probably closed my business when I had my Bargain Basket distribution business. I depended strictly on foot traffic going into stores. I also sold small items wholesale on eBay. I would guess that business would have grown substantially, maybe even paid my bills. When my partner Sandro Piancone and I operated a $100 million distribution and export company, we depended entirely on our wholesale distribution business. In this business, we carried over two thousand products, selling to distributors, restaurants, bars, and supermarkets all across Mexico. Around thirty percent of the company was food service; the rest were supermarkets. Maybe we would have survived with the supermarket business, but maybe not. Even though we owned many of our brands, mostly specialty brands, to make sushi, Italian food, and other imports, we had no plan outside of our supply chain. We didn't have an online store, didn't sell on Amazon, and never shipped to consumers.

Looking back, I can see all the mistakes we made. Luckily, there was no pandemic back then, but we had another large economic problem, the economic meltdown of 2008. Sandro and I took a company public to build the largest wholesale distribution company in Mexico, a roll-up strategy where we acquired large brands and distributors.

The problem? We only sold to the supply chain, in this case, food service, supermarkets, and convenience, not directly to consumers. The other big problem was that we were backed by two companies, a large Hedge Fund in New York and an Investment Banking firm in California. We needed an additional ten million dollars to close our acquisitions, and our backing went under from one day to the next. What happened? Everything happened; we received calls from suppliers, customers, and investors. It wasn't fun, and we learned our lesson many times over.

When I work with other brands, I ensure we're pursuing both the traditional supply chain and wholesale distribution channels, as well as direct-to-consumer models and any out-of-the-box ideas they might have. For my own business, at the moment, I'm marketing Hemp Cigarettes to master distributors, distributors, wholesalers, and wagon jobbers, selling on Amazon and selling directly to the consumer. In doing this, I try to establish relationships with decision-makers on every one of the channels listed. This promotes good business, but it also has a built-in contingency plan. We don't have to close the manufacturing plant if something goes wrong. By the way, we also produce white-label hemp cigarettes for the largest companies in the world, further shielding ourselves from a national crisis. Suppose something goes wrong with a US supply chain partner in the USA, or maybe regulation changes. In that case, we have distribution all over Mexico and produce for companies in Australia, Europe, and Asia. We also export our brand, adding more protection and contingency plans to the business model.

Multiply Your Salespeople

"If you train and support your distributors and retailers, it's like having a fleet of free salespeople selling your products."

Multiplying your sales is probably one of the most critical factors in modern wholesale distribution. It's what makes this business attractive. It's not just you and your team visiting stores, merchandising, and selling. You can have dozens of salespeople for every distributor you have. This can be thousands of salespeople, delivery workers, merchandisers, brokers, account managers, and sales managers all working hard to make their numbers by selling your product. This is leveraging at its best, but it doesn't happen alone. If you don't have outstanding distribution support models, this will not occur, so make sure you have them. Would you like to multiply your sales and grow your brand with wholesale distribution and sales? Go to WholesaleMBA.com and work with us in all aspects of your brand, retail, or wholesale company.

In the following few chapters, you will learn the different types of distribution businesses, different distribution channels, and how to sell your products to each distribution channel, including wholesalers and retailers. All of this is what you call your business model.

You'll start getting into the specifics of every business model out there; when you do, take notes on how you would leverage that distribution channel with your products. For example, consider how your product would fit this model if we're going over warehouse programs to sell to supermarket chains. How would you price your products, support the retailers, and develop push programs to run traffic to the stores and get more and better real estate in the store? Even if you're an executive with a Fortune company, go over the exercises of plugging your brands into the business model. For example, if you're the largest vitamin company in the USA, why aren't you selling in the convenience channel or hotels? Bayer owns some of the largest brands in medicine, including One a Day, the largest vitamin company in the USA. You can find Bayer aspirin in hotels and liquor stores and get them by mail; they are everywhere with their aspirin. Why aren't they everywhere with their vitamins? Even the most significant player in a vertical can benefit from a new idea, new partners, or new channels.

As I write this book, I attempt to disrupt the Tobacco Industry. Sandro, my partner, and I even trademarked Disrupting Tobacco™, among other brands, and we're going after the industry with all we've got. Indeed, we can't compete with an industry that is close to nine hundred billion dollars, or can we?

Do you know Tesla is now the most valuable car company in history? As I'm writing, Tesla's valuation, or market cap, is more significant than that of giants like Toyota,

Mercedes-Benz, and Ford. Today, Tesla's market cap is $664 Billion, with sales of $24.5 Billion in 2019. It's the seventh most valuable company in the United States. Tesla doesn't even sell half a million cars per year. In 2019, they only sold 368,000 vehicles, compared to $278 Billion in sales for Toyota the same year with ten million vehicles sold. Ford sold 5.9 Million cars in 2018. Toyota's market cap is $231.4 Billion, half that of Tesla's, and Ford's is $34.1 Billion. Remember that Tesla is a new company, unveiling sales of its first cars in 2008 and selling only $14.7 Million. Why didn't Toyota or Ford build an electric car twenty years ago? How can a small company with only $14.7 Million grow to rival the S&P largest companies in twelve years? Tesla is a perfect example of a company that is disrupting the market.

Over here at the San Diego Hemp Cigarette manufacturing company, we're not fixing the world's energy problems as Tesla wants to do. However, we're still aiming for a noble cause to help people stop smoking tobacco and prevent tobacco companies from using plastic-based filters, the number one plastic polluter globally. It's tough to compete with the tobacco industry, their lobby, advertising dollars, and their army of salespeople and distributors, not to mention an addictive substance. So, how can we compete with these giants without the giant piles of money? We'll compete with wholesale distribution, marketing, and timing. Alright, we can call the timing luck, with a lot of luck.

The wholesale distribution and marketing part comes with a lifetime of studying, learning, and experimenting in the marketplace with consumer goods, marketing, and distribution. We're using a traditional form of wholesale distribution for our hemp cigarette sales, which is getting the product next to the cash register in convenience stores. So, what is the other part, the secret sauce? This is where timing or luck was on our side.

The timing and luck came in a tobacco factory, a bill passed in the USA, and new legal restrictions against flavored tobacco.

Let's start with the first thing on the list: a tobacco factory. A few years back, a shady-looking gentleman approached me to import his brand of cigarettes to Mexico. I didn't trust him, nor did I like the idea of selling cigarettes, so I declined. He then went to Sandro, and Sandro accepted the offer. Soon after, Sandro opened a cigarette manufacturing company in Tijuana, Mexico. The first problem was getting a permit to start a manufacturing company in Mexico, as they're not legal anymore. The second problem was hiring a team to make cigarettes, as it's not a plug-and-play manufacturing process.

It turns out, by luck, that one of Sandro's companies had a grandfathered permit for tobacco, so he opened the first manufacturing plant in fifty years in Mexico. To run the plant, Sandro hired Alfredo Garcia, a plant manager for BAT, where his father and grandfather worked for BAT, one of the largest tobacco companies in the world. Alfredo moved from Monterrey to Tijuana with his family and brought an entire team of engineers to run the plant.

The tobacco plant ran smoothly for years, making private-label tobacco cigarettes for clients until something extraordinary happened. In 2019, the US passed the Hemp Bill, a comprehensive law that made Hemp legal for farming and any industrialized or consumption use in all fifty states. What does this mean? You can now farm hemp and make hemp products, including hemp cigarettes.

Most entrepreneurs in the USA didn't jump into creating consumer packaged goods as you or I would do. After all, we know that the value is in the brand, not farming, but most entrepreneurs didn't listen to my rant, and most went into Hemp Farming. Thousands of new entrepreneurs farmed hemp for the first time, and the first crop sold at $300 per pound, compared to $2 per pound of tobacco. However, this trend didn't last long, and it went down to $50 in a few months. By the end of 2019, it was already at $40 and went down where we could buy the best hemp in the world for less than ten percent of its original price. In other words, hemp became a commodity, and the value was in the brand.

After many attempts to cross the plant into Mexico to make hemp cigarettes, Sandro and I decided to start a hemp brand in San Diego, California. As of this writing, hemp and cannabis are legal in Mexico; however, exporting hemp is still not easy. We couldn't wait, so we quickly got some funding and started a two-million-dollar operation in San Diego to make hemp cigarettes and sell them nationally.

Manufacturing hemp cigarettes is not easy. You need around a two-million-dollar plant just to get started, plus a team of experts to run the machine and others to prepare the hemp to run in the manufacturing machines, as they were made for tobacco, not hemp. After months of trial and error, we were able to patent the process for preparing and manufacturing hemp and infusing our hemp cigarettes with flavors and aromas. This is when the second legislation hit, and we were ready and able to hit the market running.

In November 2019, Massachusetts became the first state to restrict flavored tobacco products, including cigarettes and electronic cigarettes. California became the second, and Rhode Island, New Jersey, and New York announced a ban on flavored electronic cigarettes. We're betting all other states will follow, leaving consumers without a flavored cigarette and opening our flavored hemp cigarettes market.

The ban on flavored tobacco products is incredible, but it's not our only advantage. We can sell our products on the convenience store counters, next to the checkout, where tobacco can't. This makes our products an impulse buy, an immediate consumer purchase, especially after discovering their favorite tobacco products are illegal in their state. I like to say, "If a smoker goes into their corner convenience store and asks for a pack of menthols, the clerk will tell them they're now illegal. The guy has two choices: either he quits smoking right there and then, or he tries our new hemp menthol cigarettes."

As far as quality, it was vital to us only to use the very best hemp we could find. With it, we made a customer experience entirely biodegradable, where the paper, filter, and box are made out of hemp.

In our quest to Disrupt Tobacco™, we need to get more funding, distribution, and marketing. We will help the environment and help tobacco smokers quit smoking, using hemp as a transitional product. To stay on top of all the case studies I share in print, audio, and video, go to WholesaleMBA.com and subscribe to the free newsletter.

Chapter 7 - The History of Wholesale Distribution – The Most Disruptive Business Ever

---

"The history of wholesale distribution is exciting because it created the middle class, independent wealth, modern affluence, and new millionaires and billionaires."

Wholesale Distribution disrupted business, society, and the economy and launched the United States and modern history. Christopher Columbus commercialized his mistake, looking for a shortcut for the spice route; he landed in America in 1492, unofficially ending the Middle Ages and launching the modern era of international connectivity and commerce.

In America, the first British permanent colony was established in Jamestown, Virginia, in 1607. However, the Spanish crown commercialized their colonization since their first arrival. The crown of Spain still behaved as a standalone, undisputed monarchy, where all the riches, land, minerals, and even peoples of the Americas belonged to the crown and them alone. In contrast, the UK, Dutch, and other European countries already shared the risk and reward of exploration with merchants and entrepreneurs who could invest in voyages of discovery and profit from them.

Without consumer goods, especially silk, and spices, there would be no modern wholesaling, no modern consumer goods, and no wealthy or merchant class—only aristocracy with inherited wealth in the form of land and taxation.

The trading of consumer goods created wealth on earth. Before this, the only wealth in large societies, such as Europe and Asia, was inherited. Different monarchies and dynasties maintained wealth and political power because they were monarchs appointed by divine power and, therefore, entitled to land and taxation of non-royalty. These royals could grant their friends and family land and wealth and maintain the status quo. At the time, there was no other form of wealth outside of the court.

Let's transport our imagination to the Middle Ages. This period, also known as the Dark Period, lasted for one thousand years, from 500 to 1500. Rome no longer controlled the economy, trade, and culture in Europe and

North Africa. The main political and economic structure after the fall of Rome was that of the Feudal System.

The Feudal System of the Middle Ages had two main economic classes: the rich and the poor. The wealthy class was the nobility, and the poor class worked for the nobles in one way or another. Imagine the large castles and beautiful landscapes of the Middle Ages where the King and Queen held court with their nobles. We see this in movies and read about it in books. The nobles were the minority of the population. Where is everyone else? Everyone else is a subject.

In the Middle Ages, wealth was connected to the land, and only the King and Queen could own or assign the land. This land was given to their friends, family, and other nobles in exchange for loyalty and taxes. Farmers didn't own land; instead, they worked on land controlled by the feudal lords. The Feudal System, which dominated from the 9th to the 15th century, required farmers to cultivate land for the landowners.

The middle class initially consisted of merchants, skilled laborers, and tradespeople. Later, it expanded to include the bourgeoisie, who lived within the city walls, unlike the lords' farmers, soldiers, or servants.

In those days, wealth was synonymous with the King. Suppose you're not the King, royalty, or part of the feudal system, the inner circle. In that case, you're a commoner, a peon, and even if you managed to accumulate wealth, you were at the mercy of the plutocrats who could strip your wealth away. All of this changed with consumer goods and wholesale trade.

The Silk Road was not new to merchants in the Middle Ages. It had been in place even before the Roman Empire. After the empire fell, nobody controlled the distribution channels of all the products bought and sold along the Silk Road. European entrepreneurs stepped in to fill this gap and became wealthy, accumulating more wealth than many Kings. It was not only the birth of the new merchant-rich class but a change of the baton of who controlled commerce. It went from the King to the state to private enterprise, and the countries that followed this new way of doing business succeeded and created new empires after the Middle Ages. The ones that didn't follow suit failed. The top loser of the new Colonialism Age was Spain. The winners included England, Belgium, Netherlands, and France.

What spark unleashed the new class of wealthy non-landowners that did not belong to the royal society?

Silk and spices started this economic transformation in Europe. This new era of commerce catapulted the new wealthy class and ended the Monarchy and Feudal system. At the same time, it gave birth to colonialism. Silk was purchased in China and transported to Europe. Spices from North Africa using the same trade routes were the cause of the new rich, discovery, and colonialism.

Christopher Columbus was looking for Asia when he left Spain. He wanted to find a quicker way to transport silk and spices. This was the old channel of wholesale distribution. This new age of discovery was sparked by commerce, and it changed the world forever, bringing us colonialism, imperialism, the industrial revolution, prosperity, and the information revolution.

Europeans thought silk was grown in trees as a fruit; spices were purchased primarily in India and were worth their weight in gold. When this organized trade began, it was not done by governments or kings but by enterprising merchants who wanted to explore new businesses. This was a raw wholesale distribution model – they bought products unavailable in their region and transported them to the region without labor, transformation, or manufacturing.

Trade produced the first upper class; it introduced the concept of the new rich and changed the world forever. What would become of this new class of people who seemed to produce wealth from nothing, without land, cattle, or owning gold or silver mines? This is you; this is the new you. This is your journey into the wonderful world of consumer goods and the wholesale industry. It was and will remain the most disruptive business in history. It changed the definition of business, but it also changed the definition of economy and wealth and shifted authority from the absolute control of the King to the economic power of the merchants.

Merchants stop being just innkeepers, blacksmiths, and stoneworkers. They were now large, powerful families that even Kings used to finance growth, infrastructure, and wars. This same power is available to you. Use it to create, discover, introduce, and market consumer goods into a marketplace, regardless of consumer type, distribution channel, or retail store.

Just like the first visionary merchants that ventured outside their city walls, crossed deserts, and even discovered a continent in search of new ways of doing business, you too must learn to create new products, even outside the walls of a convenience store or supermarket, with or without mainstream distributors. You will learn to think differently, discover needs in the market, and understand that you have more than retailers and distributors at your disposal. With the help of this book, you'll find a new blue ocean of possibilities for commerce.

No, this is not a history book, and it's not a textbook, either. It's a step-by-step guide showing you how to create or find products and sell them. You do need to know some of the basics of the industry. No, not the first 5000 years of trade or The Wealth of Nations by Adam Smith. I'm talking about merchandising, sales, marketing, product development, and wholesale distribution basics.

Controlling distribution channels can bring great wealth, topple empires, and change society forever. Yes, having a product is very important. However, without a supply chain or a distribution channel, your product can be the best idea that never made it to your consumer's hands. Pay as much attention to your product as you do to your distribution.

Chapter 8 - What is Wholesale Distribution?

"Wholesale Distribution is the Secret World of Selling Products!"

Many years ago, I realized that not all wholesale distributors are alike. Still, I learned that there are many structures and strengths to every type of wholesaler, distributor, broker, account manager, or category buyer. You mustn't bunch all distributors into one category because this will not serve you well or help the distributor selling your products. Depending on what you're selling, you might have to control a channel, such as the natural channel. Maybe you have food products and want to be careful about marketing them to foodservice distributors, who sell them to hotels, restaurants, and other on-location consumption locations.

I worked with a brand of food products for Latino consumers, specifically Mexicans and Mexican Americans living in the USA. These were not from Mexico but from

USA-made products like beverages and salty snacks, including potato chips. Our target was Mexican-owned and specialty Mexican stores, mainly in California, Texas, New Mexico, and Illinois. To do this, we employed Mexican-owned distribution companies and distributors with Mexican salespeople selling to Mexican stores. This strategy worked well, but it wasn't our first strategy.

Our first strategy was to sell to pockets with a large Mexican and Mexican American demographic, cities, and towns like mine. I live in southern San Diego, Bonita, with many Mexican ex-pats and Mexican Americans. I thought that even if our target market goes into Kroger, Walgreens, or 7-Eleven, they can buy the product. It doesn't need to be in a Mexican supermarket, right? Wrong! That strategy failed miserably.

Name-brand supermarkets carry a few Mexican items, but they are in the Hispanic aisle. They sell name brands, not start-ups; we needed awareness, merchandisers, signs, and maybe sampling at the store to introduce people to our products. The mainstream stores didn't allow any of these strategies, so our products failed, and we were kicked out of the stores. We could do sampling events in the Mexican supermarkets and have racks, signs, posters, poll signs, etc. This, combined with the target audience being our Avatar or perfect consumer, gave us a recipe for success. The products never crossed over to the mainstream but remained a solid player in these ethnic stores.

A word of advice: spend the most time and effort knowing and then reaching your Avatar or perfect consumer. After all your research is done, start developing an emotional connection to the consumer using social media, advertising, books, whitepapers, articles, videos, and face-to-face with your team or brand ambassadors. Don't ignore who they are, what they want, their pain, and how they prefer to buy. I made the mistake of assuming my target market for Mexican food in dense Mexican areas was the right move, and in hindsight, I ignored the facts. I overlooked the consumer. In this case, a housewife, thirty-five to fifty-five years old, speaks Spanish and visits two or three stores to get what she needs, usually a natural store, a mainstream supermarket, and a Mexican supermarket to get those unique ingredients and specialty foods.

Once you know your consumers are already connecting with them, it's time to go after your supply chain and your wholesale distribution strategy. I'll say this repeatedly throughout the entire book because it's so important. It's so important that I repeat it in lectures, keynotes, courses, articles, and on my soapbox.

As you decide on your business model and imagine the best type of customer for your product, you'll also have to consider the best retailer, wholesaler, or distributor to carry your products. Sometimes, I hear partners, other brands, or clients say, "I want every type of distributor," but this is a recipe for disaster and sends red flags to people in the industry who know about wholesale distribution. A quick example from the beverage industry is that beverages require large trucks carrying a lot of weight. Imagine that each beverage case weighs 30 pounds, and the distributor carries 20 brands. You need a particular distributor to take your beverages into the stores. The beverage industry has very specialized distributors to cover their territory. Not only that, but these Direct Store Delivery full-service distributors offer full service, and they have a fantastic relationship with convenience stores and independent supermarkets in a specific territory. Like any other distributor, they also have weaknesses, such as their limited geographic territory; usually, they only sell in one city at a time.

"But I want national distributors," you may say. Well, I'm sorry to disappoint you; those don't exist. Sure, some companies are national and can take your product to stores throughout the USA. However, these large companies don't have a sales team ready to sell your product; they just deliver the product or only offer it to large stores or franchised chains. I don't think that's what you have in mind. You want a distributor with a sales team that can take your products to stores like FedEx, sell them, collect the money, handle merchandising, maintain relationships with buyers, managers, and owners, and pay you on time. Sounds amazing, right? Unfortunately, that's not how it works in reality.

More likely, you'll need to develop your business model based on your target consumer, where they buy, and the best distributor and sales team for that channel, at least to start. After that, you'll be able to explore new channels, with their specialty wholesalers and distributors catering to that new channel. Your national or international channel will be a collection of different wholesalers, distributors, importers, and exporters selling to other channels. But where do you get all of this information? Well, here, let's go over all of it.

Words matter, so let's define some of these terms and industry jargon to be on the same page. This is more important than you think. My partner refers to Wagon Jobbers as "micro-distributors." Wagon Jobbers are small distributors serving a limited territory, selling novelties, candy, sunglasses, and other products, typically sold at convenience stores. Sandro calls them micro-distributors because they're small, and he thinks people outside of the industry won't understand the term wagon jobbers. As it turns out, you still need to explain what a micro-distributor is. The problem occurred when buyers, distributors, or wholesalers came across any of our materials that said micro-distributors. Sandro had to describe these distributors, to which they asked, "You mean Wagon Jobbers?"

What is a Wholesale Distributor?

A wholesale distributor is a person or business that sells or delivers the product to retailers or other wholesalers for resale. It might be an importer, manufacturer, reseller, or inventor.

Wholesale Distribution has evolved from just delivering goods in your van or fleet of trucks from store to store. You can sell and deliver products in diverse ways. You could sell in person, via phone, or online and deliver in person using trucks or drop-ship products by the case or truckload. There are also new stores like Cash and Carry and superstores like Costco and Sam's Club.

Wholesale Distribution is not only about getting the product to your consumers through retail stores. It's evolved from this to many types of sales, such as MLM, direct sales, sales to offices, drop shipping, catalog, cruise ships, and even social media sales, to name just a few.

For example, the person selling to your local convenience store or supermarket is certainly a wholesaler. They might sell soda, candy, sunglasses, cookies, milk, janitorial products, soap, etc. This company could be a small independent one-person operation or a national wholesale distributor with a fleet of trucks. In most cases, it's both. Most convenience stores buy from different suppliers; some are very large, and some are a one-person show.

In most of our examples, retailers will sell using wholesale distribution. Still, I want you to have multiple distribution channels, not just the traditional supermarkets, convenience stores, food service, and other old-school methods. Think of all the new and exciting ways to build your brand, communicate with consumers, and reach international markets.

One of my clients sells products only through Instagram. He sells Hemp Cigarettes and collects money with the Venmo App. His name is Carlos, and he has a few thousand followers on Instagram at last count, so he's not famous or an influencer by any means. He posts about his product five times per day; he shares videos and photos and talks about his day in his posts. That's enough for him to make a living from his products. He offers people packs, takes their shipping address from Instagram, and uses the Venmo App for payment. That's it, that is his entire sales funnel. Why does this work? Because his followers are customers, not just followers. If paying customers buy every week, you don't need millions to make a living.

Distributors come in many shapes and sizes and can sell the same things to the same customers. There is business for everybody. It's time to add your sales channels to your business model. You need to see what's available to you and then decide what your consumers want and how you'll get products into their hands. Do they prefer to buy on Amazon? Do they go to natural stores or pharmacies? Do they buy subscriptions where you ship products to their home every thirty days?

So, what do wholesale distributors sell? Everything! Just look around your home, office, retail store, or restaurant. Wholesale distributors sell everything you see in these places. The question is, what type of product and consumer do you have?

PART 2 - Find, Sell, and Support Wholesalers and Distributors

Chapter 9 - Wholesale Distribution Hacking

"Hack wholesale by thinking beyond tradition."

When my business partner Sandro and I started our first project together, we used our business and wholesale distribution experience to grow a food and beverage distribution company to $100 Million and took it public. We had to use our previous experience selling to convenience stores, supermarkets, pharmacies, restaurants, and bars, using our trucks, warehouse programs, and direct store delivery. It was quite a challenge, as we also used sales brokers, our sales team, trucks, and third-party logistics companies. We sold in the USA and Mexico and had trucks and distribution centers in Miami, San Diego, and five cities in Mexico. We also had to use our own merchandisers and third-party companies to merchandise our products inside all the large supermarkets across Mexico. This is an example of an all-in strategy, and most of you will not have to do this, as you probably don't have such a large-scale operation running across multiple channels of distribution simultaneously. Oh, by the way, while we were traveling through Mexico and the USA selling, we were also acquiring distribution companies and brands.

At this time, we had our own brands that we started or through companies we procured, Miller Beer for the entire state of Baja California, a portfolio of European and American beverages that we sold to every channel, including on-premise, mass, and convenience, and products we didn't own, but represented exclusively and non-exclusively as well as commodity items such as sugar and flower.

At the moment, Sandro and I are growing several companies owned by Green Globe International, Inc., and Hempacco, Inc. (both public companies). However, we're concentrating on convenience stores in the USA, followed by E-commerce and Mass Retail. We currently have master distributors that allow us to reach over one hundred thousand stores across the USA and partnerships in international markets. Sandro and I decided to go over the convenience store vertical because it's the most difficult channel to sell into, providing our companies with a very high bar to follow and separating us from other brands, and because our target market, what we call our Avatar, buys products in convenience stores. It doesn't hurt that I have a lot of experience producing, selling, and marketing to stores and consumers in this channel.

As for you and your efforts to identify and sell to the best wholesale distribution channels, let's get started by identifying where you'll place your attention and how you'll find and sell into your channel. In this part of the book, you'll discover several types of wholesale distributors and sales channels, both mainstream and not, so you can understand your options as you decide your niche. For example, suppose you're starting a beverage company. In that case, you might want to sell into 7-Eleven and other C-stores or to the natural channel, such as Whole Foods stores, all using DSD beverage distributors such as Budweiser or Miller. However, this channel requires the most time and investment on your part. Hence, it's good to know about alternatives to only selling to large beverage distributors, such as direct sales to consumers, office buildings, or schools.

If you're selling vitamins, you might think of selling them to gyms or GNC stores, maybe even Pharmacies such as CBS or Walgreens, and again, it depends on your funding and the time you want to spend penetrating these stores in several markets across the country. Sandro and I sell and manufacture nutritional supplements and beauty products in our fifty-thousand-square-foot facility in San Diego. We've sold to large pharmacies and the natural channel, and we decided not to go after this market in our first stage, opting to sell directly to consumers using TikTok and other social accounts through our eCommerce stores instead. We launched several brands this year. Our brand, "Lucky To Be," a wellness and self-help-inspired brand, currently sells online and later in mass accounts. We also launched Hemp Bar, a brand of products sold in convenience stores, together with The Real Stuff and the Snoop Dogg, Rick

Ross, and Cheech and Chong brands. There is some crossover between convenience and e-commerce; however, we developed some brands specifically to sell into convenience and others to sell online.

What are you doing right now? And what are you planning to do with your products? Do you already have your perfect consumer? Where do they buy? Do they buy online, and if so, where and how? Do they buy in physical locations? Where and how? As you read this part of the book, take notes on every type of distributor and if it fits into your business model. It’s alright to change or pivot as you go. This is a large part of the equation; whether you’re a start-up or an experienced entrepreneur doesn't matter. Even the largest brands pivot to find their consumer, only it’s more difficult for those large companies to pivot, as their supply chain is already established. This is where the smaller brands have the advantage, and it’s all about speed.

Be sure to follow us on social media and subscribe to our newsletters at WholesaleMBA.com. Stay updated on our business activities, including the trade shows we attend or exhibit at and the reasons behind our choices. You’ll also get insights into the types of distributors we’re seeking for our various brands and access to a calendar of events. Stop by our booths at upcoming shows and hang out with us—we’d love to connect!

To successfully hack your wholesale channels, you need to think beyond traditional distribution methods. Don’t limit yourself to online sales or focus solely on store shelves or distributors. Instead, consider alternative channels, innovative marketing strategies, and unique hooks that can capture the attention of both distributors and consumers.

For example, selling beverages in the refrigerator at 7-Eleven requires a lot of investment, and you're competing against a trillion dollars in economic power. Maybe try to sell subscription cases directly to consumers, drop-ship to their house, or partner with event organizers to sell your beverages at raves or independent concerts, creating demand and a cult following even before one bottle or can is placed at retail.

Chapter 10 - What do Wholesale Distributors Sell?

"Almost Every Single Product in Stores is Sold Wholesale or Through Distributors."

Today, I visited a coffee shop where I wrote a few words for this book. I then stopped at a gas station next to Circle K, and in the evening, I did a quick hop into a Walgreens pharmacy for a case of bottled water, all of this in San Diego, CA. I have this habit of observing everything when I visit stores. I look at the displays, signs, pricing, store merchandising, artwork, floor, impulse buy items, everything.

Sitting in the coffee shop, I saw they sell cookies, pastries, freshly squeezed orange juice, have a refrigerator with sodas, and prepare food. Their products were delivered by a foodservice distributor, beverage distributor, beer distributor, wine distributor, small local baker, and coffee roaster. They also receive drop-shipped merchandise. This is just a small, independent local coffee shop. When things run out, the owner sometimes walks in with boxes from the restaurant depot or Costco. All of these items are a distribution opportunity. You could sell to any of these wholesalers and generate significant business from coffee shops.

When I had my distribution company in San Diego and started selling beverages, we introduced our product into coffee houses, delis, restaurants, and bars, increasing our beverage distribution by 100%. The same was true when Sandro and I had the Miller Distribution company and sold foodservice products all over Mexico. Selling to on-premise or foodservice accounts was a new opportunity for me because I had only sold to retail stores before.

Stopping at the Circle K gas station felt familiar. As I filled up my tank, I glanced at the advertisement displayed above the pumps. I located the window posters promoting their daily and weekly specials. They also sell natural gas and ice outside the store, with two Redbox machines. Did you know these Redbox Video Vending Machines make fifty thousand dollars per machine annually? Yes, Redbox sells a billion dollars per year from vending machines. I entered the store to check if they carried my hemp cigarettes, and they did. I asked the store manager how they were selling. I also saw all the candy, beverages, beef jerky, toys, sunglasses, auto supplies, and many items I used to deliver to these stores twenty years ago. This store also has a walk-in refrigerator where you can buy cases of beer and soda. Do you sell products to chained, franchised, or independent convenience stores? Again, you could sell them through wagon jobbers, wholesalers, or local DSD distributors. Maybe you could even drop ship products to the store and skip the distributor altogether.

The Walgreens store I visited is one of the largest ones. I often visit their vitamin section to see if I can spot any new products or trends. I picked up my case of water and headed out. Years ago, I sold private-label bottled water to supermarkets by the truckload. I made little money per case and only two hundred dollars per truckload, but I didn't have to do much more than a few phone calls to sell it. I also used to sell truckloads of soda to Wholesalers in the USA and export to Mexico. My cousin and former partner Eduardo imported truckloads of Proctor & Gamble Mexican products. They sold them to large Mexican Wholesalers in Los Angeles, making around one thousand dollars per truckload. Again, not much, but he didn't drive the truck! He only made the phone calls.

Our world has a supply chain for most products; even if you don't use the supply chain, it still exists. Maybe you grow your vegetables, are self-sufficient, and never go to the store to buy them. Have you thought of the supply chain to get vegetables to consumers? Think of the seeds, the land needed, the water, the full-time farmers and temporary workers, the refrigeration costs, trucking, storage, and merchandising. Those sellers have a unique supply chain even if you buy vegetables at Farmer's Markets. You have a supply chain for electricity; you have it for gasoline, houses, and prescription medicine. However, in this book, we're interested in some unique distributors serving a particular supply chain. For this book, the primary industry, or the products we want to sell, is primarily Fast Moving Consumer Goods and Durable Goods, which are secondary categories.

This is where it gets very general because wholesalers and distributors can sell almost everything. Nearly every product made can be sold at wholesale prices, even cars, houses, businesses, planes, trees, art, debt, etc.

You can find importers, wholesalers, and distributors marketing and selling every single product available to you at retail prices. What they or you sell depends on your wholesalers, retailers, and consumers' needs. You might sell specialty vitamins only at gymnasiums instead of large retailers or sell hand-made jewelry in high-end boutiques in Los Angeles. You might sell products found in every store across the US or even abroad.

As you look at products, opportunities, or sales channels, try to find products and channels that are scalable, in other words, that you can quickly grow and expand, such as selling to retail or online stores. Here are a few of the products I've sold in the past:

- Food and Beverage
- Vitamins and Nutraceuticals
- Tools
- Toys and Novelties
- Clothing
- Books

- Jewelry
- Housewares
- Electronics
- Personal Care
- Fashion Accessories
- Health and Beauty items
- Sports and Recreational
- Pet Supplies
- Cleaning Supplies
- Business Supplies

Wholesale Distributors sometimes sell to everyone, including the end-user or consumer. They also sell to other distributors, businesses, cash and carry's, retailers, wholesalers, and exporters. I like to ask my distribution partners about their entire business and channel:

1. How many inside and outside salespeople do they have?
2. How many routes or delivery trucks do they have?
3. Do they have cash and carry?
4. Do they have an online store?
5. Do they sell to sub-distributors or wagon jobbers?

Knowing what they do and how they do it helps me help them sell more products. Knowing their territories and accounts helps me geotarget their territory with online and cable television advertising.

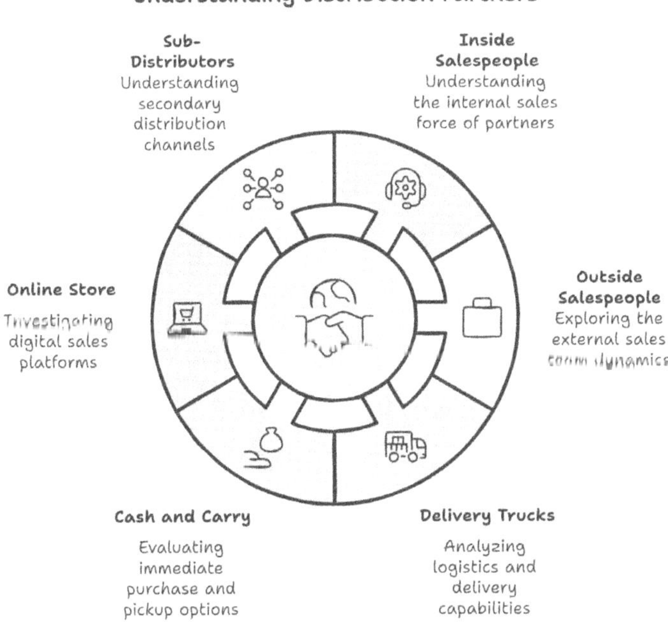

Figure 10 - Understanding Distribution Partners

Chapter 11 - Choosing Your Sales & Distribution Channels

"Get to Know Your Customers – Retailers, Distributors, Wholesalers."

Let's get to know your customers, from consumers to retailers and wholesalers. Write down the types of distributors you want and how you can sell your products to them and through them. Analyze how they think, what they want, how to support them, and how they will help you and your company sell more. Use this chapter to start developing your channel support strategy!

The name of the game here is "Channel Strategy." You might be new to sales or distribution or a CEO or veteran of the industry. It does not matter where you are; you will know more about being a better supplier and salesperson when you finish the chapter. Most importantly, you will be able to plan your sales and distribution channels according to your product, distributor, and consumer needs. Ready?

It does not matter where you are in your business venture. You can be a Start-Up, small or medium company, Global 5000, Fortune 500, or Fortune 50 company. You can be a private or public company, an analyst, a prominent hedge fund, or a small investor. You need to understand your business, your customer's business, and your competitors.

Let's list the different types of wholesale distributors and how they interact with their customers. If you are a distributor, buy or sell to them, you will now be better equipped to conduct business, have better service, and expand your operation.

Take Action

Take action after learning about how your customers work, sell, buy, and do business! Change or adapt your business models and sales channels to provide more products, better service, or proper customer promotion. This book empowers you with information. Even though I try to make it as specific as possible, I don't know you or your business at a level where I can tailor marketing plans, sales programs, commission structures, or promotions. You'll have to do that on your own. Now that you have the information, take action. Make a bullet point plan to sell more, adopt new products, and reach more customers.

If You Sell to Distributors

If you sell to distributors, you might be a manufacturer, an importer, a broker, or a master distributor. Learn all the distributor types and ensure your product is distributed through the correct channels. Learn how your distributors work, how they operate, their service to the retailer, and what products they want to sell.

Get to know your distributors as people and as a business. First, you need to determine what type of distributors they are and how they work. Are they local DSDs? Are they Cash and Carry Wholesalers? How about a buying association or club? Once you know this, you can dive into the specifics. To learn more about how they work, follow this guideline:

Accounts

- What territory do they cover?
- How many accounts do they have?
- What accounts do they service? For example:
  - Franchised convenience stores
  - Independent convenience stores
  - Liquor stores
  - Smoke shops
  - Chained supermarkets
  - Ethnic supermarkets
  - Restaurants
  - Bars

    - Hotels

Infrastructure

- What is their warehouse size?
- Is it dry, refrigerated, or frozen?
- How many outside salespeople do they have?
    - How many accounts do they visit per day?
- How many inside salespeople do they have?
    - How many accounts do they call per day?
- How are salespeople compensated?
- Do they have merchandisers?
- Do they have promotional teams?
- How many delivery trucks or vans?
    - How large are they?
    - Are they dry, refrigerated, or frozen?
- Do they have sales managers, directors, or VPs?

What are their top products or specialties?

- What are their top sellers?
- Why do they think they are top sellers?
- How many products do they carry?
- Are they mostly selling one category? Such as beverages, vitamins, sunglasses, novelties, or ice cream? Maybe they specialize in refrigerated products or the natural channel.

Trade Organizations they belong to:

- Local trade organizations
- National trade organizations

- What trade shows, expos, or buying shows do they attend?
- Do vendors sponsor or accompany them?
- Do the trade organizations have magazine or sponsorship opportunities?
- Do they have buying clubs or programs?

If You Sell to Retailers

If you sell to Retailers, you could be a manufacturer, importer, broker, sizeable national distributor, or a one-person wagon jobber. Or maybe you have a call center or sales team selling to national or regional retailers. Learn about your competitors and all the other distributors, and you can perhaps apply some of their techniques for your business and service retailers better.

Some of the questions to ask retailers might seem basic, but they're not, as I discovered from some of my accounts and salespeople not asking the right questions. Remember, these questions are not just for you to ask but for your salespeople, account managers, or marketing team. I visited a gas station in San Diego with a large convenience store attached. I checked on our Bargain Basket selling tools. It was packed, clean, and had proper signage, so I headed out. The clerk intercepted me, "Are you looking at the basket?" he asked about our large metal wire rack. "Yes," I said, chatting with the clerk, a young, delightful man. After talking, he asked, "Why are you not in our other stores?" He was the owner's son and had nine stores in San Diego and five out of town. We ended up selling to all stores and even dropped ship products to the out-of-town stores. This conversation made me wonder how many opportunities we missed in San Diego and nationally. It turns out we were missing a whole lot. Since then, I have added some new questions to my sales scripts. What are sales scripts? The dialog salespeople use when engaging with retailers. You can develop your sales scripts. I've used mine over the years with my outside sales teams, DSD salespeople, brokers, call centers, account managers, etc.

Here are some of the questions you can ask your retail accounts:

Retailer information

- Are you a franchise or an independent operator?
- Do you belong to an association or buying club?
- Does the owner own other stores or businesses?
- Can you buy for other stores or accounts?
- Can the manager make buying decisions?
- Do you have a preferred distributor?
- What are your best-selling products in my category?
- Can I merchandise my product off the shelf?
- Can I hang pole signs, stickers, and posters?

If You are a Retailer

See how your suppliers get products to you and find new distributors that provide different services and fill various needs. You can also ask your suppliers if they can run promotions sending people to your store. These could be online promotions or contests, advertising, special events at your store, sampling, or giveaways for your clients.

As a retailer, your primary focus is ensuring you have the right products, at the right price, from the right suppliers. The suppliers you work with—and the distribution models they use—can greatly impact your store's profitability, efficiency, and customer satisfaction.

Many retailers only rely on a handful of trusted distributors, but expanding your supplier network can give you a competitive advantage. By working with different types of distributors, you can:

- Find better pricing options and increase profit margins.
- Gain access to exclusive products not available through major distributors.
- Negotiate better payment terms.
- Expand your selection and attract new customers.

How to Improve Your Supply Chain

Retailers should actively seek out new distributors, wholesalers, and manufacturers that align with their product needs. Here's how:

- Explore trade shows and buying groups. Many niche distributors and direct manufacturers offer better deals at trade shows, where they showcase new products and negotiate directly with retailers.

- Leverage cash and carry wholesalers. These suppliers offer flexible purchasing terms and allow retailers to buy in small quantities, reducing excess inventory risks.
- Consider working with jobbers for smaller, high-turnover items. Jobbers offer quick restocks of fast-moving inventory, allowing you to test products without large commitments.

Questions Retailers Should Ask Their Suppliers

To ensure you're getting the best service and pricing from distributors, ask:

- Do you offer volume discounts?
- What are your best-selling products?
- Do you provide any promotional or marketing support?
- What is your minimum order quantity?
- Can you accommodate seasonal fluctuations in demand?
- Do you offer private-label or white-label options?

Leveraging Your Suppliers for Promotions

Many retailers don't take full advantage of their suppliers' marketing and promotional programs. If you're already buying from a distributor or manufacturer, ask them how they can help drive traffic to your store. They may offer:

- Co-op advertising funds to help cover marketing costs.
- In-store signage and displays to boost sales.
- Product sampling programs to attract new customers.
- Social media or influencer marketing support to drive online and in-store sales.

Diversifying Your Supplier Base

Retailers who rely on a single distributor can run into supply chain disruptions if that distributor has shortages, price hikes, or delays. To protect your business:

- Work with at least two or three distributors for essential products.
- Explore regional suppliers who can deliver faster than national wholesalers.
- Keep an eye on direct-from-manufacturer opportunities that cut out middlemen and reduce costs.

Whether you're a new business or a retailer, choosing the right sales and distribution channels is critical for long-term success. By expanding your network, testing different suppliers, and negotiating better deals, you can create a more profitable and resilient business.

Stay flexible, keep learning, and don't be afraid to adapt your strategy as your business grows.

If You are a New Business

If you are new to the business, this part of the book will give you a particular view of the different types of wholesalers and distributors out there. You can then pick the one you like the most and start your business using that distribution style or model.

Starting a new business in wholesale distribution or retail means navigating a complex network of suppliers, distributors, and sales channels. If you're new to the industry, understanding these different types of wholesalers and distributors will help you determine which model best suits your business.

One of the biggest mistakes new business owners make is assuming that one-size-fits-all when it comes to distribution. The reality is that distribution channels vary significantly based on product type, target market, and logistics. Whether you're selling beverages, health supplements, or novelty items, your approach to distribution will shape your company's success.

Finding the Right Distribution Model

First, identify which type of distribution model works best for your business:

- Are you a manufacturer looking to sell in bulk to a master distributor?

- Do you want to work directly with retailers, bypassing traditional wholesale?
- Would a hybrid approach—selling online while also targeting wholesale buyers—be more effective?

Understanding your product, consumer demand, and available capital will help guide your decision. For example, if you're selling a high-demand product like energy drinks, working with a DSD (Direct Store Delivery) distributor could be a smart move since these distributors specialize in convenience stores and supermarkets. On the other hand, if you're selling specialty gourmet food, your best bet might be cash and carry wholesalers or specialty food distributors who cater to niche markets.

Testing Your Market & Building Relationships

As a new business, your first priority should be learning from your customers and distributors.

- Start small and test different sales channels. Rather than committing to large orders, test your product by selling to a handful of retailers, a few local distributors, or directly to consumers online.
- Visit wholesale trade shows. These are excellent for finding the right partners, understanding current market trends, and negotiating better deals with suppliers.

- Talk to store owners, jobbers, and distributors. Understand how they buy, what challenges they face, and how your product fits into their existing inventory.

- Keep your business model flexible. It's okay to pivot if a certain distribution channel isn't working. Many successful businesses evolve their approach based on market response.

Common Pitfalls New Businesses Should Avoid

- Choosing the wrong distribution channel. If you go after big chain retailers too soon, you may face delayed payments, low margins, and overwhelming order volumes that strain your cash flow.

- Underestimating the role of logistics. Whether you're using third-party logistics (3PL) or shipping directly from your warehouse, shipping costs and inventory management will significantly impact your bottom line.

- Ignoring price structure. You must calculate your margins carefully to ensure you're making a profit at every stage—from manufacturing to wholesaler pricing to retail markups.

Ultimately, the key to success as a new business is learning to adapt. As you go through this book, take notes on different distribution models and test which ones align with your product, goals, and budget.

Many Types of Distributors

"There are many distributor types, like convenience stores, even when selling to one channel."

Many distributors are servicing many types of sales and distribution channels. Aside from Wholesale Distributors selling to Retail Stores, retailers sell cars, jewels, chemicals, gas, scales, floors, etc. We'll focus on those distributors selling to convenience stores, superstores, department stores, restaurants, bars, specialty stores, supply stores, supermarkets, and pharmacies. We will also explore other wholesalers, including distributors, jobbers, cash and carry, general wholesale stores, and exporters. Furthermore, we will highlight some unique distribution opportunities like eCommerce, Amazon, direct sales, and other creative structures.

These distributors or customers – or sales channels - are broad and will include many subcategories. For example, the essential Convenience Store category is one of the largest in the country, and it could consist of liquor stores, markets, gas stations, candy stores, car washes, auto parts stores, and minor corner stores.

Some channels or categories are similar, and one company can fit into more than one category. For example, a company selling candy can be a route distributor because they have their own route. They can also be DSD (Direct Store Delivery) because they deliver to each store individually and service the account. Finally, they can be a rack jobber if they place their candy in their display rack.

Chapter 12 - Set Up Example Companies

"These examples will help us understand the wholesale distributor categories in later chapters."

There are many types of products to be sold through all the listed channels we will explore. In this chapter, we will set up two companies. These companies will help as examples when explaining the different distribution channels studied in the following chapters.

We will explore food and nonfood distribution to all types of distributors and retail stores and even food consumption or foodservice accounts with these companies. These are just examples. I wanted to list every product for this book, but it would be one thousand pages long! I decided to choose two relevant products that are applicable across the board. To stay on top of examples and case studies, don't forget to visit www.WholesaleMBA.com to find videos, photos, and other information on marketing and sales strategies.

Now, let's set up our two sample companies and follow them through every example of wholesaling and distribution. We'll see how these two example companies can sell to distributors and retail stores.

For our examples, we will concentrate on the Wholesale and Distribution part of the business. We will discuss branding, promotions, pricing, and strategy, but this book focuses on wholesale and distribution.

Example of Company 1

"Paris-Line Sunglasses"

This company is a sunglass brand that is manufactured in China and France. It imports the products to the USA and sells them to wholesalers, distributors, exporters, and retailers.

The company has two main product lines: high-end and low-end. The high-end line sells by mail order, internet, department stores, and specialty boutique stores—the low-end sells in pharmacies, convenience stores, and supermarkets. The high-end sunglasses sell at a retail price of $120, and the low-end glasses sell at $10.

Example of Company 2

"Superior Energy Drink"

This Beverage Company outscores the production of its energy drink to different bottlers around the USA. They sell the product to Beverage Distributors, Wholesalers, Jobbers, Food Service Distributors, and sometimes directly to retailers. The product is distributed to stores, clubs, and restaurants.

They have one main product line, a 16-ounce energy drink selling at a retail recommended price of $2.00.

Brand Name Companies

As you can see, the two companies in our example are "Name Brand Companies." This means they create their brand and products, market them to create a demand or satisfy a need, and sell them to wholesalers and distributors.

As our examples progress, we'll follow all their customers, including distributors, sub-distributors, jobbers, wholesalers, and exporters. No matter where you are in your business or career, these examples will relate to you and your company.

Chapter 13 - Route Distributors

"I started as a route distributor in San Diego, delivering to convenience stores, pharmacies, car washes, and supermarkets."

I recommend using route distributors if you sell to convenience stores or your products require merchandising. I started as a route distributor and then transitioned to a beverage distributor, doing routes and full service. In my opinion, route distributors, many being full service or DSD, are the best type of distributors. They can give you more space in the store, build relationships with the store managers and employees, and keep you on top of any problems or opportunities.

Route distributors sell to several accounts in one city or a smaller location (maybe a small town or even several square blocks) and typically have their vehicles covering those routes. These distributors could sell many products from many different companies, or they could sell their products. We call them route distributors because they follow a specific route every day. These distributors can include DSD, Wagon Jobbers, Foodservice, and Liquor.

The Route Distributor will likely sell products from other companies and not their brands, although I've seen small brands distribute their product. A perfect example could be your local coffee roaster selling coffee to local coffee houses and some hotels and restaurants. In this case, they would have their trucks and salespeople, but most likely, they will not represent other brands unless you can strike a very handsome agreement or out-of-the-box relationship. I can tell you that none of the brands I know or have worked with are going after this niche market.

Route distributors can come in many sizes, from tiny distributors selling from the trunk of their car or van to large national distributors with a fleet of eighteen-wheel delivery trucks. Today, we call the small distributors Wagon Jobbers, going back to when distributors used horse-pulled wagons.

Sometimes, the distributor can just sell their products, although it often does not happen. A good example is milk. Milk distributors typically handle their brand and nothing more or distribute for only one brand. Maybe they have other milk-derived products like butter or yogurt but don't normally sell other people's products. I once worked with a distributor with four trucks delivering milk and other products, "do you think I can sell other products?" he asked me. This, again, is another opportunity for you to work with distributors nobody is calling, partnering with, or selling other products.

As a boy, I met the first route distributor in Tijuana, Mexico. My neighbor's friend had a Volkswagen van filled with candy. I remember vividly because, in my wildest imagination, I considered eating the entire van. My neighbor would cross the border, head to Costco, and drive back with a van full of candy. He then distributed them around the city. The route was enough for him to support his entire family.

The second route distributor I met was my cousin Arturo Sandoval. He worked with his uncle in a tortillería (tortilla shop). He would make tortillas in a small retail spot near my house, sell them at a retail store, and later deliver them to small retail stores and restaurants. It was a small delivery operation, and his drops, or store deliveries, didn't yield much. He needed more products to sell to get more per drop, but like many others, he didn't know what to sell, and nobody approached him with different products.

If you remember, I mentioned my first business in the USA was Bargain Baskets, a route business that was also a rack jobbing and DSD business.

A route distributor selling many products could be a candy distributor selling many candy brands or a food distributor selling different types of food. This distributor could also sell just one product. Let's say the local newspaper. This distributor goes to many retail locations and only delivers a single product. For me, routing was critical, and when I turned in my old, beaten-down vans for brand new fourteen-footer trucks, routing became a priority for saving time, optimizing sales, and lowering gasoline bills.

When I bought the new trucks, I installed GPS to save on insurance and learn about routing systems. It turned out I had no routing systems and wasted a lot of time and money. Sure, I had routing folders and materials back then, but I didn't think about implementing efficient routing systems. I thought my salespeople would stick to the route every day and only sell within that route. I organized my routes geographically. For example, you drove to downtown San Diego, and you only delivered to stores downtown, usually a few blocks away from each other. If the salesperson had additional time, they would visit new stores in the same route to grow their route, sell more, and make more money, as they only made a commission, no base salary.

What was really happening in my San Diego routes was far from what my imagination had planned. Salespeople did not drive to one route, deliver the product, and open new stores in that one route. Instead, they visited the high-selling stores from the very first day to maximize their commission for that day, without thinking of tomorrow or the next day. This practice only increased when I held promotions or contests, as salespeople wanted to earn the special incentive. I figured it out only after one day of reviewing the truck's trajectory. My salesperson drove twenty miles in one direction to deliver to a large account, only to drive forty miles in the opposite direction to deliver to a different account, and this happened repeatedly. The stores in the heart of the route suffered and were unhappy with us, as we often didn't serve them. Our salespeople ignored the small accounts and the accounts that gave them a hard time or tried to negotiate a better deal.

Alternative Route Opportunities

We know many types of route distributors sell to retail stores. Now, let's talk about other opportunities in routes entirely outside the retail channel. As we list these different opportunities, add them to your business model and brainstorm how to utilize them in your sales and distribution. After all, the more outside the box, the more of a barrier to entry you develop against competitors.

Dry Cleaning Routes

There is a strip mall near my house with a tiny dry cleaner. I'd never thought about it until I saw two cars and a van parked outside their retail store. The vehicles had a pole across the back seat from end to end, stacked with hung clothes wrapped in plastic. Next to the car, a man with a company polo shirt was loading his van with clothes next to the vehicle. Curious, I asked the man, "Is that for delivery?" "Yes," he said, "this is half a day of deliveries." "Half a day?" I asked, "You have more to deliver?" "Yes, I'll come back and pick up the rest later. It turned out these were independent contractors, not employees of the dry cleaning business. They had their clients where they picked up clothes to wash, iron, and dry clean. This is also a route business with great potential for business opportunities. What is the opportunity? It's a fantastic opportunity for brands that sell household items, clothing and accessories, and even local services or products. For example, you can add a flyer to each hanger, advertising your product, or how about a trial size of your product to every home they visit? The opportunities are vast. You could reach hundreds, even thousands of people at their homes for pennies.

Bill Pay Routes

Have you heard of bill delivery in routes? Oh yes, it's a real thing; maybe not in your town or even in the USA, but it's the only way companies can deliver their invoices to millions of households worldwide. The route is easy; probably by foot, a router goes house to house, delivering the water, electricity, gas, and phone bills. These utility companies visit every single address in a country. I witnessed this growing up in Mexico and never thought twice about it. In my mind, it was the only way to deliver bills. It amazed me when I moved to San Diego and received my bills by mail.

Mexico is not the only country that delivers bills by hand in a routing system. It happens in every country that has an unreliable postal service. It's not just for utilities. Companies like American Express also hand-deliver statements in Mexico and other countries. Most delivery people don't work for American Express but for a third-party company that could directly deliver your promotions or products to high-income households in other countries.

Office Routes

My partner Sandro has a large building in San Diego with many employees. We often order water, sodas, coffee, tea, snacks, cleaning supplies, and other items in the mail. We order from catalogs, Costco online, Amazon, or Office Depot. We do this because nobody is delivering to our building. It's in an industrial park southeast of San Diego, next to the border with Mexico. There is no density of offices, primarily warehouses; however, you have a concentration of employees. If I had a delivery service bringing everything I needed, I would buy it from them and probably buy more if they had other products in their truck. If I felt like drinking iced tea, I would buy that; if I wanted to treat employees to candy, I would buy a few cases.

When I worked in large office buildings in and around Mission Valley, we had a delivery service offering coffee, tea, water, snacks, cleaning supplies, and other products. I remember a young entrepreneur doing it; it was his own business, and he built his route himself. He had excellent service and grew his route fast, adding employees to get to more office buildings. I always thought this business was perfect for Fast Moving Consumer Goods, especially beverages, vitamins, snacks, and cleaning supplies. When I worked on a project with 5-Hour ENERGY, part of their strategy was sending brand ambassadors to office buildings to educate office workers and give them samples. 5-Hour

ENERGY's target market is not extreme sports teenagers; they target office workers.

Imagine your product in office buildings, consumed by office workers. Do you need to offer a new package or more sizes? How will you contact these office route companies? Can you drop-ship directly to office buildings while looking for a route rep? How will you reach these offices? There is usually an office manager buying supplies for the company. You can do a telemarketing campaign, send them a mailer, or visit them.

Not all office building route distributors are small operators. You can probably find large operators in every metropolitan area, with substantial regional operators. It will be harder to get into the larger businesses and remember, you'll need to educate the sales team, delivery team, and most importantly, the consumer. It's one thing to sell a few cases to a route owner. It's quite another for the consumer to know what it is, buy it, and consume it. I recommend starting in your territory and educating consumers, possibly with brand ambassadors, to ensure you'll have sales at the stores.

Another possible homerun opportunity for brands is to sell directly to large companies. Yes, companies like Google have their snacks and beverages buyers. Can you imagine selling your products directly to Google and giving them away for free to their nearly one hundred thousand employees?

Vending Routes

As part of our Hemp Cigarette business, Sandro and I own six hundred smart vending machines, Redbox-type machines with a computer inside, a screen to choose and buy, and up to three additional large flat screens for education and advertising. A sister company owns four thousand more of these smart vending machines. What will we do with them? We'll place them in retail locations and sell CBD, CBG, Hemp, and similar products. Each machine can hold two hundred products and sell up to twenty thousand dollars per month per machine. This is not a typical vending machine, at least not your old soda and potato chip machine. These are machines with products ranging from twenty to eighty dollars each. Do people pay that much off vending machines? Oh yes, they do.

Consider the Best Buy machines selling two-hundred-dollar noise cancelation earphones at the airport or machines selling hundred-dollar beauty care creams at the mall. In our case, we don't need a traditional route to service our vending machines. Because of the high value, we can afford to ship the product to the store or machine location, or if density permits, we can send it to someone's house. They can service a few machines.

Selling your products to vending companies is a great idea. You even have national vending companies like Vistar, owning thousands of machines all over the country. You can find hundreds of vending routes and operators in every major city in the country, some selling snacks and beverages, others selling masks and hand sanitizer, and others selling high-end products for hundreds of dollars.

Newspaper Routes

You're probably thinking of the kid throwing rolled-up newspapers into people's front doors on his bicycle. There are also more extensive operations delivering hundreds of newspapers every single morning. Can you imagine partnering with some of these part-timers to deliver your advertising directly to these doors? You could target houses by zip code or block to find your perfect consumer and provide information right to their hands.

There are many routes similar to the ones delivering newspapers. For example, I get two phonebooks delivered every year. Yes, they still deliver phonebooks door to door. There's also an advertising package delivered by hand, an envelope with local specials in my neighborhood. I'm sure you can think of another three or four opportunities around your business or home. Don't forget to do a quick video or write a paragraph and send it to me if you do. I want to hear about all the new and creative ways you use wholesale distribution to market and deliver your products to consumers. Go to www.WholesaleMBA.com and share your story.

Invent your Route

There are many more routes and route entrepreneurs. Think about how you can disrupt the consumer goods industry using your own route, hacking the system, or piggybacking on others' routes.

How about a specialty route? For example, I took my car to the mechanic at an independent shop in San Diego. I noticed a large truck parked outside with the sign Mac Tools. Mac Tools is a franchise that sells to mechanics at car shops. When I sold my tool program, I mainly sold in convenience stores, but I had a few car washes and auto dealerships that sold my tools. They didn't sell my $1.98 tools; they sold a higher-end program with tools from $9.99 to $19.99, and they were some of my best customers. I never developed a route to sell to car dealerships, but that market is wide open. Here is the opportunity for you: the dealership didn't have a small rack filled with tools. They had a big metal table with metal wire on the perimeter to make it into a bin. The table was six to eight feet long and four to five feet wide, and it had a sign, "Clearance," to push scarcity and opportunity. You don't have to sell tools to see this is a great opportunity. Usually, you have large metropolitan areas with car dealerships all on the same street. A route there could yield high returns per stop, and you could sell snacks, auto accessories, sunglasses, toys, or anything else you can fit in the store. My tables were in the waiting room or the dealership's retail floor, so customers could see my tools while waiting for their car to get fixed.

When I was in college, I tried to start a yard cleaning route and a carpet cleaning route, and a college friend, Henry, had a pool cleaning route. All of these can be successful, although mine wasn't. My friend was successful; he had a pickup truck filled with chemicals and giant brushes, but this was his only job. He had to turn people away because he didn't have enough time and didn't want to grow his business or hire employees.

My business failed because I didn't know how to market correctly. I just went door to door, knocking and asking if I could clean the yard or carpet, without realizing they used larger, better-equipped companies to do this. Because I wasn't committed to the business, I just gave up after a few weeks. This time wouldn't be the first I failed in a business or a route.

In high school, my mother started a little magazine; calling it a magazine is an overstatement. A few thick pages were stapled together, including a few articles, the monthly local television programming, and some advertising. My mother received the programming by writing to American television stations like NBC, CBS, ABC, and KPBS. Yes, they sent her the television programming every month with plenty of time to produce the magazine. We announced US television programming because we lived in Tijuana and could see some local San Diego channels.

The advertising from the magazine was not much, but enough to eat and pay the bills in Mexico. I helped transcribe the programming because we got it by mail, on paper, and not electronically. I also had to run to the graphic designer, the printer, or San Diego to buy paper. Our tiny operation had two routes: delivering the actual magazine to businesses. Ours was a free magazine that we placed on companies' counters with good traffic. It was also a way to get these businesses to advertise. My mother made the sales, sometimes just cold calling businesses in person and selling them a twenty-five-dollar ad or a one-hundred-dollar ad when she got lucky. The other route was collections, and I had to go business by business and collect the advertising money. This was not my favorite route. Collecting money in Mexico wasn't fun; it's not fun anywhere, but I had to go multiple times to collect the money from our advertisers. This is standard practice in many third-world countries. I would go on my route, and the receptionist would say, "The accountant is not here," or "We only cut checks the second Thursday of the month." I would show up the second Thursday of the month, and they would say, "We forgot to print your check today, but you can come back next month."

I bet you can think of many other routes that you can use for your business or at least consider and explore before you launch your next product. Bottled drinking water delivery is still a thing. I see many houses in my neighborhood, and businesses get weekly deliveries near my office. Free newspaper or magazine is another one. In San Diego, The Reader is a perfect example. It comes out every week, has excellent specials and announcements, and usually has a good feature article on the cover. The Reader is delivered to businesses only; they're placed on metal wire racks and fly off the racks. They charge advertising to be in the magazine, but you could start your magazine, just like my mother did back in the day.

When I lived in Tijuana, I tried to start a general merchandise route; you guessed it, it failed miserably. I used all my savings to go to Los Angeles and buy general merchandise, like houseware, kitchenware, toys, and gift ideas from an importer. My lifetime friend Amilcar Pasos went with me, and we filled his trunk and back seat with the product. I didn't have a car, and my friend always indulged in my crazy ideas, never telling me, "That's not going to work." I brought my haul home and placed ads on the paper for route people or salespeople. I got a few, and one of them had a large van and an existing route, selling to convenience stores and gift shops; it seemed like a perfect fit. I gave the sales guy the product and explained my prices and his cut. He left that day, and I never saw him again.

I lost all my savings and was heartbroken. I didn't understand how somebody could do this; it was dishonest. I had the guy's address and phone number, called every day, took the bus, and looked for his house to collect, but I never found him. I couldn't let it go and probably tried collecting for the next two years. Now, I was stuck with the loss, out of money, and discouraged from starting another business. Don't think this only happened to me when I was young or in the minor leagues. I had large, reputable companies do the same to me, including the largest beverage distributor in the United States. I had to learn them, lessons you don't have to learn because you can read about them here, look at my videos, audios, and other material, and share stories from other entrepreneurs on my social media channels.

Losing all your money, being heartbroken, starting from scratch, and not giving up are the foundations of entrepreneurship. Sure, please try to avoid any of these problems, but in the end, they're obstacles you'll overcome, just like any other obstacle. The key is to stay on point, pivot, and continue. Many entrepreneurs come into FMCG or CPG from different industries: doctors, lawyers, former beverage executives, and investors. My point is that most of the people I've mentored, coached, or consulted with aren't seasoned veterans in wholesale distribution or consumer goods. They're jumping into the industry for the first time. Big soda execs tell me they managed a team that executed the plan, but as a start-up, they must do absolutely everything when they start, which overwhelms them.

When you launch new products, create your business model, select your distribution method, answer all the questions you read in this book, and then present your finished business model to people who can help you. Maybe your friend is an online marketing wiz; ask for their comments on your online strategy.

If you're in the consumer goods industry or just starting, remember that everything you do and what happens is an investment in your business. If you fail, it's still an investment. If you do something wrong, run out of money, and pick the faulty distributor or retailer, you will still learn from experience. The worst thing I see is new entrepreneurs entering the marketplace, failing, and bowing out. No! You just learned what not to do. You're more competent and bankable now that you have that experience. Don't leave; pivot and try again until you get it right.

Route Management

"My salesperson was driving twenty miles to see one client, then forty miles in the opposite direction to see another."

Route management is planning and executing the route, from documentation to technology and best practices. The big picture of route management is arranging the different sales and service stops in a route. For example, expect your salesperson to visit twenty stores daily, five days per week.

A retail route can involve different types of delivery methods. Sometimes, the salesperson takes on multiple roles, acting as the delivery person and merchandiser during a single visit. Picture a van or truck stocked with your product, stopping at store after store. The sales rep presents the products, takes the order, retrieves the items from the truck, and stocks them on the shelves. In some cases, the same delivery driver-turned-salesperson even collects payment on the spot.

Route Management is the trick to any route. Route Management considers these questions and more:

1. How often do you visit the route?

2. How do you report on the route?
3. How many stores do you see per day?
4. How much money do you make from every route?
5. How do you profit from the route?
6. How do you collect the money?
7. How do you track invoices?
8. How do you load the vans or trucks?

Usually, you load up the truck according to the store visit order, so whenever you open the delivery truck doors, the following order is ready to be unloaded and delivered.

You can still manage your route the old-fashioned way with paper and folders, but you can also use inexpensive software that includes on-the-spot invoice printing, placing orders with phone apps, and linking it all to your accounting. QuickBooks has software for wholesale distribution companies and software extensions to manage routes. Part of the challenge is managing truck inventory, not just the warehouse. Developing and following a system can be time-intensive if the person doing the route is the same person doing the selling.

After you have a grip on your route, whether you do it yourself or have an entire staff of trucks and drivers doing it, it's time to maximize the sales for the route. Ensure you have enough products to sell, enough new products to show, and enough specials and displays to "wow" your customers.

Maximizing your route sales can make the difference between making substantial net profits at the end of the day. Most of your profit will come from your up-sell or "extra sales."

Two Categories of Retail Routes

There are several categories of retail routes, but we can separate them into two large categories: Straight Sale and Pre-Sale.

Straight Sale

The Straight Sale is when you carry the products in the van or truck, make the sale, return to the truck, and deliver the merchandise on the spot. Sometimes, you even place the merchandise on the shelves and collect the money, all on the same trip. Easy!

Wagon Jobbers, Rack Jobbers, DSD distributors, and other small distributors make the straight sale.

Pre-Sale

The Pre-Sale is when you sell in at least a two-step program. You visit and sell to the account, and someone else delivers later. So, if you go to the store, you take a catalog, reorder form, or samples and take the order down. A delivery truck will deliver the merchandise in the future.

There can be more steps to both processes. You could have a merchandiser come to the store and merchandise the product or a promotion team to help sell the product at the point of sale. You could also send someone to collect the money if you offer store credit. Using “collectors” is especially popular in third-world countries where check payments are rarely used, the mail system is inefficient, or the accounts are too small and always pay cash! Mexico, again, is a great example. The market for convenience stores is extensive, with more than half a million tiny convenience stores (we call “changarros” in Spanish). Still, only the prominent players, like the retail chains, use checks or bank transfers. When they pay with checks, they don’t mail them. You still have to go and pick them up!

How can you add your products to every single type of route distributor?

Businesses can have different types of distribution. A sunglass distributor could sell in a DSD route and drop ship to other customers. They could even have other distributors as customers.

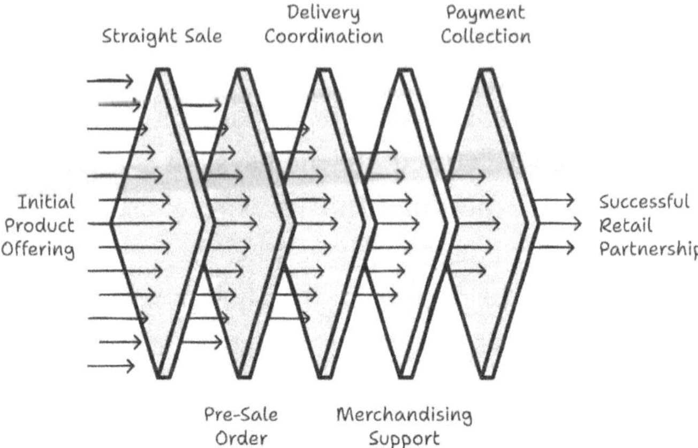

Figure 11 - Retail Route Process Funnel

Chapter 14 - DSD or Direct Store Delivery

"DSD is the most crucial term in Wholesale Distribution to Supermarkets and Convenience Stores. Make sure you know it."

Is DSD the best way to sell your products? I think DSD is the best way to sell products at retail; however, it has many limitations. For example, there is no national DSD distributor, so getting distribution will require you to search, sell, train, and deal with hundreds of nationwide distributors. As always, you should also be creative when looking for DSD distributors. Just because a distributor doesn't currently sell products like yours doesn't mean they won't take your product. A large beer distributor usually only sells beverages, but there's no law against them selling your vitamin packs. You must be innovative, change paradigms, and constantly consider disrupting the market.

Direct Store Delivery, or DSD, is among the most used terms in Wholesale Distribution and Retail. This implies that you deliver products directly to each store. In addition, Full Service DSD means you provide the product to each store, clean it, merchandise it, stock it, and take back any damaged product. Most retail stores favor this kind of delivery. In contrast, the favorite delivery method of suppliers is the Warehouse Program, where you deliver your products to only one place, typically a central distribution warehouse owned by the retailer, and it's up to the retailer to get the product to each store. We'll cover this in the following chapters.

Research this chapter and understand everything about DSD because retailers and wholesalers will throw this term around. Remember, a DSD distributor is also a Route Distributor and could include a Jobber, Beverage Distributor, or Foodservice Distributor. You could get creative and embrace other hybrid distributors.

"Large retail chains love DSD because it means they get great service and free merchandising at each location."

DSD is the most critical type of delivery for the small wholesale distributor, so we'll spend more time explaining what it is and how to benefit from it.

Direct Store Delivery is a term retailers use to specify products brought to the retail stores by a distributor. They refer to this as DSD. When speaking with customers, you'll often hear them ask, "Do you have DSD? or 'Do you have DSD Distributors in every city?"

When you have DSD products, you do not mail your products to the store or deliver them through warehouse programs (explained later.) They are delivered directly to each store and frequently shelved and merchandised by the distributor, as with "Full-Service DSD."

Selling to a national chain like Walgreens with a Direct Store Delivery (DSD) promise doesn't mean you need to purchase trucks to cover the entire country—it simply means someone needs to handle the delivery. To achieve this, partner with distributors in major cities who can service your accounts.

Landing a big chain like Walgreens or other national accounts also provides valuable leverage with DSD distributors. If you've already secured partnerships with these large chains in a specific city, reach out to the top distributors and offer them your accounts. Once they start delivering your product to the large chains, they're likely to introduce it to their other accounts in that city as well.

In the beverage industry, brands often aim to partner with major distributors to carry their products. These top distributors, such as MillerCoors, Budweiser distributors, or large non-alcoholic beverage distributors, are inundated with pitches from new brands seeking to work with them. However, these distributors have strict criteria, and store placement is one of the biggest hurdles.

If you don't already have accounts to offer, they'll likely pass on the opportunity. On the other hand, if you approach a distributor and say, "I have 200 accounts carrying my product in your territory. Are you interested?" you're far more likely to secure their support. I call this the "today is your lucky day" conversation.

Offering accounts to your distributor and providing merchandising, sampling, or advertising is part of your Distributor Package. Your Distributor Package is what you will do for your distributors to help them sell your product. If you are a distributor, request this of every brand before giving them that first meeting.

"Think outside the box, change paradigms, and constantly think of disrupting the market."

Where do you see DSD?

Typically, Direct Store Delivery, or DSD, is offered in these types of stores in the USA:

- Convenience Stores: ARCO AM-PM, 7-Eleven, Circle K, Independents, etc.
- Supermarkets: Safeway, Ralphs, Albertsons, Independents, etc.
- Pharmacies: Walgreens, CVS, Sav-on Pharmacy, etc.

- Gas Stations with Stores: Shell, Exxon, Station 76, etc.
- Superstores: Walmart, Target, Kmart, and more
- Auto Part Dealers: Auto Quest, Auto Zone, Advanced, New Car Dealership Part Stores, etc.
- Restaurants and Coffee Shops
- Bars
- Liquor Stores
- Hardware Stores: Independent and corporate stores
- Gift Shops
- Department Stores
- Boutiques

You also find this type of delivery in non-retail accounts, accounts that require products, sometimes to manufacture, or other times to provide a service. These accounts could include:

- Auto Mechanics: Delivering parts, supplies, and tools
- Businesses: With office and cleaning supplies
- Manufacturing Plants: Getting anything from raw materials to chemicals, equipment, paychecks, and more
- Beauty Shops: Buying supplies to cut hair or do nails

Suppose you are selling your new sunglasses brand to different kinds of stores: large retail supermarkets, superstores, convenience stores, gas stations, independent liquor stores, and independent mini markets. How would you offer DSD to these stores? Well, let's say they are already your customers. You or your distributor would visit a store, look for your sunglass rack or display, see what has been sold, determine the condition of the glasses and display, clean the display, stock it with new sunglasses, and arrange the name or pricing signs as needed. This is typical for a DSD full-service sunglass operation, and because you have a display or rack, it would fall into the category of rack jobber. If you're this sunglasses company's brand owner, you want DSD. If you're in the store, you also want DSD because the sales rep or merchandiser will ensure the display is always filled with best sellers, clean, and with pricing and signage.

My operation in San Diego had sunglasses, not my brand or name brand, but we sold sunglasses. We had our own displays and different display sizes for different stores and sold many sunglasses. It never occurred to me to produce my brand, and I was already importing products from China. It would have been effortless to carry my brand, get it into mass distribution, and then sell the brand itself. However, as I've revealed before, my radar was not on brand building at the time. I had the wholesale distribution channels, the hard part, but lacked the brand, which I now consider the easy part.

The bizarre fact is that no other sunglass brand owner ever called me to offer their sunglasses for distribution or offered stock in their company to build their brand in my stores. I would have accepted in a second, allowing the brand to grow, get funding, and even go public. This lesson is for you and me to concentrate on building brands in the wholesale distribution channel, not just selling other people's brands.

How can you benefit from DSD for your products?

With DSD, you have two primary choices: sell to a distributor that has DSD or provide DSD on your own. If you offer it independently, you need your vehicles, employees, and warehouse. If you use distributors, you will ship the product to their warehouse, and they have their trucks and employees.

There are two main types of DSD Services.

There are two main types of DSD Delivery: case droppers and Full-Service DSD. Case droppers is not an industry term; it's a term I've come to use over the years to refer to a non-sales or merchandising distribution company.

Case Dropper DSD

The disclaimer: "I consider case droppers DSD because they deliver directly to a store without servicing it, but technically they are DSD."

Case droppers are distributors that show up at the retailer's door, drop a few cases or pallets in their back door, and leave for their next drop. They don't serve by opening the cases, stocking the shelves, merchandising the product, or promoting and selling. The largest of these wholesalers are Core-Mark and McLane Company for convenience stores and UNFI for independent supermarkets. Other large distributors sell to other channels, such as chain supermarkets, natural stores, and large convenience stores in the USA. If you have your product and sell it to them, you will have close to national coverage with just two distributors, but this does not mean they will help sell your product. Visit the chapter on Selling to Distributors to learn how to sell to distributors and ensure they sell out of your products. Different types of DSD case droppers sell to channels like food services.

Before looking for these distributors online, let me explain how case droppers work. These distributors might deliver your product to stores, but they will not sell your products in these stores. Think of them as freight companies, UPS, or FedEx. They do a great job at delivering, but they will not sell your products for you.

Some may think case droppers are not DSD because they lack service, but technically, they are because, as the name says, they deliver directly to stores. To dive into this, let's explore the anti-DSD, or the warehouse program, a form of distribution where you ship your products to the retailer's warehouse, and it's the retailer's responsibility to deliver your product to the stores. Convenience store chains don't typically do this, although we have a few exceptions, like 7-Eleven in Dallas or small gas station franchises with a pseudo-warehouse program.

Drop shipping to stores is not considered DSD. Even though you're shipping directly to the store, we call this drop shipping, not DSD. So DSD is when you deliver directly to the stores using your or a distributor's truck.

Case Droppers Don't Sell

Another name we use for these very large case droppers is wholesalers. Although the term wholesalers is also attributed to other types of large distributors that don't sell to chained accounts but to many independent stores. Let's say wholesale distributors can fall into more than one or two categories.

Full-Service DSD

"Of all the distributors in the country, I think DSD is the best wholesale distribution you can get for your products."

Full-service DSD distributors deliver your products and stock, merchandise, and maybe, as meaningful, develop personal relationships with the store's employees, manager, or owner. They visit their stores in a route and sell, deliver, stock, and ensure they have the correct pricing. If they do a great job, they will also arrange Point Of Sale (POS) or Point of Purchase (POP) material like posters, racks, and stickers and rearrange your product for the best possible placement on the retail floor.

I just can't say enough good things about full-service DSD. I've tested every other form of wholesale distribution, and this is by far the best. In the DSD world, the leaders, in my opinion, are the beverage distributors, specifically the three-tier beverage distributors. Usually, they are MillerCoors and Budweiser distributors, although other regional independent distributors have the same best practices.

I was always overly impressed when I visited Budweiser and MillerCoors distributors and went on a ride-along with salespeople. I went on these visits because I was selling them a beverage, and I knew they had an advantage because the stores wanted to carry Budweiser, Miller, Coors, and their other name-brand beers like Peroni, Tecate, and Heineken. These name brands drive traffic. I know the beverage I represented was not a traffic generator, but they will let my brand come into their store because Miller is distributing it. If I show up alone, it would be a challenging climb without these brand-name distributors. By the way, these large beer distributors also carry non-alcoholic brands, not just beer.

Representing a brand name gives these beverage DSDs a decisive advantage, but their procedures make them the DSD Champions of the world. The salespeople do a great job, as do the delivery people who come in with the product and merchandise, organize, place pricing, and other points of sale material. There is an entire chapter on Beverage Distributors because there's so much we can learn from them.

There are two main delivery categories for DSD.

The same categories you read about in "Route Distributors" apply to DSD. There is the "Pre-Sale Delivery" category, where a salesperson goes to the stores without the merchandise, sells the product, and then delivers the product at a later date. You also have the "Immediate-Sale Delivery," where you sell and deliver the merchandise simultaneously because you have it in your truck. You can go back to the chapter on Route Distributors to read this in more detail.

Both types of delivery work well, and the one you use will depend on your product and operation. It's the same if you are the manufacturer selling directly, selling to distributors, or the distributor selling and distributing third-party products.

What are the key differences, benefits, and challenges of these distribution types? Well, it's simple. Obviously, at first glance, it's better to have the product with you when you sell it, like in Immediate-Sell Delivery. That way, you may sell, go to the van or truck, get the product and merchandise, and maybe even collect the money all at one stop. Again, at first glance, this is the way to go. The problem is when you sell two thousand products! Imagine keeping two thousand products in your truck; it's a headache. In this scenario, the Pre-Sale Delivery is helpful and all about picking. You sell, select the products in the warehouse for customers on a route, and then deliver the ordered products.

Immediate-Sell Delivery *is good when you only have one or a handful of products, and you can keep a complete stock in your delivery truck or van. You can sell, deliver, and service your account and collect the money all in one stop.*

Pre-Sale Delivery *is best when you have many products and can't keep them all in the delivery vehicle. You must pick up orders in the warehouse and deliver them precisely for the route or individual customer.*

Advantages of DSD

The advantages of DSD depend on the type of DSD and who is doing it. Are you or your company doing the DSD, or are you selling to a distributor who does DSD? This is important because you will place all your attention on your product if you do it. If you use a distributor, it will depend on the type of distributor you are using. How many products do they have? How many stores does each salesperson visit per day? Do they merchandise the stores?

How do they merchandise? Does the salesperson do it, the delivery person, or a merchandiser?

I sold to many DSD operations when I had my wholesale distribution companies and developed my products. Still, they sold nothing close to what my salespeople could do, and the distributors I trained and put in business also sold more than the large distributors. This is because the large distributors had hundreds of different products and never minded our products.

The primary advantages of full-service DSD are the relationships with the store owners, managers, or employees and the cleaning and merchandising of the products and displays. These two things create a significant barrier to entry and give brands with full-service DSD a competitive advantage over brands that dropship or deliver to the warehouse.

Disadvantages of DSD

Yes, DSD also has its disadvantages. For example, case droppers deliver to stores but don't merchandise; they don't even sell your product. They only deliver after you sell it.

Full-service DSD sells and delivers to stores, but don't assume they will open many stores for you. You still need to develop a go-to-market strategy and a business model to open and support your DSD distributor's open stores. Once you help open stores to let consumers know you're in that store, these are "pull programs," you can do this with sampling, advertising, and other consumer marketing strategies.

The other major disadvantage of full-service DSD is that these distributors are regional, not national. So you need to go to all these distributors individually, city by city, sell, train, support, conduct push and pull marketing programs, and then go to the next town. One failure I see is when brands sell to a distributor, promise they will support them, get another distributor that takes their attention, and four months later, the first distributor returns the merchandise.

Full-service DSD is not a great option for entering a market quickly, as you have so many distributors that you'll need to convince and support.

Figure 12 - Pros and Cons of DSD

Chapter 15 - Rack Jobbers

"Rack Jobbing is one of the best kinds of distribution because you own your little piece of real estate in the store. You are the only one who can place products on your rack."

I mentioned before I purchased Bargain Baskets. This business was the epitome of rack jobbing. After all, I had racks, lots of racks. I had small and large floor racks with tools, pet supplies, and houseware. I had spinner racks with electronics, counter racks with lighters, pens, toys, wall-mounted racks, sunglass racks, and even corrugated tables and shippers with socks, hats, and tools. We had twenty programs with over one thousand different products sold at convenience stores, supermarkets, pharmacies, car washes, auto parts stores, and anywhere I could place my racks.

The bread and potato chip distributors are also more famous rack jobbing operations with plenty of store frequency. You also have the milk distributor, who makes daily visits to stores. However, they don't have their rack, but they merchandise one in the refrigerator, so we'll give them credit even if they don't own it.

Rack Jobbers are a type of DSD distributor. A Rack Jobber can be any size and have its displays in the stores. I love this type of distribution because you own your little real estate in the stores, and nobody else can place products on your displays.

Rack Jobbers usually service convenience stores, although they also have a few large stores like supermarkets. These Jobbers typically have a good relationship with stores because they always have a "foot in the door" with their displays. They invested in that rack they left in the store, and a rack can be anywhere from a few dollars to a few hundred dollars in price.

The other advantage to Rack Jobbing is that it's easy to get into, and you only sell once when you place the rack in the store. After that, it's just a matter of stocking your shelf every time you visit the store.

Rack Jobbing also allows you to up-sell more items to stores. When you are a rack jobber, service is the key to success. You must provide outstanding customer service by keeping your rack stocked and clean and ensuring you have the newest products. If you provide good service, you can upsell more products. You can place another rack, more seasonal items, clip strips, and other smaller display items or counter racks. You often have to speak with the store manager to get things in. Even if it's a large chain with a category buyer, you can still get things directly to the store with the store manager.

For example, let's say you decide to sell sunglasses from store to store. You go into the store and most likely have your sunglasses displayed in the store. You then proceed to fill your sunglasses in the sunglass display. You clean the display and ensure all sunglasses have a visible price, maybe even a sign with special pricing or a catchword to attract customers. Signage is essential in retail, and it's vital in jobbing. Your signs have to be bright and colorful. Ensure that the item description and price are on the sign, for example, "Sunglasses for $9.99."

If you have not done it already, go to www.WholesaleMBA.com and sign up for the course to become a wholesale distributor. It covers everything you need to be a Rack Jobber.

The rack jobbing operation I owned was a bit dismembered when I bought it. My vision was to develop sales and distribution procedures, standardize, and repeat the same results elsewhere to scale the operation from one city to national distribution. When thinking of how to use rack jobbing in your business, think of how you'll train salespeople and distributors to sell and merchandise your products. I'm currently using my procedures to sell hemp cigarettes at convenience stores and create scripts, forms, and best practices to turn it into a jobbing operation and reach fifty thousand stores.

Here are some of the best-sellers I used to carry as a rack jobber into convenience stores. Supermarkets, pharmacies, and other stores had different products:

- Tools
- Lighters
- Small Toys
- Small Radios and Headphones
- Seasonal items
- Laser Pointers
- Sunglasses
- Auto Accessories
- Bath and Beauty items
- Pet Supplies
- Novelty Bottle Openers
- Hats and Caps
- Die-Cast Cars
- Houseware
- First aid and medicine

I sold most of these items in counter displays, either a large spinner rack, clip strips, counter display, or wire baskets. Tools were the main thing I sold, accounting for over 50% of my sales. I sold the tools in metal wire baskets in about five hundred stores. These great baskets allowed me to own my little piece of real estate in over five hundred stores. Once I placed the basket in the store, I just had to go back and refill it regularly. We placed baskets in liquor stores, convenience stores, gas stations, auto parts stores, supermarkets, pharmacies, independent and large chain accounts. Since I was there to "fill up the basket," I took the opportunity to up-sell the store with novelties, lighters, toys, auto accessories, and more. Have you ever heard of this Bargain Basket concept? It has been in more than seventeen thousand stores in the USA!

Learn from Jobbers

Maybe you're not a Jobber but have a product brand you import or manufacture. This does not mean that jobbers are not necessary to you. You can sell to Rack Jobbers and learn a lot from jobbers. You can use this concept even if you drop ship your products or deliver them through distribution centers. I've done it with the largest chains in the USA. I've shipped cardboard and metal displays all around the USA, taking the Jobber model as an example, using racks and displays.

Racks are great POS (Point of Sale) displays. In my experience, they sell more than just placing items on the shelves. It does not matter what types of products you sell; try to put them in racks and not just on shelves. You must be creative and use metal displays, cardboard, clip strips, and stack products or cases on the floor or pallets. Try to figure out how to place products on or close to the counters.

You don't need small products to succeed in rack jobbing. I've used my expertise to innovate across different categories and place my products in high-traffic areas. Walgreens didn't want my wire metal racks. Sometimes, they would let me in with a rack or two in a few stores, but they would call and ask to pick them up two months later. I realized Walgreens had large six-foot tables in the middle aisle and a high-traffic section of the store that cut the halls down the middle. I asked the manager if I could place some of my products on an empty table, and they said yes because they didn't have a product, so a new business model emerged. I started developing programs for the middle isles, and sometimes, I had two or three tables stacked high with my products and brand-new signs that I'd designed especially for these tables. In the chapter on warehouse programs and drop shipping, I expand on how I scaled what started as a small Walgreens jobbing operation of a handful of stores into four thousand Walgreens stores. Now, Walgreens has over nine thousand stores, so you could take my old concept, copy it, and double the number of stores.

Rack jobbing allowed me to hack into corporate stores with a small operation, helping make personal relationships with store managers, regional managers, and buyers. They taught me how to sell and work with their store policies. I listened, and they shared their internal procurement secrets. With this, I scaled my products and now teach my clients how to do the same. The lesson here is not to get into Walgreens or any other chain. The message is to change your brain and adopt new ways of wholesaling, not accept the status quo, and compete in a blue ocean, an ocean your competitors are not swimming in.

I recommend you read the book Blue Ocean Strategy. The authors W. Chan Kim and Renée Mauborgne illustrate how we've been competing and incorrectly reaching customers by competing with the rest of the world on their turf or red ocean. They propose that we create a new competition field that is not crammed with competitors; this is the Blue Ocean Strategy.

For example, when selling tools to retailers, I realized they already carried them. Walk into a 7-Eleven, Circle K, or Valero, and you'll see tools on display. Visit a supermarket like Kroger, CVS, or Walgreens, and you'll find an aisle dedicated to tools, with shelf after shelf of products similar to the ones I was selling. These tools were already slotted in their established tool program, making it difficult for me to break in and sell the quantities I wanted. Instead, I focused on positioning my tools as impulse buys—something customers weren't necessarily looking for but would pick up on a whim once they saw them.

If I called the buyers of any of these stores, they would tell me, "Our tool section is full," or, "You need to call the category manager at corporate," or even, "We only sell our name-brand." So, how was I able to sell my tools and programs? The buyers and managers also thought and placed me in the red ocean. I wanted to be in the Blue Ocean, not on the shelves, not talk to the category manager, but instead in my metal wire basket, next to the cashier, as an impulse buy. The strategy is simple in hindsight, but nobody did it back then. Now, I notice the same strategy being used in stores—it looks like others have caught on. I took a business that works on the shelves and turned it into a rack jobbing operation.

Billionaire Rack Jobbing 101

"How did a young and frustrated fax saleswoman use rack jobbing to be the first self-made woman billionaire in history?"

Do you listen to audiobooks? I've been listening to audio content since I was a teenager. I had books on tape, an old, cheap Walkman, and collections of philosophy, history, and business audiobooks. Yes, I was a weird kid, and because my commute to school was three or four hours each way, I would endlessly listen to books on tape. I still have this audio habit, and I dutifully listen to audiobooks all the time, everywhere. This, as well as my other books, are available on audiobook. My love of audio content brought the story of Sara Blakely to my ears. I listen to a few curated podcasts, and "How I Built This" is worth listening to. Guy Raz, podcast host and author, introduces incredible stories of entrepreneurs. The podcast is part of NPR, and Guy does a brilliant job interviewing mega-successful entrepreneurs on how they started their businesses and took them to success. I see it as a step-by-step template for success, and I recommend you add the podcast to your weekly audible routine. Please share your favorite episode at www.WholesaleMBA.com

I have plenty of favorite podcast episodes, and hearing the story directly from the founders is incredibly uplifting. Nothing seemed easy for ninety percent of the most successful businesses. On the contrary, as you listen to the podcast, you question entrepreneurs' sanity or insanity. I always wonder, "How did they overcome so much? How did they continue after so much failure? What were they thinking?"

The billionaire Sara Blakely started her company, Spanx, with five thousand dollars. The product was a mix of underwear and nylons. The company is described as a maker of shaping briefs and leggings designed to smooth one's figure.

Sara Blakely finessed her way into the Neiman Marcus buyer's office. Sara was immediately rejected until she showed her figure in the bathroom with and without the Spanx. The buyer was sold! Sara was now in seven Neiman Marcus stores as a test. Sara's story is fantastic, as you'll hear on the podcast; however, the big bang for me was what followed.

Sara Blakely walked into Neiman Marcus and searched for her product. Can you imagine the excitement of seeing your product for the first time in a store? She couldn't find it. She continued searching and found her product buried in a nylon shelf. Sara knew her product would not sell there. What did Sara do? She searched for a small upright display merchandiser, filled it with her product, dragged it through the store, and placed it next to the cash register. "Are you allowed to do that?" the store clerk asked her, "Yes, I am," said Sara Blakely. Drop the mic! Billionaire.

Well, it took a bit more than a rack in the cash register, but that's how she thought. How can I be out of the shelf and in the face of my target consumer? The answer was turning her supply chain from a warehouse program to a rack jobbing operation. How can you do the same? It doesn't matter if your product is not intended to sell in a rack; make it.

Rack Jobber or Wagon Jobber Distribution Examples

Example Company 1: Paris-Line Sunglasses

You know all store-to-store distributors, including DSD, Route, and Rack Jobbers. You want all three types of distributors for your lower-end sunglasses. You especially want the Rack Jobbers. They will have a sunglass display in every store and service it frequently, cleaning, re-stocking, rotating, and placing the best sellers in every store. You are looking for distributors who offer outstanding service to their customers.

You probably would not sell your high-end sunglasses through DSD distributors. Those would probably be drop-shipped to retail stores. Maybe follow up with merchandisers or account managers to ensure the sunglasses are displayed correctly.

Example Company 2: Superior Energy Drink

You would probably choose Rack Jobbers in small cities where you can't land a big beverage distributor. Rack Jobbers are good candidates for beverages because they are often in the store. Still, they are not beverage specialists and probably don't have much experience selling the product or giving service. You will have to hold their hand in the sales and service process.

Chapter 16 - Beverage Distributors

"Beverage Distributors have the best distribution I've ever seen; you can copy them or sell to them."

Not all beverage distributors are the same way, but what I learned from Miller Beer and Budweiser distributors was invaluable. Their DSD is one of a kind, and their three-tier system with salespeople, delivery, and merchandisers is efficient and keeps competition at bay.

Doing business in other countries has also given me an interesting perspective on wholesale distribution. In this case, I also want to highlight the distribution systems by FEMSA, the owner and second most profitable Coca-Cola distributorship in the world, located in Mexico. FEMSA has an incredible distribution network with different sales styles depending on the region, fantastic merchandising inside and outside the stores, ownership of their refrigerators in stores, and selling them to other accounts. While diving into FEMSA's financials, I found they sold more than half a million refrigerators per year.

Most large beverage distributors just sell beverages. There is the exception where large companies in food service or other distribution types sell multiple products and drop off drinks at their customers' locations. For the most part, you see beverage distributors distributing beverages. My book Build Your Beverage Empire details beverage distribution and the beverage industry.

I started my venture into the beverage distributing business while researching the market for products that sold quickly and often. At that time, I still had my novelty distribution business, selling to many accounts all over town. I was pleased with the company but discovered I had missed an opportunity. When you sell novelties in a convenience store, such as a novelty watch, you can’t sell it repeatedly to the same customer. That was the opportunity that I was missing.

I wanted to find items that the same person could purchase every day, and after researching the market, I found beverages to be the best bang. When you go into your corner store or coffee shop to buy a soda or cold drink, you could do it daily, often selling to the same consumer. This concept was not true of my novelty business. This is when I discovered and transitioned to the beverage industry.

There was a boom in the New Age Beverages industry, including energy drinks, vitamin water, and alternative sodas. It was the dawn of companies and brands making news, like Vitaminwater, Sobe, Rockstar, Red Bull, Monster, Fuze, Jones, and many more. The valuations for beverage companies were high, and investment was available for new and existing ventures.

For Beverage Distributors

The largest beverage distributors in the USA are soda, beer, and liquor distributors. Most are independent distributors and don't work directly for the soda or beer company. They may have a franchise or be a sub-distributor. They own and hire their people and own their trucks even though they say Coke or Miller on the side.

Beverages are a great product to distribute because of the turns in the store. In other words, they sell out! Let's forget about Coke. Chances are, you will not get a Coke distribution contract. Let's say you sell Snapple, Orange Crush, or another second-tier beverage brand. If you place five cases in a store, you will return in a week, and the product will be sold out. That's called a "turn." The number of times your product sells out in a store is the turn it has in the store. Beverages are one of the best-turning products with decent margins. There are other fast-turning products like name-brand chocolates (Hershey's, M&M), but you don't make much money on them, and there is significant competition.

One of the keys to becoming a successful beverage distributor is getting the best brands. When looking for a distributor, most large successful brands go with big beer distributors, so you have difficulty landing one of those accounts. It would be hard for you to get exclusive access to Snapple, Vitamin Water, Red Bull, Coke, or any drinks if you don't already have them. What can you do? Well, you can either get a remote territory or search for new products with no distribution.

"The great thing about the Beverage Business is the number of products you can sell. You can drop five to ten cases per week per account if you can get a name-brand item."

Selling Beverages in a Remote Territory

You must first contact your local distributor if you decide to get a remote territory with existing brands. Let's say you would like to distribute Snapple. Search for the major distributor in town (just ask a store manager who delivers their Snapple drinks) and give them a call. Ask them about the territory they cover and whether you can supply products to areas on the outskirts or locations they don't serve. There are advantages and disadvantages to this approach. If you don't live in that remote area, you'll have to drive to it daily, and it can take a long time. On the other hand, if you are the go-to guy for Snapple drinks or some other name brand, you can make lots of money.

Finding New Beverages

Discovering new, up-and-coming beverages isn't as complicated as you might think—but finding the good ones is! Hundreds of new drinks hit the market each year, including energy drinks, sodas, iced coffees, teas, juices, and more. These products often appear in trade magazines and at trade shows. However, you don't have to spend money traveling to trade shows when you're just starting out. Instead, start by researching opportunities closer to home.

Start by visiting all of your local supermarkets. Don't limit yourself to major chain stores; check out healthy alternative supermarket chains as well. Avoid single independent supermarkets for now. Why? Many new beverage brands sell directly to large and medium-sized chains, bypassing traditional distributors. These brands often ship to a single warehouse owned by the retail chain, which means they may not yet have broad distribution in your area. By exploring health or specialty stores, you'll likely discover new and unique brands you haven't seen before.

Selling your Beverages

If you are not looking to distribute but have a product yourself, you must find the proper channels, including retailers, wholesalers, and beverage distributors. Your first choice will be to land the large beverage distributors or very large "DSD case droppers" like Core-Mark. The beverage distributors will give you a presence wherever they sell the product, and the large DSD will provide you with a national presence. It will all depend on your strategy, capital, and product.

What's your strategy? No matter what your plan is, it revolves around sales. Yes, you have to build brand equity, and you will need promotions, but all will come with sales and distribution. I will say it again and again: the name of the game is sales and distribution. Focus on getting retail accounts first and distributors second. Yes, you heard me right; retail accounts are first!

How to Land the BIG Distributors

There are large distributors out there, especially in the USA. Large liquor distributors like Southern Wine and Spirits are strong in liquor stores and on-premise accounts with wine and liquor. You have Core-Mark and McLane, which are distributed nationally to convenience store chains and regional city-wide distribution with beer distributors. You also have large non-alcoholic distributors, wholesalers, and jobbers. If you want to land the big boys, distributors in the largest cities in the USA with thousands of accounts, you need just one thing: customers.

Yes, you heard me right. These distributors get hundreds of calls from energy drinks, sodas, beers, and beverages. They all say they have the best-looking, best-tasting products, but you know what? It does not matter. They don't care about your beverage's look, feel, or taste; they care about sales.

Your best bet to get the BIG distributors is to give them accounts. So open accounts with them or open chains and hand over the distribution. Some even tell you, "Bring me 100 new accounts, and you're in." So how do you do this?

You have several options. You can go to supermarkets and convenience chains and open a few in a particular territory or region, or you can go and open one account at a time with independent stores. I've done both! The fastest way is to open chains in a territory. Yes, national supermarkets and convenience store chains purchase by region. You just have to visit the regional sales manager. Sometimes, an area is considered a city; occasionally, it's several cities or even several states.

Sales Packages

When selling your beverages to distributors and retailers, you first need a "Distributor Package" and a "Retailer Package." These packages include product and point of sale photos and specifications and everything you will provide your distributor and retailer. You detail things like commissions, ride-a-longs (when you go and ride with the salespeople to help them sell), posters, stickers, coolers, refrigerators, product discounts or specials, pricing, profit margins, and everything you will provide to help increase sales. These packages are critical, and you should have them before you even call a distributor; otherwise, you will not look professional.

No Promotions Without Distribution

I have a saying that especially applies to New Age Beverages: no promotion without distribution. Don't spend money on sponsorships, club events, or other promotional activities that don't bring you distribution. It's all about getting the accounts. That's the name of the game.

It's great to be part of the beverage industry. You can sell many products in a small city. Besides energy drinks and new-age beverages, new beverage companies are seen as great investment opportunities, with many landing funding from investors.

"Large beverage distributors like beer distributors are some of the best Full-Service DSD Distributors. They have good salespeople, delivery trucks, and even merchandisers."

Beverage Distribution Examples

Example Company 1: Paris-Line Sunglasses

You don't want Beverage Distributors to sell your Sunglasses!

Example Company 2: Superior Energy Drink

There are many beverage distributors, and they can specialize in different beverages. You have beer, soda, juice, and liquor distributors, and some who do a little of all the non-alcoholic drinks. You also have some that might specialize in convenience stores only or even food service to restaurants and bars.

Your business plan has to specify all the types of distributors you want to reach and a strategy to reach and support them. This includes all kinds of distributors listed above. If you have a beverage or food company, you need different distributors through several channels like the convenience store and foodservice channels.

Chapter 17 - Foodservice and On-Premise Distributors

"Foodservice distributors are the backbone of the food and hospitality industry."

In the food and beverage industry, foodservice and on-premise distributors play vital yet distinct roles in the supply chain. While they both connect manufacturers to businesses, their focus, customer bases, and methods of operation are quite different. Understanding these differences is essential for effectively selling to and working with each type of distributor.

Foodservice distributors are the backbone of the food and hospitality industry. Their primary role is to supply businesses that prepare and serve food to customers. These businesses include restaurants, hotels, catering companies, hospitals, schools, and corporate cafeterias. Foodservice distributors typically offer a wide range of products, from fresh produce and frozen goods to kitchen supplies and cleaning products. They are known for their ability to deliver large quantities of products on a regular schedule, often just in time to meet the needs of high-volume kitchens. This reliability is key, as many foodservice customers depend on consistent supply to avoid disruptions in their operations.

On the other hand, on-premise distributors focus on establishments where products are consumed on-site, such as bars, nightclubs, coffee shops, and event venues. Their primary emphasis is on beverages, ready-to-eat items, and other products designed for immediate consumption. Unlike foodservice distributors, on-premise distributors often deal with smaller, more frequent orders and provide a more personalized service to their customers. Many on-premise distributors go beyond delivery, offering promotional support such as branded merchandise, point-of-sale displays, and event sponsorships to help boost sales within their venues.

While foodservice distributors prioritize efficiency and bulk pricing, on-premise distributors concentrate on creating brand visibility and enhancing the customer experience at their venues. For example, a foodservice distributor might supply cases of beverages to a corporate cafeteria, while an on-premise distributor would work with a nightclub to introduce a new energy drink, complete with branded glasses and signage.

The relationship between manufacturers and these distributors is equally important. Foodservice distributors often establish long-term contracts with their customers, ensuring stability and consistent sales. In contrast, on-premise distributors build closer, more dynamic relationships with their clients, helping them tailor their offerings to match the preferences of their patrons. This distinction makes it essential for manufacturers to adapt their approach when working with each type of distributor.

How to Work with Foodservice and On-Premise Distributors

To effectively work with foodservice and on-premise distributors, it is essential to understand their priorities and tailor your approach accordingly. Foodservice distributors are typically driven by the need for efficiency, reliability, and consistent pricing. They are focused on delivering large volumes of products to businesses that depend on steady supply chains. Manufacturers working with foodservice distributors should ensure that their products meet these expectations by offering competitive bulk pricing and a dependable delivery schedule. Providing additional resources, such as preparation guides or promotional incentives, is also beneficial to help foodservice customers incorporate the products into their operations.

On-premise distributors, in contrast, thrive on building strong relationships with their clients and enhancing the consumer experience. Manufacturers working with on-premise distributors should be prepared to offer marketing support tailored to specific venues. This might include providing branded items, creating promotional displays, or collaborating on special events to generate buzz around the product. Since on-premise distributors often deal with smaller orders, the focus should be on creating a premium experience for the end consumer rather than simply moving large quantities of inventory.

Pricing strategies also differ between the two types of distributors. Foodservice distributors generally expect lower prices due to their high-volume orders, while on-premise distributors are often willing to pay higher prices if they receive robust promotional support in return. Regardless of the channel, it is crucial to ensure that the pricing structure allows for healthy profit margins at every stage of the distribution chain.

Selling to Bars and Restaurants

In my first wholesale distribution business, Bargain Baskets, I primarily sold to convenience stores before expanding to supermarkets and pharmacies. From there, I branched out to unconventional accounts like car washes and tool stores, eventually making my way into club stores and superstores like Walmart and Target. Since my focus was on tools, electronics, pet supplies, and other similar products, I didn't sell to bars, restaurants, or similar establishments. That changed when I decided to diversify my portfolio by including beverages and adding an energy drink to the mix. This marked my first experience selling to those types of accounts.

When I loaded the energy drink cases onto the trucks, I thought they would only sell in my convenience stores; after all, convenience stores are the best market for energy drinks because the consumer is male, sixteen to thirty-four years of age. Eduardo Enciso, my cousin and salesperson, quickly discovered he could sell into clubs, bars, restaurants, hotels, and other accounts. These accounts are called on-premise in the beverage industry, and if you work for a food company, you will refer to them as foodservice accounts. The difference is that foodservice primarily sells food and supplies to the chef or maybe the general manager with the chef. The on-premise distributors are usually beverage distributors selling to bars and restaurants, and they sit down with the bar manager or the general manager and bar manager. Sure, sometimes the chef gets involved, especially if it's a wine distributor because the chef wants to ensure their food complements the wine, or vice versa!

I soon found myself selling beverages across San Diego. We then expanded, opening a distribution arm in Tijuana and selling there as well. Over time, we began working with Budweiser and Miller distributors across the U.S., a practice that Eduardo and I continued for many years, spanning various beverage lines.

This introduction to selling to restaurants and bars eventually led me to collaborate with my partner, Sandro Piancone, when he opened a food distribution center in Tijuana with plans to take his company public. Sandro invited me to join as Vice President of Marketing and Mergers and Acquisitions, where I also contributed to sales, strategy, and investor relations.

This was my first experience with a large foodservice company, and Sandro was an incredible mentor. His background in food was extensive—his entire family was deeply rooted in the industry. His father, Michael Piancone, came from Italy on his honeymoon, settled in New Jersey, and worked in his family's pizzeria before opening his own. Their family business, Roma Foods, grew into a major Italian food distribution company, thriving nationwide, especially on the East Coast.

Sandro carried on this legacy with foodservice in his blood. He owned a pizzeria near San Diego State University, operated a catering business, ran an ice cream business, and much more. His entrepreneurial spirit and deep expertise in food made him an ideal partner and mentor.

Sandro worked as a salesperson for Roma Foods and eventually decided to expand into the Tijuana market, learning Spanish along the way. After Roma Foods was sold, he chose to continue importing food into Mexico and launched his own company. This venture became my gateway into the foodservice industry and on-premise sales. Together, we distributed over 2,000 different products across Mexico to restaurants, bars, and hotels, and we also supplied Miller Beer to the same outlets.

If you have food or beverage products—or even items used in the foodservice industry—this channel could be an excellent opportunity for your wholesale distribution. Products might include drink mixers, chocolate, raw cooking materials, glassware, pots and pans, tea, and many other essentials.

In the USA, you have regional, state, and national foodservice distributors; the largest of them are Sysco and US Foodservice. A typical large salesperson for a foodservice company will sit down with the decision maker in the account and take their order. If you have a new product that the foodservice salesperson has in their catalog, you'll need to do something to sell it. In other words, it won't sell itself. Just imagine, when we had our two thousand SKUs, our salespeople wanted to sell flower and cheese, the easiest sellers, and we wanted them to sell our own brands of products because they had higher margins. If you sold a product to us, it would go on the catalog, and that's it, unless you train and give a spiff or commission to our salesperson, or you advertised it or sold it to the account, your product would just stay on the catalog, never selling anything. This is not just true of the foodservice vertical, but with any vertical. You're responsible for selling to everyone in the supply chain, even the end consumer.

Foodservice and on-premise distributors each play a unique role in helping manufacturers bring their products to market. While foodservice distributors provide the infrastructure needed to supply high-volume customers, on-premise distributors focus on enhancing brand visibility and consumer engagement at the venue level. By understanding the differences between these channels and adapting your approach to meet their specific needs, you can build strong partnerships that drive growth and success for your brand. Whether supplying large institutions or promoting your product in trendy bars and coffee shops, these distribution channels offer valuable opportunities to expand your market reach.

Chapter 18 - Drop Shippers and eCommerce

"Drop shipping and eCommerce: low overhead, wide reach, seamless sales."

The Old and New Ways of Selling

The traditional days of drop shipping through catalogs or mail-order sales are long gone. Today, drop shipping has transformed to align seamlessly with modern eCommerce platforms, social media strategies, and even innovative approaches like influencer marketing. Whether you're using a website, selling on Amazon, or leveraging social media, drop shipping allows you to build direct relationships with consumers while bypassing the need for traditional retail channels.

This evolution reflects the shift toward a consumer-focused sales landscape. By combining cutting-edge sales strategies with efficient shipping methods, drop shipping offers a scalable way to launch a product and test its viability in the market. It's particularly beneficial for startups or small businesses not yet ready to invest in mass production or traditional distribution networks.

Connecting Drop Shipping to eCommerce

eCommerce and drop shipping are natural partners. Platforms like Shopify, WooCommerce, and Etsy allow businesses to sell products online without maintaining inventory or operating physical stores. Drop shipping lets you list products on your eCommerce site, sell directly to consumers, and fulfill orders through a third party. This synergy has revolutionized how products are brought to market, providing businesses with an accessible way to reach global audiences.

Imagine you've created a new product—vitamins, electronics, or clothing—but aren't ready to mass-produce or distribute to large retailers. Instead of making a significant upfront investment, you can create a website, list the product, and start selling immediately. Social media platforms like Facebook and Instagram allow you to run targeted ads, while eCommerce integrations handle payment processing and order tracking. This modern approach ties together drop shipping and eCommerce, enabling businesses to test demand, refine marketing strategies, and establish a customer base before scaling up.

What's a Drop Shipper?

Drop shippers are businesses or individuals that sell products without holding inventory. Instead, they rely on third-party suppliers to store and ship goods directly to customers. Products are delivered via carriers like the US Postal Service, FedEx, or UPS.

While traditional drop shippers might have used their own warehouses, modern drop shipping often involves outsourcing warehousing and shipping to fulfillment centers like Amazon FBA or third-party logistics providers (3PLs). This shift has made drop shipping more accessible and cost-efficient for small businesses entering the eCommerce space.

The Advantages and Challenges of Drop Shipping

Drop shipping offers significant advantages, particularly for entrepreneurs and startups. It allows you to sell products nationally or even internationally without the overhead of maintaining inventory. By using tools like telemarketing, email, and social media, you can reach decision-makers in retail stores or directly target end consumers.

However, drop shipping isn't without its challenges. While it reduces upfront costs, it requires careful planning to ensure profitability. Shipping costs, potential product returns, and customer service needs can quickly erode your margins if not managed effectively. Additionally, drop shipping puts you in the retail business, especially when selling directly to consumers. This means handling sales tax, tracking shipments, managing returns, and responding to customer inquiries—often labor-intensive.

Drop Shipping in Practice

Consider Paris-Line Sunglasses. With two distinct product lines—a $10 wholesale line and a $120 premium line—you can approach drop shipping in different ways. The lower-cost sunglasses can be drop-shipped in bulk to retail stores or distributors, typically sold by the dozen or more. Buyers would usually cover shipping costs, making it feasible to ship significant quantities while maintaining profitability.

For high-end sunglasses, eCommerce opens the door to selling directly to consumers. At $120 per pair, you have enough margin to support online sales, whether through your own website, social media, or catalogs. However, selling directly to consumers comes with additional responsibilities, such as collecting and remitting sales tax, offering shipment tracking, and providing customer service. While this approach allows you to capture retail margins, it also requires a robust system to handle the operational complexities.

Now consider Superior Energy Drink. Drop shipping beverages presents unique challenges, particularly due to shipping costs and the fragility of glass bottles or cans. While it's technically possible to drop-ship energy drinks directly to consumers or retailers, the costs often outweigh the benefits. A better approach might involve partnering with another business that specializes in drop shipping beverages. This way, you can leverage their expertise and infrastructure without taking on the logistical burdens yourself.

Integrating Drop Shipping and eCommerce

eCommerce platforms have made drop shipping easier than ever by streamlining the process of setting up an online store, managing orders, and integrating with suppliers. Platforms like Shopify, BigCommerce, and Squarespace offer features tailored to drop shipping, including real-time inventory tracking and automated order fulfillment.

To succeed in this space, you must think beyond simply listing your product online. Building an eCommerce store that integrates drop shipping requires a solid marketing plan, including:

- Creating a strong online presence through a well-designed website.
- Running targeted ads on platforms like Facebook, Instagram, and Google.
- Partnering with influencers or affiliates to promote your product.
- Offering excellent customer service to build trust and encourage repeat business.

Combining eCommerce with drop shipping lets you quickly test the market for new products, gather customer feedback, and scale your business without heavy upfront investment.

Lessons Learned

My experience with drop shipping has taught me valuable lessons. I set up a call center in one of my businesses to contact independent supermarkets, regional chains, and national retailers. Using a combination of telemarketing, mailings, and samples, we drop-shipped thousands of orders to stores nationwide. While this strategy allowed us to scale quickly, it also highlighted the importance of managing costs and maintaining strong customer relationships.

When I transitioned to eCommerce, I realized that selling directly to consumers came with its own set of challenges. I used to receive hundreds of emails daily, and failing to respond promptly would lead to unhappy customers. Managing customer expectations and streamlining communication became just as important as delivering a quality product.

Drop shipping and eCommerce are powerful tools for building a business in today's digital marketplace. By leveraging drop shipping, you can minimize overhead and quickly expand your reach. When combined with eCommerce, this strategy allows you to create a seamless customer experience, from online browsing to doorstep delivery.

While the approach comes with challenges, careful planning and a focus on customer satisfaction can make it a gratifying way to launch and grow your business. Whether you're selling sunglasses, energy drinks, or any other product, integrating drop shipping with eCommerce opens up endless possibilities for success.

Chapter 19 - Warehouse Programs

"Warehouse programs streamline storage, logistics, and supply chain efficiency."

Warehouse programs are a pivotal component of the distribution and supply chain industry, offering manufacturers, distributors, and retailers an efficient way to manage, store, and distribute products. These programs go beyond simple storage solutions, encompassing strategies and systems designed to streamline logistics, reduce costs, and improve product availability across the supply chain.

What Are Warehouse Programs?

Warehouse programs refer to structured agreements or systems where products are stored in centralized facilities before being distributed to retailers, distributors, or end consumers. These programs often involve large-scale operations, such as those managed by wholesale clubs, regional distribution centers, or third-party logistics (3PL) providers.

The primary purpose of warehouse programs is to ensure that products are readily available to meet demand while minimizing storage costs and inefficiencies. Depending on the business model, warehouse programs can vary in complexity and scale, ranging from small regional warehouses to massive distribution hubs that serve national or international markets.

Types of Warehouse Programs

1. **Traditional Warehousing:**
   Traditional warehouses act as storage facilities where inventory is held until it is needed. Businesses may own these warehouses or lease space within them. Products stored in these warehouses are typically distributed in bulk to retailers or wholesalers.
2. **Cross-Docking:**
   Cross-docking is a warehouse program where products are received, sorted, and shipped out with minimal storage time. This system reduces warehousing costs and speeds up delivery times, making it ideal for fast-moving products.
3. **Third-Party Warehousing (3PL):**
   Third-party logistics providers manage warehousing and distribution for businesses, offering services like inventory management, order fulfillment, and shipping. These programs are popular among businesses that want to outsource logistics to focus on core operations.
4. **Retailer-Specific Warehouse Programs:**
   Large retailers like Costco, Walmart, and Target often operate their own warehouse programs,

requiring manufacturers to deliver products to their centralized distribution centers. These warehouses then handle distribution to individual stores.

How Warehouse Programs Work

In a typical warehouse program, products are manufactured or imported and then delivered to a designated warehouse. From there, inventory is monitored and managed to ensure that it meets the needs of retailers, distributors, or end consumers. Modern warehouse programs often use advanced technologies, such as barcode scanning, RFID tracking, and inventory management software, to optimize operations and prevent stockouts or overstocking.

For example, a regional distributor might store products in a warehouse near their retail customers. When a retailer places an order, the distributor fulfills it directly from the warehouse, ensuring timely delivery and minimizing transportation costs.

Warehouse programs allow you to sell directly to retail chains without using distributors. How does this work? Suppose you are selling sunglasses to large retail chains around the USA. If you sell your sunglasses through a warehouse program, you will not deliver them to individual stores but to your customers' central warehouses. Your customer then delivers the merchandise to the stores and stocks the shelves and displays.

You would start by packing your sunglasses in boxes, placing them on pallets, and shipping them to the retailer's central warehouse. The retailer then rolls out your sunglasses to their stores using their shipping. Once there, store employees open the boxes and place the sunglasses on displays or shelves. Typically, you use this program when selling to large chains with hundreds of stores, like Albertsons, Walgreens, Walmart, Target, CVS, etc. These stores have central warehouse locations and their logistics.

Every program has advantages and disadvantages. Here are a few examples of both for the warehouse program.

"Warehouse programs are big businesses. Customers will buy truckloads of merchandise delivered to one location."

Warehouse Program Advantages

The most considerable advantage of this program is that you don't need distributors or your distribution infrastructure. You use the customers' infrastructure, trucks, and employees. Another benefit of this program is that no drop shipping is involved; you only ship to your customer's warehouse. You can pull off this program with a few employees; you don't need merchandisers, large warehouse staff, or delivery people.

Here is a list of benefits:

- Low shipping costs
- Ship to a single location
- No merchandising employees
- No delivery drivers
- No picking or large warehouse staff
- You don't need any distributors

Figure 13 - Warehouse Program Advantages

Warehouse Program Disadvantages

The warehouse program may sound like the perfect way to sell to large chains. It does have significant disadvantages, the most prominent being merchandising.

When you use warehouse programs, your merchandising is left to untrained store employees with many other responsibilities. If your product sells out, they must fill the shelves, place point of purchase material, and put up displays. Merchandising is one of the most important things when selling in retail stores. If you don't have it, you're in trouble. Many companies using warehouse programs hire merchandisers just for your product in different cities to deal with the problem.

The most expensive factor in the warehouse program is slotting fees. Often, stores will ask you to "pay to play," meaning pay for the fees to place your product in their stores. Slotting fees can be hundreds of thousands of dollars.

Another problem of the warehouse program is "time to shelf," which refers to the time your product will take to hit the store shelves. When you are not using your logistics, you will be unsure when your product gets to the stores and when it gets to the shelves. You'll often find your product in the store's warehouse, waiting to be placed on the shelves. This long wait presents a massive problem for you, especially if you are running a test for a fixed period or advertising in the area and the product is not on the store shelf.

When dealing with warehouse programs, you typically pay different fees, which vary by store chain. The most common fees are for product damages and disposing of damaged products. If a store damages your product in transportation, they may charge you for it. On top of this, they charge you for throwing it in the trash. These fees can add up.

Warehouse Program Distribution Examples

Example Company 1: Paris-Line Sunglasses

You will probably not see too many sunglass warehouse programs with full truckloads unless you sell to big superstores like Costco or Walmart. You would likely ship a few pallets to a distribution center or even drop ship to individual stores with sunglasses. Sunglasses are too small to send a full container load to any chain.

Example Company 2: Superior Energy Drink

With beverages, it is prevalent to sell truckloads through warehouse programs. Many supermarket chains can buy truckloads of beverages and energy drinks. It does not even have to be a chain. For example, if you sell water, a single privately owned supermarket could buy a truckload from you, maybe even a truckload of soda.

Selling beverages in this way is common, including your Energy Drink. Supermarkets do it because they get a much better price, sometimes even lower than the distributor. You typically do this kind of deal with supermarkets, wholesalers, and cash and carries only and not with convenience stores. Convenience stores don't usually have distribution centers. It's a shame for your energy drink because most category sales happen in convenience stores.

The logistics are simple. You negotiate with the supermarket or chain to get the best price. Sometimes, they will ask you to pay for newspaper advertising or slotting (pay to place your product on the shelves.) After you agree on the price, you ship full truckloads to their warehouse, and they take care of the rest. They will distribute the product to their supermarket stores, price, merchandise, and re-stock it.

Chapter 20 - Vending Distributors

"If approached with care and strategy, vending can be more than just a dream business—it can be a profitable reality."

Vending is an excellent business model that offers opportunities to sell sodas, snacks, and other food items with minimal human interaction. Essentially, vending machines operate like a route business but without the need to visit multiple stores or manage a large sales team. It's no wonder that vending has become one of the most sought-after distribution businesses for start-ups.

However, while the potential is undeniable, there are significant risks. Vending is often marketed as a "dream business," with promises of easy profits and minimal effort, but the reality can be far more complex. Scams are prevalent in this industry, with companies selling overpriced machines, unverified routes, or "business opportunities" with no real substance. As someone who has studied the vending industry and worked with vending businesses, I strongly advise approaching this sector with caution.

The Truth About Vending: Opportunities and Challenges

The vending business can be highly profitable, but success depends on understanding its core components: acquiring machines, finding high-traffic locations, and managing operations efficiently. While many new entrepreneurs are drawn to the promise of passive income, vending requires an active effort to maintain, stock, and grow the business.

The companies I've worked with and sold to demonstrate that vending businesses can work—and work well. These companies make great money, pay their suppliers on time, and continue to grow their operations. The common thread among successful vending entrepreneurs is that they start small, focus on high-quality placements, and grow strategically.

The initial challenge lies in acquiring vending machines, which can cost thousands of dollars. Leasing is often a practical option, as major manufacturers offer financing plans that spread the cost over monthly payments. After securing a machine, the next crucial step is placement. The location of a vending machine determines its success. High-traffic areas, such as large offices, schools, or manufacturing plants, provide the best opportunity to generate consistent sales.

Securing a location involves pitching your idea to the owner or manager of the business. This process requires strong sales skills, as you'll need to convince them that your vending machine will add value to their space. Once the machine is placed, your job is to restock it regularly, collect the cash, and ensure that it remains in good working order. Over time, the goal is to duplicate this process across multiple locations, scaling your business to include dozens or even hundreds of machines.

The Vending Hybrid Model

In addition to traditional vending, there's a model I call the "vending hybrid." This approach eliminates the need for vending machines and focuses on delivering products directly to medium and large offices. With this model, you supply beverages, snacks, coffee, tea, and similar items to businesses, functioning more like a distributor than a vending operator.

The vending hybrid model is simpler to start and less capital-intensive than traditional vending. Instead of leasing or purchasing machines, you rely on direct sales to office managers or business owners. Once you've secured a customer, your primary responsibility is to return regularly to refill their orders. This model is ideal for entrepreneurs looking to enter the vending distribution space without the high upfront equipment costs.

Benefits of Vending Distributors

Vending distributors play a crucial role in the supply chain, offering manufacturers a direct route to consumers. By placing products in vending machines, businesses can reach customers in high-traffic areas where impulse purchases are common.

The scalability of vending is another major advantage. A single vending machine can generate steady sales, but with multiple machines, the potential grows exponentially. For example, imagine placing one case of your product in 20,000 machines. That's 20,000 opportunities to sell your product every day.

Additionally, vending offers an opportunity to test new products in a controlled environment. By placing a product in vending machines, manufacturers can gather valuable data on consumer preferences, pricing, and packaging.

Challenges in Vending Distribution

While vending has significant advantages, it also comes with challenges. One of the most significant is competition. Vending machine operators are often hesitant to take on new, unknown products unless they are competitively priced and offer high profit margins. Established brands tend to dominate vending machines because they are familiar to consumers and sell reliably.

Logistics is another challenge. Vending machines require regular restocking and maintenance, which can be time-consuming and costly. Additionally, the upfront investment in machines, coupled with the effort required to secure placements, can be a barrier for new entrants.

Vending Distribution Examples

Example 1: Paris-Line Sunglasses

While traditional vending machines are not ideal for distributing sunglasses, hybrid distributors could sell Paris-Line products alongside beverages and snacks in offices. By creating attractive, easy-to-display packaging, Paris-Line could target office environments where employees are likely to make impulse purchases.

Example 2: Superior Energy Drink

Superior Energy Drink offers a compelling case study for vending distribution. Beverage distributors often specialize in supplying vending companies, which range in size from a few machines to tens of thousands. Placing a single case of energy drinks in 20,000 vending machines can move a significant amount of inventory.

However, introducing a new energy drink to vending machines can be challenging. Consumers are more likely to purchase recognizable brands, so vending machine operators may only take your product if it is priced low enough to offer a large profit margin. Marketing support, such as promotional materials or samples, can help overcome this hurdle.

Tips for Success in Vending Distribution

Success in vending distribution depends on careful planning and execution. Start small and focus on high-traffic locations that guarantee sales. If you're pursuing the vending hybrid model, build strong relationships with office managers and ensure you offer competitive pricing and reliable service.

Invest in marketing to make your products stand out. Branded signage, promotions, or introductory discounts can encourage vending operators to try your product. Additionally, consider collaborating with established vending distributors to leverage their existing networks.

Finally, stay vigilant against scams. Whether you're purchasing vending machines, routes, or services, always research the seller and verify the legitimacy of their claims.

Vending distribution offers a unique opportunity to reach customers directly in high-traffic environments. Whether through traditional vending machines or the vending hybrid model, this business can be a lucrative way to scale your operations and test new products. By understanding the challenges, leveraging strong sales strategies, and building reliable systems, you can establish a successful vending distribution business that grows steadily over time.

Chapter 21 - Wholesalers to Distributors

"Wholesaling to distributors is a powerful way to scale your business, reach new markets, and move large product quantities."

In the distribution chain, some businesses act as wholesalers selling to distributors, who then supply products to retailers. This model is especially common for manufacturers, importers, or those who own their products, as it allows them to leverage distributors' existing networks to reach a broader market.

Cash and Carry businesses are a prime example of wholesalers selling to distributors. These businesses stock a variety of products, including name-brand and private-label items, and sell in bulk to jobbers or other smaller distributors who handle the final leg of distribution to retail stores.

Becoming a wholesaler to distributors offers a unique opportunity to scale your operations and sell in large volumes. By selling to distributors instead of directly to retailers, you can tap into a vast network of stores and consumers without managing individual retail relationships.

The Role of Wholesalers in Distribution

As a wholesaler to distributors, your primary role is to supply products in bulk to companies that specialize in selling to retailers. This indirect sales strategy allows you to focus on production, procurement, or importation while distributors handle the complexities of delivering products to stores.

Distributors vary widely in their size, specialization, and customer base. Large distribution companies, for example, may handle a broad range of products across multiple categories, supplying to big-box retailers or chain stores. Conversely, specialty distributors may focus on a single category, such as beverages, snacks, or sunglasses, and serve niche markets or specific types of stores.

When you wholesale to distributors, you often sell by the case, pallet, or even truckload. This high-volume sales model is akin to hiring an enormous sales team without the overhead, as distributors do the heavy lifting of marketing and selling your products to their networks.

Types of Distributors Wholesalers Work With

Understanding the types of distributors you might sell to is crucial for success in this business model. These include:

1. **Broadline Distributors:**
   These distributors handle a wide range of products and cater to large retailers, cash and carry stores, and supermarkets.

2. **Specialty Distributors:**
   Focused on specific product categories, such as beverages, sunglasses, or organic snacks, these distributors often serve niche markets or high-end stores.

3. **Jobbers:**
   Smaller distributors, often referred to as "wagon jobbers," purchase products in bulk and sell them to independent retailers, convenience stores, or other small accounts.

4. **Cash and Carry Distributors:**
   These distributors sell to jobbers and small businesses, offering products in bulk at competitive prices. They typically do not deliver, requiring customers to pick up products directly from the warehouse.

5. **DSD (Direct Store Delivery) Distributors:**
   These distributors deliver directly to retail stores, ensuring products are stocked on shelves and displayed correctly.

Advantages of Wholesaling to Distributors

Wholesaling to distributors offers several advantages, including:

1. **High-Volume Sales:**
   Selling by the pallet or truckload enables you to quickly move large quantities of product, boosting your revenue and reducing inventory holding costs.

2. **Reduced Operational Complexity:**
   Distributors handle the logistics of delivering products to retailers, allowing you to focus on production, branding, and other core aspects of your business.

3. **Access to New Markets:**
   By partnering with distributors, you can enter new geographic regions or retail segments without establishing direct relationships with stores in those areas.

4. **Scalability:**
   This model allows you to scale your operations more efficiently, as you're leveraging distributors' networks rather than building your own retail presence.

Challenges of Wholesaling to Distributors

While this model offers significant benefits, there are also challenges to consider:

1. **Pricing Pressures:**
   Distributors expect competitive pricing that allows them to maintain healthy profit margins. You'll need to ensure your pricing structure supports their needs while still leaving room for your own profitability.

2. **Relationship Management:**
   Maintaining strong relationships with distributors requires regular communication, support, and transparency. Distributors must feel confident that your products will sell and that you're committed to their success.

3. **Product Demand:**
   Distributors are unlikely to take on unproven products. You'll need to demonstrate that your products are in demand through existing sales data or compelling market research.

4. **Marketing Support:**
   Many distributors expect you to provide marketing materials, samples, or promotional campaigns to help them sell your products.

How to Become a Successful Wholesaler to Distributors

If you're a manufacturer, importer, or product owner, you're already in a prime position to wholesale to distributors. Here's how to maximize your success:

1. **Understand Your Distributors' Needs:**
   Learn how your target distributors operate, what they value, and how much they expect to make on your products. By understanding their priorities, you can tailor your offerings to align with their business models.

2. **Demonstrate Product Demand:**
   Before approaching distributors, establish demand for your product. Highlight existing sales, positive customer feedback, or market trends that demonstrate your product's potential.

3. **Provide Competitive Pricing:**
   Set pricing that allows distributors to make a profit while remaining attractive to retailers and end consumers. Consider factors like shipping costs, volume discounts, and promotional allowances.

4. **Offer Strong Support:**
   Distributors appreciate manufacturers who go the extra mile to help them succeed. This might include providing marketing materials, offering training sessions, or collaborating on promotional

campaigns.

5. **Build Long-Term Relationships:**
   Treat your distributors as partners rather than just customers. Regular communication, transparency, and mutual trust are key to building long-lasting relationships.

Wholesaling to Distributors: Distribution Examples

Example 1: Paris-Line Sunglasses

Paris-Line Sunglasses offers both a low-end line priced at $10 and a high-end line priced at $120. For the low-end sunglasses, Paris-Line could target distributors that serve convenience stores, discount retailers, or cash and carry outlets. These distributors would likely buy in bulk and resell the sunglasses to smaller retail accounts.

For the high-end line, Paris-Line could focus on specialty distributors that cater to boutiques, department stores, and high-end sunglass retailers. By working with distributors who understand the luxury market, Paris-Line can ensure its premium products reach the right audience.

Example 2: Superior Energy Drink

Superior Energy Drink is an ideal product for wholesaling to distributors. While some sales may go directly to retail stores, the majority will likely involve distributors.

Beverage distributors, DSD companies, jobbers, and cash and carry businesses are all potential customers for Superior Energy Drink.

To succeed, the brand must offer competitive pricing and strong marketing support to encourage distributors to take on the product. Additionally, Superior Energy Drink must demonstrate that it can compete with established brands in the beverage market.

Wholesaling to distributors is a powerful way to scale your business, reach new markets, and move large product quantities. By understanding how distributors operate and tailoring your approach to meet their needs, you can establish strong partnerships that drive mutual success. Whether you're selling sunglasses, energy drinks, or any other product, the key is building trust, offering value, and providing the support your distributors need to thrive.

Chapter 22 - Cash and Carry

Cash and Carry: wholesale stores for small retailers, no delivery, self-serve simplicity.

Cash and Carry businesses are wholesale stores that cater primarily to small-scale distributors, wagon jobbers, and small retail operations like liquor stores, gas stations, and convenience stores. These businesses operate out of a warehouse or storefront where customers arrive, make their purchases, and transport the goods themselves—hence the name "cash and carry." Unlike traditional distributors, they do not deliver products to their customers.

Cash and Carries bridge the gap between wholesalers and smaller retailers, offering convenience, immediate availability of goods, and access to products in manageable quantities. This model is especially appealing for small business owners because they can avoid the larger minimum order quantities typically required by larger distributors.

The most recognizable examples of Cash and Carry businesses are Costco and Sam's Club, which cater to individual shoppers and small business owners seeking wholesale pricing. However, beyond these giants are hundreds of regional and local cash and carry companies across the country, many of which focus exclusively on serving retailers rather than end consumers.

Products Sold at Cash and Carries

Cash and Carries typically stock a wide range of items, many of which are staples for convenience stores, small grocery shops, and other retail businesses. This includes:

- **Packaged Snacks**: Chips, candy, and other impulse-buy items.
- **Beverages**: Soft drinks, bottled water, and occasionally energy drinks and specialty beverages.
- **Household Goods**: Paper products, cleaning supplies, and small home essentials.
- **Imported Items**: Many cash and carry stock imported snacks and goods that appeal to niche markets.
- **Name Brand Products**: Larger Cash and Carries often carry name-brand items from major manufacturers like Procter & Gamble, albeit at prices that may not always be as competitive as those offered by larger distributors.

One of the advantages for retailers shopping at Cash and Carries is the ability to source a diverse range of products without committing to large, pallet-sized orders.

How Cash and Carries Fit into the Distribution Chain

Cash and Carries serve a unique role in the wholesale ecosystem. They cater to smaller businesses that lack the purchasing power or storage space to order directly from manufacturers or larger distributors. By purchasing from Cash and Carries, these smaller retailers can restock their shelves more frequently without tying up large amounts of capital in inventory.

For manufacturers and brands, selling to Cash and Carries can be a valuable way to reach smaller accounts that may not have been accessible through traditional distribution channels. However, it's crucial to consider the potential impact on other sales channels, particularly distributors.

Pricing Strategies for Cash and Carries

When selling to Cash and Carries, manufacturers typically price their products slightly higher than they would for larger distributors. This pricing model ensures that:

1. **Distributors remain the primary sales channel.** Cash and Carries shouldn't undercut the distributors representing your "bread and butter" accounts.
2. **The Cash and Carry can still mark up the product.** This allows them to sell competitively to their small retail customers while maintaining their profit margins.

Cash and Carry Distribution Examples

Example 1: Paris-Line Sunglasses

For customers like Cash and Carries, you would sell your lower-end sunglasses that retail for up to $10. These products are ideal for their small retail and convenience store clientele, who often focus on affordable, impulse-buy items.

The Cash and Carry would stock these sunglasses in their warehouse, targeting small jobbers and convenience store customers who frequent their store. You would sell to the Cash and Carry at roughly the same price you'd offer to a medium distributor, ensuring that they can still apply a markup while remaining competitive.

Example 2: Superior Energy Drink

Selling beverages to Cash and Carries requires careful strategy. For instance, you might sell your energy drink at a higher price to the Cash and Carry than you would to a traditional beverage distributor. In some cases, your beverage distributor may even supply the Cash and Carry directly.

Cash and Carries would likely sell your energy drink primarily to small convenience stores. It's important to ensure that these Cash and Carry customers do not compete directly with your core distributors, as the latter are your primary revenue drivers.

Tips for Working with Cash and Carries

1. **Understand Their Needs:** Cash and Carries prioritize fast-moving, in-demand products. Focus on items that appeal to their small retail clientele, such as affordable, high-margin goods.

2. **Visit Local Cash and Carries:** Researching cash and Carriers in your area can help you identify opportunities and assess whether they fit your products well.

3. **Maintain Relationships with Distributors:** If you're already working with distributors, ensure that your relationship with Cash and Carries complements—not competes with—your existing sales channels.

4. **Offer Attractive Terms:** Since Cash and Carries typically pay upfront or on very short terms, offering them favorable pricing or volume discounts can encourage larger purchases.

5. **Monitor Sales Performance:** Monitor how your products perform within Cash and Carries. If sales are strong, consider expanding your offerings or working with additional locations.

Cash and Carries may not deliver products, but they play a vital role in the distribution chain by offering convenience and accessibility to smaller businesses. By understanding their needs and strategically pricing your products, you can leverage this channel to grow your wholesale business while maintaining strong relationships with your distributors.

Chapter 23 - Exporters and Importers

"Sell by the Truckload Every Single Time."

Exporters and importers are dream customers for many businesses. They typically buy in truckload quantities, handling their own logistics, importation, permits, and sales. In many cases, they even manage marketing and promotions, reducing the burden on the seller.

If you're selling a product, you will most likely be the exporter, selling to importers in other countries. Alternatively, you could work with a third party specializing in exports to help you navigate the complexities of the process. For example, I assist U.S. companies in exporting products to Mexico, leveraging my position on the board of one of the largest importer distributors in the country.

The Catch: Proven Best-Sellers

While exporters and importers may seem like ideal customers, there's a critical catch: your product must be a proven best-seller. Importers are unlikely to take a chance on products that don't already have a strong track record of sales and demand. In simple terms, don't start by targeting exporters unless you have something exceptional to offer, such as the best price in the market or a product with a demonstrated ability to sell.

Many companies make the mistake of trying to export unproven products to other countries. While this strategy *can* work, it often means competing solely on price. This leaves little room for healthy profit margins and can make it challenging to sustain your business in the long term.

When to Consider Exporting

The best time to explore exporting is when your product has already gained traction in your home market. For example, if your products sell well in retail stores and have a solid distribution network, it might be time to expand into new markets.

However, exporting may not be the best option if you're just starting out or have minimal sales in your country. I frequently receive inquiries from businesses looking to export their products to Mexico, many of which are in their home market's early stages of distribution. My advice is always the same: "Secure sales in your own country first, then expand into other markets."

Like any rule, there are exceptions. The most notable exception is cost. If you can offer an incredible price on your products, you may succeed in selling to exporters and importers, even if your product isn't well known. This applies to both name-brand items and more generic or private-label products.

Benefits and Challenges of Working with Exporters and Importers

Working with exporters and importers can provide significant advantages for your business, particularly when scaling operations and entering new markets. One of the primary benefits is the potential for bulk purchases, as these partners often buy in large quantities. This can lead to a substantial boost in your revenue and streamline your operations by moving larger volumes of product. Additionally, exporters and importers take on the complexities of logistics, including shipping, securing import permits, and complying with local regulations, allowing you to focus on production and other core areas of your business.

Another advantage is the opportunity for an extended market reach. Exporters can introduce your products to markets that may otherwise have been inaccessible due to geographic, cultural, or logistical barriers. Furthermore, many importers handle their own marketing and promotional efforts, reducing the financial and operational burden on your business.

However, partnering with exporters and importers also presents challenges. One common issue is pricing pressure, as these partners often prioritize cost efficiency and may push for lower prices. Additionally, expanding into international markets requires an understanding of cultural differences and the preferences of customers in the target market, which can be a learning curve.

Navigating the regulatory landscape is another challenge, as import/export laws and compliance requirements can be complex and vary significantly between countries. Finally, brand recognition can be a hurdle. Without an established presence in the new market, you may need to invest heavily in marketing efforts to build awareness and credibility for your product.

Balancing these benefits and challenges is essential for successfully working with exporters and importers and leveraging their networks to grow your business.

Exporters and Importers Distribution Examples

Example 1: Paris-Line Sunglasses

Sunglasses are a great example of how you can export products to other countries. For Paris-Line, you could sell both your high-cost and low-cost lines to importers.

If your high-end sunglasses are already well known and selling successfully in your country, they could be a strong candidate for export. However, if they lack brand recognition and sales traction, it won't be easy to convince customers in another country to pay $125 or more for them.

On the other hand, your low-cost sunglasses are generic and compete primarily on price, making them ideal for export. Importers and distributors in other countries could buy, import, and mark them up for significant profits. This example highlights how generic or private-label products can succeed in export markets without strong brand recognition.

Example 2: Superior Energy Drink

Energy drinks present a unique challenge. Unlike generic products, energy drinks typically rely on strong branding, marketing, and promotions to succeed. If your energy drink isn't already a well-known name brand or doesn't offer an unbeatable price, exporting might not be a viable option—unless you or your distributor are prepared to invest heavily in branding and advertising in the target country.

Energy drinks are usually sold at a high retail price, around $1.99. Competing with established brands in a new country without a solid marketing strategy is risky and could lead to failure.

Having personally worked with and launched numerous name-brand and non-name-brand energy drinks in both the U.S. and Mexico, I've seen firsthand how critical it is to have a well-planned strategy. This includes working closely with distributors, allocating funds for promotions, and ensuring your product stands out in a crowded market.

Tips for Exporting

1. **Start Local:** Build a strong foundation in your home market before expanding internationally.

2. **Research the Market:** Understand the target country's demand, competition, and pricing.

3. **Leverage Relationships:** Work with experienced exporters and importers who understand the market and can help navigate local regulations.

4. **Offer Competitive Pricing:** Ensure your product is priced competitively, especially for generic or private-label items.

5. **Invest in Branding:** If exporting a name-brand product, allocate resources for marketing and promotions in the target country.

Exporting and importing can be highly lucrative, but success requires careful planning, market research, and partnerships. By understanding your target market's needs and leveraging your product's strengths, you can position your business for long-term success in the global marketplace.

Chapter 24 - Using Sales Brokers

"Brokers thrive on trust—pay on time, honor agreements, and value partnerships."

What are Sales Brokers?

Brokers are salespeople that you don't have on payroll. They can vary from a one-person operation to international companies with hundreds of employees covering an array of channels.

In our current companies, we write big checks to brokers; I'm talking $50,000 per month in big checks. We love brokers, I love brokers, and we never cancel their agreements. On the same note, companies have often canceled my broker agreements, avoiding hundreds of thousands in commission. Our current brokers have brought us incredible deals with Cheech and Chong, Rick Ross, and HBI Raw, to name a few. We've developed products and joint ventures and generated millions in sales.

My relationships with brokers have always been stellar. I love brokers, and I want to think brokers love me. After all,

I get them what they want, when they want it, and I pay on time, every time. However, my relationship with brands has not been spectacular as a broker, and I'm no exception. When speaking with sales brokers, they have a similar experience. Brands don't pay them, violate their agreements, use them for their connections, and immediately cancel their contracts. My first experience as a broker was devastating.

I accidentally discovered sales brokering after selling my wholesale distribution company, Bargain Baskets, and DSD Merchandising. You read part of the story in the first chapter of this book, where I took Jolly Rancher Soda to Mexico. If you don't remember, go back and read it, but I'll give you a recap to refresh your memory.

My partner in my first wholesale business, Marshall, introduced me to his childhood friend, Joe, who was now a big shot at the most prominent US beverage distributor and bottler, Honickman Group. Joe invited me to help him sell a new licensed product from Hershey's, Jolly Rancher Soda. Imagine the Jolly Rancher™ candy as a colorful, sugary soda. He offered me 5 percent of net paid sales, but there was a catch. I couldn't sell to beverage distributors, and clients had to pre-pay for the product with a wire transfer. Wait, one more thing: the clients had to buy truckload quantities, not cases or pallets. With these restrictions on hand, I decided to go after large Cash and Carry businesses, large warehouses that buy and sell wholesale to other distributors, and independent stores. I did this with my new company, Liquid Brands Management, Inc., and my partner Carlos Lopez.

To launch Jolly Rancher Soda, I created a series of sales sheets and letters for a direct marketing campaign. I had no advertising budget and zero marketing support from the bottler, so I had to improvise and do everything entirely out of the box. I couldn't promote the product on my website or raise any commotion, as Hershey's would not be happy. In hindsight, I don't know why I decided to work with Joe, Honickman Group, and Jolly Rancher Soda under those tight conditions. I wouldn't take the project now, and I would probably pre-charge them just to look at the project, but back then, I was younger, and Joe was a super nice guy and a mentor to me in the beverage industry. I was up for the challenge.

A Word on Licensing

To clarify the relationship, Honickman Group was paying a licensing fee to Hershey's for name use. I never knew the exact amount, but Joe hinted it ate up plenty of the sale price. Many ask me about licensing, and I'll address it quickly here. Yes, you can license a product; however, it must be a name brand, like Jolly Rancher. It could also be a patent or technology others can't use without paying you. For example, a famous rapper wants us to license his name and manufacture Hemp Cigarettes. We refuse because he can't guarantee the type of social media mentions and appearances. We need to make a dent in sales. A famous rock star or athlete is not enough. As far as I know, the lesson is that even if you're a celebrity, you still need wholesale distribution.

As far as licensing technology is concerned, it is easier if you have something others need or if you have a perception of need or want. I get pitched with all kinds of technology, formulas, and other things I don't need, and I would have to build a brand to sell them. On the other hand, Sandro and I started Hempacco, and the company owns Intellectual Property, or IP, including patents on manufacturing and processing for manufacturing that customers are willing to pay. We also own merchandising patents for counter displays and only license them to our customers. These patents are for counter display and customer experiences.

Direct Response Marketing

I was ready to start contacting big distributors that could buy truckload quantities but not beverage distributors, as they require exclusivity for their territory, and Joe told me not to pitch them.

I decided to start a Direct Response campaign to find new clients. Direct Response Marketing is my favorite type of marketing because you target a consumer directly using emails, letters, or online advertising. You identify your customers and send them a custom message. You can use direct response marketing if you advertise on Facebook to a specific audience. They click on your ad, go through your funnel or customer experience, and then buy from you (or not). You can still track the activity, assign a cost, track your lead or customer, and calculate how much you're paying.

Google and Facebook are two of the easiest ways to get started with direct-response advertising. Google owns YouTube and has an extensive network of website partners with which you can advertise. Facebook owns Instagram, and you can do the same there. Both companies offer analytics and an easy-to-use advertising platform. If you start advertising, please ensure that your backend is solid, that you have a great squeeze page to capture emails, and that you can capture analytics and measure conversions. Please don't just go and advertise to get some traffic; you'll throw your money away. Traffic does not equate to leads, prospects, or customers. I spend most of my time thinking of the backend, sales copy, videos, capturing emails, and the required email follow-up, and only then do I push the advertising button.

The topic of direct advertising is vast and one of my passions. You can easily use it to land wholesale distribution, retailers, or even market directly to your consumers and sell online, push them to a retail store, or even sell to them directly.

I fell in love with marketing influence when I was a teenager. Then, I was fascinated with marketing, direct response, and online marketing when I became VP of Marketing in my twenties. I also used direct response in mailing campaigns, online advertising, fax, newspaper, trade magazines, and writing articles and books like this one. I started more than twenty years ago when these strategies were maturing. If you would like to increase your direct response and online marketing IQ, visit www.WholesaleMBA.com to see my videos on the latest techniques I'm using. I'll update these strategies as I use them, so you'll always get new and fresh ideas and newly available marketing technology.

I chose wholesale grocers and cash and carries to sell them truckloads of Jolly Rancher Soda. These are categories, so I bought a wholesale grocers list with names, addresses, telephone numbers, fax numbers, and the number of employees. You could potentially also purchase lists with yearly income and other interesting categories.

After buying my list, I decided to contact them by fax, yes, fax. I know what you're thinking, "exactly how old is this guy?" Wait, don't judge. I used fax then, and I still use fax now. Many businesses use faxes, and nobody markets to them with the fax; they might get ten to twenty emails per day but no faxes. Just think about how many emails you get per day or how many advertisements you get in the regular mail. I'm betting a lot, but you don't get any faxes. Maybe you don't have a fax at all. If that's the case, you were not my target market when selling the soda. I still use faxes to market to wholesale distributors and other businesses because they have fax machines. If you do this, be mindful of the laws in your state for sending faxes.

I've also done telemarketing campaigns. My old partner and I opened a call center in San Diego, where the salespeople called distributors and retailers to sell our products and others. I know calling people takes a lot of work and dialing, so I used a shortcut and sent a fax blast or a series of faxes to everyone simultaneously. We sent hundreds of faxes with a Jolly Rancher Soda promotion.

Our phone rang off the hook from that single fax blast, and we started selling truckloads soon after. Most of the work was not buying the list, the blast, the research, or copywriting. Most of the work was on the follow-up, calling wholesalers even after placing an order. We needed to contact them constantly to see if they received their truckload, ensure it was not damaged, confirm the product was selling well, and determine the most popular flavors.

I see brand owners make one mistake: executing a campaign on social media, Google advertising, mailing, or emailing, and never following up. You should know that following up is 80% of the work. In other words, after I prepared the sell sheets and sales letters, I sent a weekly letter and followed up by phone every single week. We did not wait for them to call us. We called them and left a ton of voice messages. We slowly got some callbacks, followed by emails, quotes, wire information, and more emails and phone calls. The result is that you hopefully get great customers for a lifetime. Sure, getting the first order is a ton of work, but once you establish a relationship based on trust, you can continue selling the same or new products forever. That's what I thought Carlos, my brokering partner, and I were doing, but it turned into a nightmare overnight. Keep reading, and I'll tell you all about it.

Can you get national brokers to sell everywhere and think you're done? No, you can't. Can it be done? Not really. Even if you secure national brokering companies like Advantage Sales and Marketing, they will not cover every retail channel. They won't cover much in wholesale, as their strength is not in distribution but in selling to giant retailers, with some presence in other channels like restaurants and hotels. The real question is, why would a large national sales broker want to carry your brand? You should know there is a pecking order for brokers and brands, just like wholesalers and distributors. National or Fortune 500 brands are first in line, and if they have space or twenty million dollars for advertising, most brokers will take your product. If you don't, you need to start at the bottom with regional brokers and work yourself up from there.

Everyone can be a broker. I often tell my friends, family, and people I meet at trade shows or on LinkedIn that I will give them five percent if they can get me an account or a white-label client. Does it work? You bet it does. Maybe it won't work in a traditional sales channel like supermarkets, but newfound contacts can get your product into places you never thought. For example, one of our brokers got us into Native American Casinos. Yes, he was on the board of directors of one of the casinos and was Native American. Another contact got my products into vending machines on college campuses, a channel that wasn't on my radar.

It does not matter if you are a manufacturer, importer, exporter, distributor, or retailer. You can profit from brokers or brokering in more than one way. You can use brokers to make money and save time. You can use brokers as commission-only employees in some instances.

Brokers have evolved over the years, and you now have many different types of brokers with various sale models specializing in many channels. For example, some new broker companies require a retainer. I've seen ranges from $500 to $15,000 monthly plus anywhere from 3% to 10% of sales commission. These brokers offer more than the old-fashioned broker, such as reporting, a large sales team, price negotiation, slotting, or market trade negotiation. Just because you have a broker doesn't mean you don't spend any money. These brokers need you to have a budget per store or territory to push the product with advertising.

My first experience as a sales broker was with Jolly Rancher Soda, selling it to wholesalers and establishing a national network of distributors. Carlos and I even sold it to Mexico and established distribution there. How did this incredible opportunity turn into a nightmare?

Our company, Liquid Brands Management, Inc., poured time and money into selling Jolly Rancher Soda. We figured that if we built the brand and established a solid wholesale distribution network, we could make enough money to support our families, grow the business, and add more brands and clients. We also had an evolving beverage consulting business. Joe was thrilled, and he didn't understand how we were doing it, how we went from zero to selling monthly truckloads in the USA and Mexico, but Joe loved the results. He called us one day with the bad news that Honickman Group was cutting our commission but keeping our customers. We lost most of our income, plans, and dreams that day. It wasn't a slight loss for us as we were a tiny business. It was a significant loss, and our trust in brands took a big hit that day. I always tell my customers and you to be fair to your brokers. They will help you forever if you do.

Using Brokers to Sell

Brokers help you sell your products to importers, exporters, wholesale distributors, retailers, and other accounts. They can sell to convenience stores, supermarkets, independent stores, medium-sized chains, restaurants, and the largest retail chains in the US and even other countries.

Suppose you're low on cash because you're a start-up, or your money is tied up in inventory. In that case, brokers are a good way of getting traction as many brokers work only on commission, so you don't have to spend a lot of money upfront to hire them. However, as mentioned above, many of the best brokers charge an upfront fee or monthly retainer. Brokers do this because they are in high demand and screen potential customers, only taking the ones with money. Brokers know it is an uphill battle without money for promotions. I tell start-ups to raise capital before approaching brokers or any business.

I usually only work with the larger, well-established sales brokers and pay them a monthly fee. I expect specific deliverables from them that other no-fee brokers can't promise. That's as far as professional brokers go. My partner and I still offer commissions to everyone else. I turn my business contacts into brokers; they send business my way and get paid

I've done a lot of brokering work, and most of the time, I charge a consulting fee or retainer plus a monthly fee. I do this because most of my customers are not ready for brokers or sales, so I have a lot of work or coaching. I have to build sales specifications, Point of Sale materials, and even business plans. On the other hand, I know many brokers that don't charge a single cent upfront and do a decent job, but you need to be 100% ready for them with a sales plan, sales collateral, correct pricing, everything!

You must decide the type of broker you need, want or can afford. Start by approaching everyone you meet in the industry and offering them a commission. Be ready with a brokering agreement so they feel comfortable sending you business. Arm them with sell sheets, samples, and any other materials. Offer to send samples to their clients or prospects and pay for the mailing. This will encourage your brokers to approach more and more clients.

How to Find Sales Brokers

If you're looking for brokers to represent you and your product, you can use this strategy to search for them. First, follow the plan we discussed: make everyone you know a potential broker, offer them a commission, and don't wait for them to send you a lead or make an introduction. If you incentivize potential brokers, they'll see you as a business partner, not someone they're doing a favor with. Now, you can call them, push them, ask for contact information, and follow up.

Before you look for brokers, I recommend having a broker contract. Many established brokers will have their contracts, but non-established brokers will not. When you meet anyone you think can be a broker or can send you business, follow up by sending the agreement and telling them you don't want them to work for free and that you'll pay them from the sales. Your contract should have some language on how much you'll pay them, when you pay them, for example, two weeks after you get paid, and what they need to do for them to keep getting paid, for example, follow up, get you reports, visit clients, etc.

Don't make your broker agreement a ten-page document that they're afraid to sign or have to spend hours on legal fees to ensure no one is taking advantage of them. I use a one or two-page agreement, and I've never had to dispute or even check it.

Besides finding brokers in trade shows and with other industry professionals, you could consider looking for professional brokers or a team representing you, your business, and your products. You might want to work with only one broker house, a cooperative of brokers, or just one person. It's up to you and how you want to grow and run your business. A simple Google or LinkedIn search will give you a list of hundreds of brokers. Ensure the brokers fit your goals and that they target the proper accounts.

Brokers By Trade or Channel

Brokers are usually organized into trades, channels, or verticals, and one broker might not get you the accounts you want. One broker or an entire brokerage company might specialize in getting your products into pharmacy chains in the Midwest. In contrast, another broker could help you get accounts across major supermarket chains.

I find brokers are good at selling to chain buyers but fall short when selling to distributors, wholesalers, and independent accounts. This is normal, as selling to a buyer representing two hundred stores makes them a hefty commission. Trying to open 200 independent stores for a local distributor can be an overwhelming challenge.

Please don't just call brokers and ask them to sell your products. Make sure you're organized, and you should, at the very least, have:

- Consumer pricing
- Retailer pricing
- Distributor pricing
- Sell sheets, maybe even a brochure
- Point of sale material
- Media kit or folder with pictures and documents
- Your NDA
- Broker contract

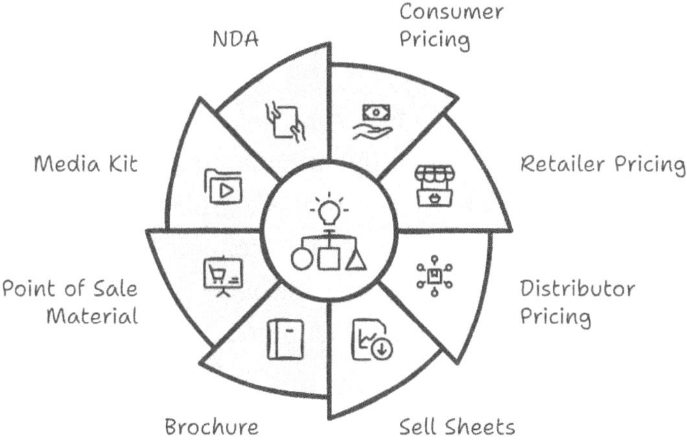

Figure 14 - Essential Elements for Product Sales

You should also have a marketing plan to support the broker. The plan should include detailed advertising, sampling programs, contests, and any other ideas you have to make people go to the store, buy the product, and come back for more. Remember, your job doesn't end when you get your product into stores; that's where your job begins.

If you're using brokers to sell into chains, you will most likely have to pay slotting, a fee you pay to get into every store. You can pay slotting fees with product or money. Either way, it can be costly when you're talking about selling to thousands of stores at a time. Let's say your slotting fee is $100 per store. It doesn't sound like a lot of money until you consider that one thousand stores will require $100,000 just to play. If you can convince the chain to take their slotting in product, your out-of-pocket can decrease by fifty or even seventy percent. It's still some big money, but it's more manageable.

It would help to reveal to the broker and the chain that you're well-funded, can produce enough product for all stores, have enough production capacity, and can withstand months of cash flow. It's essential to remember that cash flow can kill you in this industry if you're doing well, as you may need to increase production without receiving payment for at least thirty days.

I have relationships with dozens of brokers nationwide and even internationally. I invite you to visit www.WholesaleMBA.com and subscribe to the newsletter, as I often have interviews or webinars with brokers. Once you subscribe, you can send me questions to see if I can assist in choosing the broker that fits your company.

You can also find full-service brokers in specific territories. These brokers do more than meet with the chain's category manager. These rare and geographically specific brokers work in a city. They can get you a distributor, independent accounts, chains in this territory, and even go to the stores to chat with the managers and merchandise your products on the shelves. Sounds great, right? I bet you want these for every city in every state. They don't exist; you can get them only in particular locations, and they only take on a few brands.

Furthermore, they charge a commission and a retainer starting at $5,000 for their city. Some companies merchandise for you or take the product to stores, and you can scale with them. However, they don't sell your product, and sales and account management are the two most essential things once you launch your business.

How to Work with Sales Brokers

I was invited to chat at Alacer Corp., the company that owned Emergen-C (before they sold to Pfizer). Ron Fugate, the CEO, asked me to drive up to their offices in Orange County, which is only a ninety-minute drive from San Diego, CA. Ron wanted me to chat about selling to convenience stores, a much-wanted vertical where Emergen-C had no market share.

"Come and train the executive and sales team," Ron told me. "We rule the natural channel and mass, but we want to get into convenience stores." Alacer Corp also wanted to enter the beverage business, producing a ready-to-drink Emergen-C beverage. Ron read my book "Build Your Beverage Empire" and called me first to chat about their drink.

I drove up to their offices. Ron gave me the nickel tour, introduced me to his team, and took me to the conference room to start the presentation. I prepared a slideshow with sales numbers and statistics and gave away handouts and a few copies of my book. I was expecting a room filled with at least twenty or thirty salespeople, as that was my smallest audience when visiting sales organizations, brands, or even distributors.

"Let's start," said Ron. I looked around; only he and two other people sat around the oversized table with their drinks in hand. "Alright," I said as I set up the projector and started the presentation. I changed it from a keynote presentation to an intimate, more custom presentation. I included their brand in all my examples and explained how to sell their powder and newly planned beverages into convenience store chains and independents.

After the presentation, I asked Ron, "Where are all your salespeople?" Alacer is one of the largest vitamin companies in the country, and I was expecting an army of sales associates with their corresponding sales managers, directors, and maybe a VP or two. "We only sell with brokers," said Ron, "we have two broker houses, and that's it."

That was an essential lesson for me, and I hope you consider it in your business model. Brokers can be your best partners, helping you scale your company to a point where a global powerhouse will want to buy it.

I recommend treating your brokers as valued partners—your best friends, stakeholders, and investors in your business. Build strong relationships with them by communicating regularly. If you're working with a large brokerage company, make it a priority to speak with your account manager weekly. Establish rapport with the salespeople who are making the calls and actively selling your product.

Gather feedback from them, especially during the early stages. Ask what buyers think about your product, including its price, presentation, and how it fits into their stores. This insight is invaluable for refining your strategy.

Send product samples to your brokers and encourage them to use and experience your product. Ensure they have enough to share with their families or colleagues—familiarity breeds enthusiasm. Additionally, consistently send them branded merchandise like hats, t-shirts, polos, pens, notebooks, or any other thoughtful company gifts. This helps keep your brand top of mind.

Include your brokers in your email and mailing lists to keep them updated and engaged with your company. You can apply these same strategies to build strong relationships with your salespeople, wholesalers, distributors, importers, and exporters. Keeping these key players invested in your success will ensure long-term loyalty and collaboration.

I like to prepare small, branded gift boxes with your logo, colors, and products. You can custom-make them or buy them from Uline and slap a large color sticker to stamp the entire front. I use these for various mailers. For example, I send samples to brokers, sales teams, retailers, and distributors. In this case, it's a sample box with product, point of sale material, stickers, posters, sell sheets, a brochure, and usually a book, whitepaper, or case study I wrote about their industry. If they compliment my Polo shirt or the hat one of our employees wore, I send them a couple. Pay attention to your partners and what they like—a few of my partners, clients, and investment bankers like cigars. I have a cigar collection, so I might put a few in the box or send them individually. My partner Sandro owns an olive oil brand with his mom, so we send that as a gift when appropriate.

One of my clients was a professional MMA fighter. We could chat for hours about fighting and fighters when he visited. He even brought his pads to the office once, giving me an incredible lesson and insight into boxing. I printed some unique t-shirts with "martial ability" and gave them as gifts. They were a hit with him. You can never go wrong by sending a thoughtful gift.

Chapter 25 - Selling Your Products to Distributors and Retailers

---

"Always remember: success starts with the end consumer in mind."

Hempacco just shipped one full truckload of Snoop Dogg gummies under the Dogg lbs brand to our master distributor, with another one going out next week, totaling one million dollars. Yesterday, we met with three sales and business development team members.

"It's time to change from hunting and gathering to brand managing," said Sandro to them. Sergio Oliveros, our COO and CTO, was there as well, closely observing their behavior. After six years of struggling and trying to get any business anywhere, their role would change to managing distributors, wholesalers, and selling to convenience stores.

The chat didn't go as smoothly as I thought, and I had a migraine halfway through our first meeting. Our sales team was still in "getting new business" mode.

"I don't want any new business," Sandro said. "I need you to support our current distributors."

Sandro, Sergio, and I met about our wholesale distribution strategy, and it was now time to pass it over to the team. We had a great broker who helped us land master distributors who would pre-pay for products as we supported them in selling to their wholesalers and distributors. The goal? To reach 100,000 convenience stores around the country. At the same time, we were launching the Snoop gummies, producing the next products in our portfolio, and developing two other brands: *Hemp Bar*, with 15 products ready for labeling, and *Lucky to Be*, a beauty and nutraceutical line I created 12 years ago and was now resurrecting.

Develop Your Wholesale Distributor Strategy

Armed with the knowledge of how the industry works, it's time to put everything into action with sales and distribution. You need sales, whether you're a manufacturer, brand creator, or wholesaler. While online and direct-to-consumer sales are great, scaling your company often requires leveraging wholesale distributors and retailers.

This chapter addresses how to sell your products to both distributors and retailers, including how to support retailers in selling to end consumers. Always remember: success starts with the end consumer in mind. Identify where they're most likely to buy your product—whether in convenience stores, supermarkets, Amazon, or your own eCommerce store—and build your distribution strategy from there.

Selling to Distributors

Distributors are the bridge between you and the retailers. They handle logistics, warehousing, and often even sales, making them a critical partner for scaling your business.

Finding Distributors

- **Start with Your End Consumer:** Identify where your target customer shops, such as convenience stores, supermarkets, gift shops, or coffee shops. Then, determine how these retailers source their products.

- **Research Distributor Networks:** Once you've identified retailers, find the distributors that service them. Use trade directories, industry events, or referrals to locate potential distributors.

- **Tailor Your Pitch:** Highlight your product's demand and margins. Distributors want proven best-sellers that are easy to move.

Marketing to Distributors

1. **Active Marketing:**
    - Telemarketing, direct mail, and referrals are cost-effective ways to target distributors.

2. **Passive Marketing:**
    - Trade shows, trade magazine advertising, and press releases help build awareness over time.

Supporting Distributors

Distributors thrive when they're well-supported. Provide them with:

- **Marketing Materials:** Ensure they have access to brochures, product samples, and promotional items.
- **Sales Support:** Offer training sessions or webinars to help them understand and sell your products.
- **Regular Communication:** Keep them informed about product updates, promotions, or changes in strategy.

Pricing for Distributors

You've already conducted extensive market research. You know the retail pricing of your competitors' products and who sells the products to the retailers. Now, it's time to set your pricing to the distributors.

You decided on the retail price for your product, and you calculated the cost to produce your products. You can settle on a distributor price once you add other expenses like shipping, warehousing, repackaging, labeling, and commissions. Ensure you know your distributors well and how much they usually make on products like yours.

Each product and industry is different. Maybe your distributors make 10% of the sale, and perhaps they make 20% or even 40%. Even for your same products, other distributors can make different margins depending on how they operate and how much they buy from you.

Ensure you consider all expenses when calculating your profit and always have a good margin. It's better to lose a sale because you are too expensive than to win a deal, tie up your capital, spend a lot of time, and not make any money.

Selling to Retailers

While distributors are your gateway to large-scale distribution, selling directly to retailers gives you greater control over how your products are presented and sold to consumers. Retailers range from large chains to independent stores, and your approach should vary depending on their size and structure.

Finding Retailers

1. **Start Small:** Begin with independent retailers or small chains that are more accessible than national chains. Local stores are often eager to support regional products.

2. **Build Relationships:** Attend local events or trade shows to meet retailers face-to-face. Use these interactions to showcase your product's benefits and appeal.

3. **Leverage Distributors:** Distributors often have established relationships with retailers, making getting your product on shelves easier.

Pitching to Retailers

1. **Know Their Customers:** Retailers care about what sells. Research their customer base and tailor your pitch to show how your product fits their needs.

2. **Demonstrate Demand:** Use sales data, customer reviews, and testimonials to prove your product's popularity.

3. **Offer Attractive Margins:** Retailers need to make a profit, so ensure your pricing allows for competitive retail prices.

Supporting Retailers

Retailers are more likely to reorder if you make selling your product easy. Here's how:

- **In-Store Support:** To highlight your product, provide point-of-sale displays, signage, or shelf-talkers.

- **Promotions:** Run store-specific promotions or discounts to drive sales.

- **Training:** Educate store staff about your product so they can effectively recommend it to customers.

Selling to Large Chains

1. **Start Locally or Regionally:** Pitch your product to a single location or regional buyer to prove its value before scaling to national accounts.

2. **Prepare for Rigorous Requirements:** Large chains often have strict vendor requirements, including packaging, shipping, and compliance standards.

3. **Be Persistent:** Breaking into national chains takes time and effort, so don't get discouraged by initial rejections.

Balancing Distributors and Retailers

Many businesses face the challenge of balancing direct retail sales with distributor relationships. Distributors might view direct retail sales as competition, so it's crucial to:

- **Be Transparent:** Clearly define which accounts you'll handle directly and which will go through distributors.

- **Offer Support Across Channels:** Whether selling to a distributor or retailer, ensure each partner feels valued and supported.

- **Monitor Overlap:** Avoid undercutting distributors by offering retailers better prices. Maintain consistent pricing across channels.

Selling to distributors and retailers requires different strategies, but both are essential for scaling your business. Distributors help you reach a broader market, while retailers provide direct consumer access. By understanding the unique needs of each, tailoring your approach, and offering strong support, you can build lasting partnerships that drive growth and success.

PART 3 –
Building a Business as a Jobber

Chapter 26 - The Life of a Jobber

"Jobbing: Where hustle meets opportunity—build your business one stop at a time."

Jobbing is one of the fastest, easiest, and most flexible ways to become a wholesale distributor. Among the different types of jobbing, **wagon jobbing**—selling products directly to retail stores from your car or van—is particularly accessible for entrepreneurs looking to get started quickly with minimal investment.

In this chapter, we'll dive deeper into what jobbing entails, how to get started, and how to scale your operations. Whether you're selling your products, importing items, or buying and reselling, jobbing offers numerous opportunities to work with convenience stores, supermarkets, restaurants, and bars.

What Is Jobbing?

Jobbing involves buying products in bulk and reselling them to retailers or other small businesses. Unlike rack jobbing, where you manage product displays and restock them over time, wagon jobbing focuses on immediate sales during store visits. You bring the products to the retailer's door, present them, and secure sales on the spot.

For many entrepreneurs, jobbing is an attractive entry point into wholesale distribution because of its low barrier to entry. It doesn't require significant capital, expensive equipment, or large facilities. You can start selling within days with a reliable vehicle, some initial inventory, and a bit of hustle.

Key Questions to Consider

Before jumping into jobbing, it's essential to answer a few foundational questions:

1. **What products can you sell?**
   Jobbing works best with smaller, easy-to-transport products like sunglasses, novelties, snacks, or lighters. Bulkier items can be sold too, but they require larger vehicles and more storage space.
2. **How much time do you need to invest?**
   Success in jobbing depends on consistent effort. Whether part-time or full-time, you'll need to dedicate hours to visiting stores, pitching products, and restocking inventory.
3. **How much money can you make?**
   Profits depend on your product margins, the size of your route, and how many stores you visit daily. Many jobbers report earning between $2,000 and $10,000 per month, depending on the scale of their operation.

4. **How much money do you need to start?**
   The start-up costs vary based on the size of your operation, vehicle type, and inventory you plan to carry.

Starting as a Jobber

Vehicles:
Your vehicle is your mobile warehouse. While you can start with any car, larger vehicles like minivans, vans, or pickup trucks are better suited for jobbing. These allow you to carry more inventory, reducing the need for frequent restocking.

When I started jobbing, I used a minivan because it was affordable and offered enough space for both small and bulky items. You don't need to spend a fortune on your vehicle; reliable used options are sufficient.

***Warehouse Space**:*
While your vehicle acts as your mobile warehouse, you'll still need a base of operations. For most jobbers, a garage or mini-storage unit works perfectly. A garage offers the advantage of zero overhead costs, but if that's not an option, a small self-storage unit is an affordable alternative.

Staying organized is critical, even if your storage space is small. Shelves or pallets can help keep your inventory accessible and efficient to manage. Remember, a messy warehouse is often a sign of good sales—but regular cleaning and restocking are essential for long-term success.

***Startup Cash**:*
Starting as a jobber requires enough capital to purchase inventory. A bare minimum start-up could involve as little as $1,000 in inventory if you plan to sell part-time. However, a more robust operation targeting $5,600 in monthly profit would require an initial investment of around $4,000 to $8,400 in inventory.

Daily Operations

Your daily routine as a jobber revolves around visiting stores, pitching your products, and making sales. On average, you might visit 10 to 20 stores selling anywhere from $700 to $2,000 worth of products. Assuming you maintain a profit margin of 40%, your daily earnings could range from $280 to $800.

Successful jobbers maintain a consistent schedule, often visiting the same stores weekly or bi-weekly to restock inventory and introduce new products. Building strong relationships with store owners and managers is key to securing repeat business.

Scaling Your Jobbing Business

While jobbing is an excellent way to start in wholesale distribution, it also offers opportunities to grow. Here's how you can scale your operation:

1. **Expand Your Route:**
   As you become more efficient, you can increase the number of stores on your route. Adding just a few

more stops each day can significantly boost your earnings.

2. **Add New Products:**
   Diversifying your inventory allows you to appeal to a broader range of customers. For example, if you start with sunglasses, consider adding complementary items like lighters, phone chargers, or snacks.

3. **Hire Employees:**
   Bringing on additional jobbers allows you to cover more territory and increase sales. Start by hiring one or two part-time employees to manage specific routes.

4. **Invest in Larger Vehicles:**
   Upgrading to a larger van or truck enables you to carry more inventory, reducing the need for frequent restocking trips.

Challenges and Tips for Success

While jobbing offers numerous advantages, it also comes with challenges. Managing inventory, finding reliable suppliers, and navigating fluctuating demand can be difficult. Here are a few tips to ensure your success:

- **Build Strong Supplier Relationships:**
  Partnering with reputable manufacturers or wholesalers ensures that you get quality products at competitive prices.

- **Focus on High-Margin Products:**
  Prioritize items that offer a strong return on investment. Even small increases in margin can significantly impact your profits.
- **Stay Consistent:**
  Regular visits to stores build trust and establish your reputation as a reliable supplier.
- **Monitor Your Costs:**
  Keep track of your expenses, including fuel, vehicle maintenance, and inventory purchases, to ensure your business remains profitable.

Jobbing in Action

Example 1: Paris-Line Sunglasses
Paris-Line is an ideal product for jobbing. The small, lightweight sunglasses can be transported in large quantities, making them easy to sell to convenience stores, gift shops, and gas stations. Starting with a few dozen pairs of sunglasses, a jobber could quickly expand their route, targeting stores in high-traffic areas.

Example 2: Superior Energy Drink
While beverages are bulkier than sunglasses, energy drinks are still a popular product for jobbing. Selling directly to convenience stores, jobbers can introduce Superior Energy Drink as a premium alternative to established brands. Building relationships with store managers and offering promotional materials, such as posters or samples, can help boost sales.

Jobbing is a flexible and rewarding way to enter the world of wholesale distribution. With minimal start-up costs and the potential for significant earnings, it's an excellent choice for entrepreneurs who are willing to put in the work. Whether you're selling sunglasses, energy drinks, or novelties, the key to success lies in consistency, strong relationships, and smart product selection.

By starting small and scaling strategically, jobbing can evolve from a part-time side hustle into a full-time business with limitless potential. Let this chapter be your guide as you embark on your journey in the exciting world of jobbing.

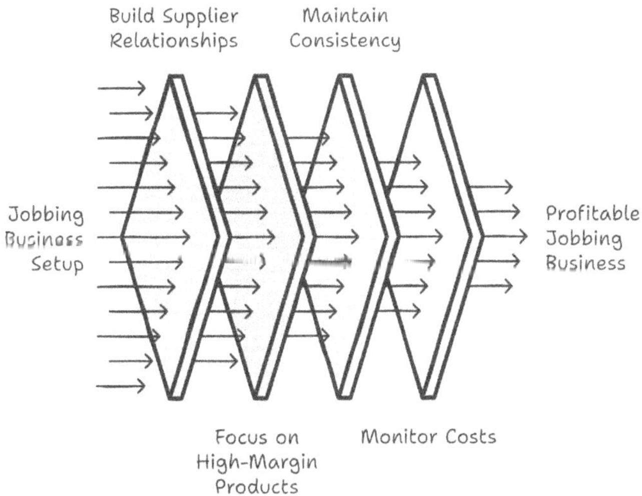

Figure 15 - Achieving Success in Jobbing

Chapter 27 - Your New Business Case Study

"Starting a business involves more than just logistics and sales."

In the last chapter, we explored jobbing and provided an example of how this type of business operates. Now, we'll dive deeper into a case study for starting a jobbing business called **Novelty Distributing**. This detailed example outlines the practical steps, financial planning, and strategies needed to launch and grow a successful wholesale distribution business. By breaking down the components of starting and running a business like Novelty Distributing, you'll better understand what it takes to build your own venture.

Business Description: Novelty Distributing

Novelty Distributing supplies convenience stores with popular items like tools, novelties, sunglasses, toys, and lighters. The business will be based in a medium-sized town of about 250,000 people, providing plenty of potential customers. Neighboring towns may also offer expansion opportunities as the business grows.

As a new business, Novelty Distributing starts with no customers or merchandise. The goal is to establish a route with 100 high-quality accounts. While you may have more customers overall, these 100 accounts will form the core of your business, generating most of your revenue.

Setting Goals

The first objective is to generate **$20,000 in monthly sales** with an average sale of $200 per store per month. Some stores may purchase more and others less, but this average will guide your operations. Achieving this sales goal means keeping **$8,000 in profit** before taxes and overhead expenses.

Start-Up Capital

To generate $20,000 in sales each month, you'll need approximately $12,000 worth of inventory every month. However, getting started requires more than just one month's worth of stock. A safe estimate is to invest $20,000 in merchandise for sufficient products to begin building your route and servicing accounts.

You can start smaller if you're not ready to invest this much upfront. For instance, you might launch with $5,000 to $10,000 in inventory, initially targeting fewer stores and scaling as you gain experience and revenue. Alternatively, if you have more capital, you could aim for larger sales volumes, such as $50,000 per month, by opening more accounts and stocking more inventory.

Building Your Customer Base

Opening new accounts is straightforward if you have the right products at the right prices. Here's how to approach it:

1. **Identify Potential Customers:** Start with convenience stores, gas stations, and small independent retailers in your area. Create a list of prospects to visit.
2. **Make the Pitch:** Walk into stores, talk to decision-makers, and show them your products. Explain the pricing, their potential profit margins, and why your products will sell well in their stores.
3. **Follow-up:** Once you've opened an account, maintain a strong relationship with the store owner or manager to ensure repeat business.

Servicing Your Accounts

Once you've established your route, your primary tasks will be servicing and keeping these accounts well-stocked. You'll likely visit 10 to 20 stores per day, depending on your route size and the demand for your products.

Some stores will require weekly visits, while others may only need servicing every two weeks or monthly. The frequency depends on the store's sales volume and your relationship with the retailer.

Your time will primarily be spent visiting stores, but you'll also need to allocate time for other tasks, such as:

- **Inventory Management:** Ordering, organizing, and stocking products in your warehouse or storage space.
- **Bookkeeping:** Managing accounts payable, receivable, and taxes. Using tools like QuickBooks can simplify this process, requiring only 30 minutes per day or a few hours per week.
- **Logistics:** Planning efficient routes to minimize travel time and fuel costs.

Managing Overhead Expenses

Starting a business comes with overhead expenses, but these can be kept relatively low in a jobbing operation. Common costs include:

- **Gas and Vehicle Maintenance:** With a well-organized route, stores are typically close together, reducing fuel consumption.
- **Insurance:** Business liability insurance and vehicle insurance are essential for protecting your assets.
- **Storage:** If you're not using your garage, a small self-storage unit can be rented for a reasonable cost, such as $350 per month.
- **Printed Materials:** Business cards and invoices are necessary, and you may also want brochures or sales sheets.

Additional Recommendations

Starting a business involves more than just logistics and sales. Consulting with professionals early on can save you significant headaches later. Speak with a lawyer, insurance agent, and certified public accountant (CPA) to address the following:

- **Legal Requirements:** Ensure you have the proper permits and licenses to operate in your city or state.
- **Tax Strategies:** Work with a CPA to develop a plan for managing taxes, including sales tax collection and filing.
- **Insurance Needs:** Protect your business with appropriate insurance coverage for liability, vehicles, and inventory.

Scaling Your Business

Once you've established a solid foundation, you can scale Novelty Distributing in several ways:

1. **Expand Your Product Line:** Introduce new items, such as seasonal novelties or branded merchandise, to increase sales and attract more customers.
2. **Grow Your Route:** Add neighboring towns to your territory to expand your customer base.
3. **Hire Employees:** As your business grows, consider hiring part-time or full-time employees to manage specific routes, freeing up your time to focus on strategy and growth.

4. **Invest in Marketing:** Use digital tools, like social media or email campaigns, to promote your products and attract new customers.

Case Study: How Novelty Distributing Operates

Step 1: Initial Setup

- Inventory Investment: $20,000 in merchandise, focusing on high-demand items like lighters, sunglasses, and small tools.
- Storage: A home garage is used initially, with minimal shelving and basic organizational tools like pallets and a hand truck.

Step 2: Building the Route

- First Month: Open 20 accounts, each purchasing an average of $200 worth of products. Focus on high-traffic convenience stores and gas stations.
- Second Month: Expand to 50 accounts, refining the route for efficiency and identifying top-performing customers.

Step 3: Daily Operations

- Average Sales: $1,250 daily across 10 stores, yielding $500 in daily profit.

- Weekly Routine: Four days of route sales and one day for inventory management, bookkeeping, and administrative tasks.

Conclusion

Starting a jobbing business like Novelty Distributing is a practical and rewarding way to enter the wholesale distribution industry. With a clear plan, the right products, and a commitment to building strong customer relationships, you can achieve consistent sales and scale your business over time.

Whether you're starting small or aiming for rapid growth, the principles outlined in this chapter provide a roadmap for launching and managing a successful jobbing operation. Let this case study inspire you to take the next steps toward building your own business.

Novelty Distributing Operational Sequence

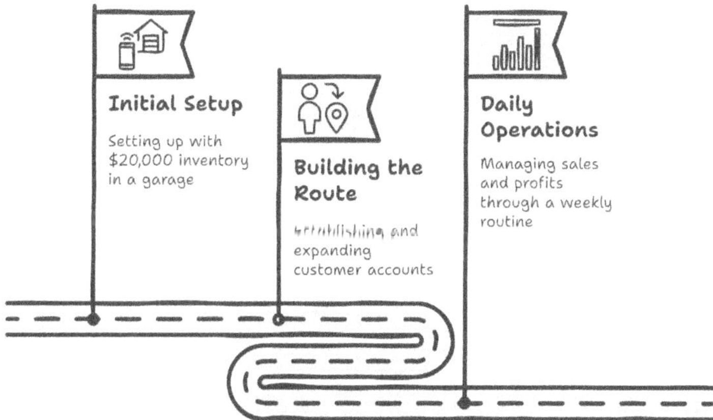

Figure 16 - Novelty Distributing Operational Sequence

Chapter 28 - The Art of Choosing Best Sellers

***"Finding Best Sellers is Easy;
Just ask, "What are your best sellers?"***

When building a distribution business, the key to success lies in selecting products that already sell well—best sellers. This concept may sound simple, but it's crucial to understand why and how to identify these winning products to ensure your business thrives.

Finding Best Sellers Is Simple

The easiest way to identify best sellers is to ask one straightforward question: **"What are your best sellers?"** Whether you're dealing with a supplier, store owner, or distributor, this question will often yield valuable insights. Avoid guessing what might sell or relying on personal preferences. Your likes and dislikes are not a substitute for market research. Instead, trust proven data and established trends to guide your decisions.

How to Find What Sells

Identifying best sellers doesn't require years of market research or extensive resources. Here are practical ways to determine what sells:

1. **Ask Suppliers Directly:** Always ask your supplier for their best sellers. Don't settle for vague answers like "what's new or trending." Instead, dig deeper by asking about specific products with consistent sales records.
2. **Observe Local Stores:** Visit convenience stores, supermarkets, gas stations, and pharmacies in your area. Take note of items that are sold out or frequently restocked. Speak with store owners or managers and ask targeted questions like, "How many units of this product do you sell weekly?" or "Which category moves the fastest for you?"
3. **Research Retail Pricing and Suppliers:** Once you identify what sells, investigate who supplies these products and the terms they offer. Knowing the retail price and understanding the margins stores work with will give you a better sense of your potential profit.

The Importance of Sticking to Best Sellers

Selling proven products eliminates the guesswork and reduces risk. Many distributors make the mistake of trying to introduce untested items, only to find themselves stuck with unsold inventory. Focus on established winners with a proven track record, particularly in convenience stores where space is limited, and turnover is essential.

What Types of Products Can You Sell?

Based on years of experience in distributing and jobbing, here's a curated list of perennial best sellers that perform well in almost any town:

- Laser Pointers
- Brand Name Candy
- Watches and Watch Sets
- Individually Packed Vitamins
- Small, Inexpensive Toys (Under $5)
- Novelty Lighters
- Sunglasses
- Auto Accessories
- Hand Tools
- Name-Brand Beverages
- Coffee Services
- Small, Inexpensive Electronics
- Houseware Items
- Pet Supplies
- Bath and Beauty Items
- Cell Phone Accessories
- Seasonal Items
- Car Air Fresheners
- Bottle Openers
- Hemp Cigarettes
- Nutraceuticals

These categories represent products with consistent demand. They are staples for many convenience stores and small retailers, ensuring steady sales year-round.

Packaging Matters

The presentation of your products can make or break a sale. Choose products with clear or blister packaging that allows customers to see exactly what they're buying. Avoid items in opaque boxes or packaging that hides the product. The more visible and appealing the product is, the better it will sell.

Why Stores Buy from You

Stores often buy from distributors like you because they can't afford to purchase directly from importers or manufacturers. Large minimum order requirements and long lead times make it impractical for small retailers to source products directly. For example, while you may purchase $4,000 worth of vitamins to distribute across 100 stores, a single convenience store is unlikely to spend $4,000 on one product. Instead, they prefer to buy smaller quantities from you, even at higher prices, to manage their cash flow and reduce risk.

How to Buy Best Sellers

Once you've identified the products you want to sell, it's time to find reliable suppliers. Here are the best ways to source your inventory:

1. **Local Cash and Carry Stores:** These wholesalers cater to jobbers and often sell in smaller quantities than importers or manufacturers. They can be an excellent starting point for new distributors.
2. **Trade Shows:** Attending trade shows allows you to connect with top suppliers and discover new products. While trade shows can be expensive, they are invaluable for building relationships and securing competitive pricing.
3. **Build Relationships Online:** While buying products online is often more expensive, you can use online platforms to connect with suppliers and establish long-term partnerships. Focus on finding reliable sources who can provide consistent stock.

What to Avoid

To maximize profits and avoid pitfalls, steer clear of these common mistakes:

- **Buying Online Retail Prices:** Most online "wholesale" listings are marked up significantly. Avoid purchasing inventory from these sources, as it will eat into your margins.
- **Buying from eBay:** While eBay can offer deals, it's rarely a source of true wholesale pricing. Sellers often resell items they've purchased from real wholesalers.
- **Liquidations and Overstock:** While liquidation deals may seem tempting, these products are often unsellable. Popular items rarely end up in liquidation. Stick to products with proven demand.

The Secret to Success: Proven Winners

The key to thriving as a distributor is simple: stick to best sellers. Don't waste time or money trying to reinvent the wheel. Instead, focus on products with a strong track record and consistent demand.

If you're looking for inspiration or guidance, visit **WholesaleMBA.com**, where you'll find resources, examples, and a curated list of products developed and sold across the U.S. and internationally. By leveraging proven strategies and reliable suppliers, you can build a profitable and sustainable distribution business.

This chapter is your roadmap to making smart product decisions and maximizing your sales potential. Stick to what works, focus on best sellers, and watch your business grow.

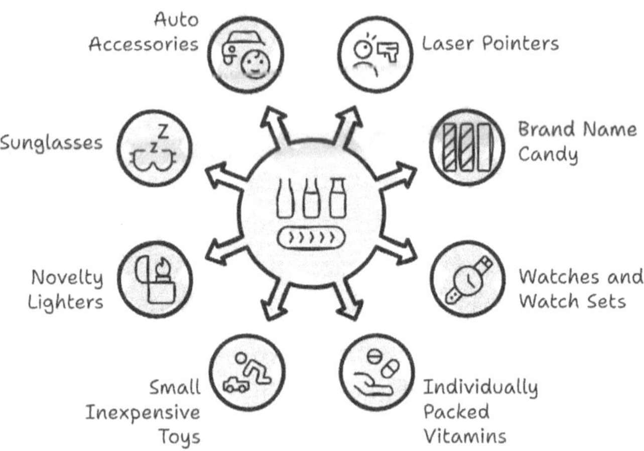

Figure 17 - Rack Jobber Product

Chapter 29 - Cash Flow Management for Jobbers

"Cash flow is the lifeline of distribution—manage it wisely to thrive."

Cash flow management is arguably the most critical aspect of running a successful distribution business. Without adequate cash flow, even a thriving business can quickly find itself struggling to stay afloat. Selling products, opening new accounts, and servicing stores may seem straightforward, but the real challenge lies in ensuring you have the money in hand to keep the operation running smoothly.

In this chapter, we'll explore the importance of cash flow, strategies to maintain liquidity, and essential formulas to help you make informed financial decisions.

The Reality of Cash Flow

In an ideal world, you could buy $600 worth of product today, sell it for $1,000 the same day, and pocket $400 in profit. The next day, you'd repeat the process and steadily grow your business. Unfortunately, cash flow rarely works this smoothly.

In reality, your sales cycle may involve delayed payments, especially when working with larger accounts or offering credit terms. For example, selling $100,000 of merchandise to a large retail chain every two weeks sounds promising, but if the chain pays you 45 to 60 days later—despite taking a 2% early payment discount—it can put a significant strain on your cash flow.

When products are shipped to multiple distribution centers or stores, the complexity increases, with invoices being processed at different times. This can leave you waiting for payments while your inventory and operational costs continue to pile up.

Strategies to Improve Cash Flow

1. Collect Cash at the Time of Sale

One of the best ways to maintain a healthy cash flow is to collect payment immediately upon delivery. Whenever possible, resist giving customers credit terms. While many stores will request 30-day payment terms, agreeing to this can quickly drain your cash reserves.

For example, if you buy $10,000 worth of products and sell $1,000 per day, it will take 10 days to recover your initial investment if you collect cash upfront. However, if you give customers 30 days to pay, you could find yourself out of money while waiting for payments to come in, requiring additional capital to purchase more inventory.

2. Be Cautious with Big Sales

Large sales to big accounts, such as chain supermarkets or independent retailers, can be lucrative but often come with credit terms. Before taking these deals, carefully assess your cash reserves and ensure you can handle the delayed payments without running out of operating capital. If you can't afford to wait, it's better to pass on the deal than risk financial strain.

Inventory and Investment

Inventory is one of the largest investments for any distributor. Managing your inventory effectively is crucial for maintaining a healthy cash flow. Think of inventory as cash tied up in your warehouse. The more inventory you have sitting on shelves, the less cash you have available to run your business.

To minimize risks:

- Keep your inventory lean by ordering only what you can sell within a short period.
- Avoid overstocking, even if discounts for bulk purchases are tempting.
- Prioritize selling your inventory before purchasing more.

The Money Formula

While ROI sounds impressive, wholesale distributors should focus on Gross Margin instead.

Understanding key financial formulas is essential for making informed decisions about pricing, profitability, and cash flow. Let's break down four important metrics for distributors.

1. Return on Investment (ROI)

ROI measures the percentage return on the money you invest. While it's commonly used in other industries, it's less relevant in wholesale distribution.

Example:

- You buy a product for $20 and sell it for $40.
- ROI = (Profit / Investment) × 100 = ($20 / $20) × 100 = **100% ROI.**

---

2. Gross Profit (GP)

Gross Profit is the dollar amount you make from a sale, calculated as the difference between the sales price and purchase price.

Formula:
GP = Sales Price – Purchase Price

Example:

- Sales Price: $40
- Purchase Price: $20
- GP = $40 – $20 = **$20 Gross Profit**

---

3. Gross Margin (GM)

Gross Margin represents the percentage of sales revenue that exceeds the cost of goods sold (COGS). It's the key metric for evaluating profitability in wholesale distribution.

Formula:
GM = (Sales Price – Purchase Price) / Sales Price

Example:

- Sales Price: $40
- Purchase Price: $20
- GM = ($40 – $20) / $40 = 0.50 = **50% Gross Margin**

Breakdown:

- Subtract the purchase price from the sales price to calculate Gross Profit ($40 – $20 = $20).
- Divide the Gross Profit by the Sales Price ($20 / $40 = 0.50).

- Multiply by 100 to express the result as a percentage (50%).

---

4. Markup

Markup is the percentage added to the cost of a product to determine its selling price.

Formula:
Markup = (Gross Profit / Purchase Price) × 100

Example:

- Purchase Price: $20
- Gross Profit: $20 (Sales Price $40 – Purchase Price $20)
- Markup = ($20 / $20) × 100 = **100% Markup**

Conclusion

Cash flow management is the backbone of any successful distribution business. By collecting payments promptly, managing inventory effectively, and understanding key financial metrics like Gross Profit and Gross Margin, you can build a sustainable and profitable operation.

Remember, cash flow is not just about making sales; it's about ensuring that money flows back into your business at the right time to keep operations running smoothly.

Whether you're handling small daily transactions or large-scale deals with extended payment terms, the strategies outlined in this chapter will help you navigate the complexities of cash flow management and grow your distribution business with confidence.

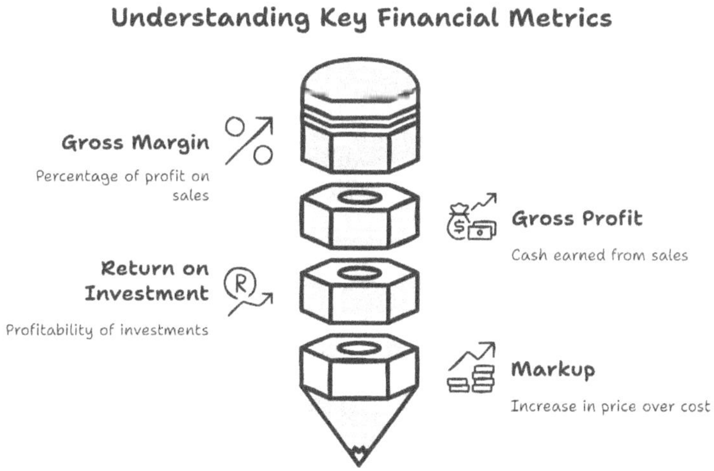

Figure 18 - Understanding Key Financial Metrics

Chapter 30 - Other Distribution Channels

"Distribute to Warehouses and Offices."

When we think of distribution, we often picture products being sold to retail stores for resale. However, a significant and often overlooked opportunity exists to sell directly to businesses that use these products in their operations. This approach opens up a world of potential customers, ranging from offices and warehouses to factories and schools. By distributing directly to these entities, you can diversify your business, maximize your routes, and increase your profitability.

Beyond Retail: Selling for Business Use

Not all products need to be sold to retailers to generate income. Many businesses require supplies and materials for their daily operations. Think about the wide range of products businesses use:

- **Office supplies:** Paper, ink, pens, and envelopes.
- **Industrial supplies:** Packing tape, stretch film, gloves, and cleaning chemicals.

- **Janitorial equipment:** Mops, brooms, soap, and paper towels.

By targeting businesses directly, you can turn operational necessities into consistent sales. Even if retail distribution is your primary focus, adding business-use sales can complement your existing routes and provide additional revenue streams.

The Practical Benefits

Selling directly to businesses has several advantages:

1. **Steady Demand:** Businesses need these products regularly, creating an opportunity for repeat sales. Once a company relies on your products, they are likely to reorder consistently.
2. **Large Orders:** Many businesses purchase supplies in bulk, such as cases of paper or pallets of packing tape, making each sale more substantial.
3. **Flexible Delivery:** If a business is on your route, delivering their order adds minimal time or effort. You can arrange warehouse pickups or schedule dedicated delivery days for larger, less frequent orders.
4. **Diversified Revenue:** Selling to businesses allows you to reduce dependence on retail sales and maintain steady income during seasonal fluctuations or slow periods in retail demand.

Strategies for Selling to Warehouses and Offices

You'll need to approach businesses differently than retail stores to succeed in this distribution channel.

1. **Identify Potential Customers:** Start by researching the types of businesses in your area. Large offices, warehouses, factories, and schools are excellent prospects for products like packing tape, janitorial supplies, and office essentials.
2. **Make a Targeted Pitch:** When approaching a business, focus on how your product can save them money, time, or effort. For example, highlight your competitive pricing, fast delivery, or the convenience of buying locally rather than ordering online.
3. **Adapt Your Product Offering:** Cater your inventory to meet the needs of businesses. For example, instead of selling individual rolls of tape, offer cases or pallets. Bundle related items like gloves and cleaning supplies to encourage larger purchases.
4. **Streamline Your Delivery:** Efficient delivery is key. Offer flexible options, such as adding smaller orders to existing routes or requiring minimum quantities for out-of-the-way customers.
5. **Build Relationships:** Like retailers, businesses appreciate reliability and excellent service. Follow up regularly to check on their needs, offer promotions, or introduce new products.

Real-World Example: Packing Tape

When I ran my route business, packing tape was one of my most profitable products. While tape was not my primary focus, I realized it was necessary for many local companies. I sourced tape at excellent prices from importers and factories, even importing directly from China.

By making a few targeted calls, I opened a new revenue stream. I sold tape by the case to shipping companies, factories, and warehouses. For customers near my existing route, I delivered small orders directly. For those farther away, I required a minimum purchase of five cases or asked them to pick up their orders from my warehouse. This simple strategy boosted my sales and improved my profit margins with minimal additional effort.

Thinking Outside the Retail Box

The key to success in this channel is creativity and flexibility. Think beyond traditional retail sales and consider how your products might fit into the operations of local businesses. For example:

- **Seasonal Products:** Sell seasonal items like hand warmers in winter or fans in summer to offices or warehouses that require them for employee comfort.
- **Custom Packaging Solutions:** Offer customized packaging materials, like branded tape or specialty boxes, to businesses with unique needs.

- **Collaborations:** Partner with local offices or schools to supply their ongoing needs, building long-term relationships.

Leveraging Modern Sales Channels

In addition to traditional business-to-business sales, modern sales channels can help you expand your reach. Consider these:

- **Social Media:** Platforms like TikTok and Instagram can be surprisingly effective for B2B sales, particularly if you use video content to demonstrate your products.
- **Email Campaigns:** Send regular updates to local businesses, highlighting your products, promotions, and new offerings.
- **Cold Calls and Visits:** Sometimes, the most direct approach is still the best. Visiting businesses in person allows you to establish trust and build a relationship.

Challenges and Solutions

While selling to warehouses and offices can be lucrative, it comes with unique challenges:

- **Taxes:** Unlike retail sales, you must collect and remit taxes for business-use sales. Work with a CPA to ensure compliance.
- **Minimum Orders:** Balancing the profitability of small orders with the effort required to deliver them

can be tricky. Set minimum order requirements for deliveries outside your route to maintain efficiency.

- **Product Customization:** Some businesses may require specific features or branding, such as custom tape or packaging. Be prepared to offer these options at a premium.

Conclusion

Expanding into business-use sales is a smart way to diversify your distribution channels and increase your profits. You can build a steady and reliable customer base by thinking creatively and targeting warehouses, offices, and other local businesses.

Whether adding a few extra stops to your route or selling full pallet loads, distributing to businesses allows you to maximize your resources and grow your operation. Don’t limit yourself to traditional retail sales—use your imagination, explore new opportunities, and discover the untapped potential of this often-overlooked channel.

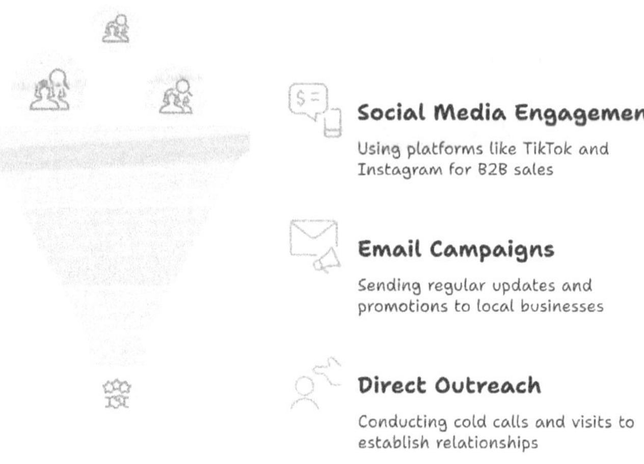

Figure 19 - Modern Sales Channel Strategies

Chapter 31 - Conclusion

"Chart your path to success!"

As we approach the end of "Wholesale MBA," reflecting on your extensive journey is important. This book has been a comprehensive guide designed to equip you with the knowledge, strategies, and ideas needed to excel in the dynamic world of wholesale distribution. Whether you're an aspiring entrepreneur, a seasoned executive, or somewhere in between, the principles and practices outlined here are meant to serve as your roadmap to success.

Reflecting on the Journey

From the initial stages of product development to the complexities of distribution, marketing, and sales, we've delved into all the critical aspects of the wholesale business. We've explored how to identify and develop winning products, create effective distribution models, and build strong relationships with brokers, distributors, and retailers. We have emphasized the importance of understanding your market, consumers, and unique value proposition.

Throughout this book, we've shared real-world examples and practical strategies that have been tried and tested in the field. These stories and case studies serve as inspiration and how-to guides, illustrating how theory translates into real-world wholesale distribution practice.

The Power of Innovation and Adaptability

One of the recurring themes in this book has been the power of innovation and adaptability. The wholesale distribution landscape is constantly evolving, driven by changes in consumer behavior, technological advancements, and market dynamics. To stay ahead of the curve, you need to adopt a mindset of continuous improvement and innovation.

Whether it's leveraging new marketing techniques, adopting cutting-edge technology, or finding creative ways to interact with consumers, your ability to adapt and innovate will set you apart from the competition. Remember, the most successful companies are those that can anticipate change and respond proactively.

Building Strong Relationships

Another key point of this book is the importance of building strong and mutually beneficial relationships. In the world of wholesale distribution, relationships are everything. Its success depends on the strength of its partnerships with distributors, retailers, brokers, and, ultimately, its end consumers.

Invest time and effort in nurturing these relationships. Understand the needs and challenges of your partners and work collaboratively to find solutions that benefit everyone involved. By fostering a culture of trust, transparency, and collaboration, you can create a network of allies committed to your success.

Emotional Connection with the Consumer

At the center of everything we have discussed is the consumer. The ultimate goal of any business is to meet the needs and exceed the expectations of its customers. In wholesale distribution, this means understanding your consumers' preferences, behaviors, and buying patterns, and using this knowledge to deliver value at every touchpoint.

Whether you're selling through traditional retail channels, online platforms, or direct-to-consumer strategies, always keep the consumer at the center of your efforts. Build your brand around their needs, communicate effectively, and create experiences that resonate with them. A satisfied and loyal customer base is the most valuable asset any business can have.

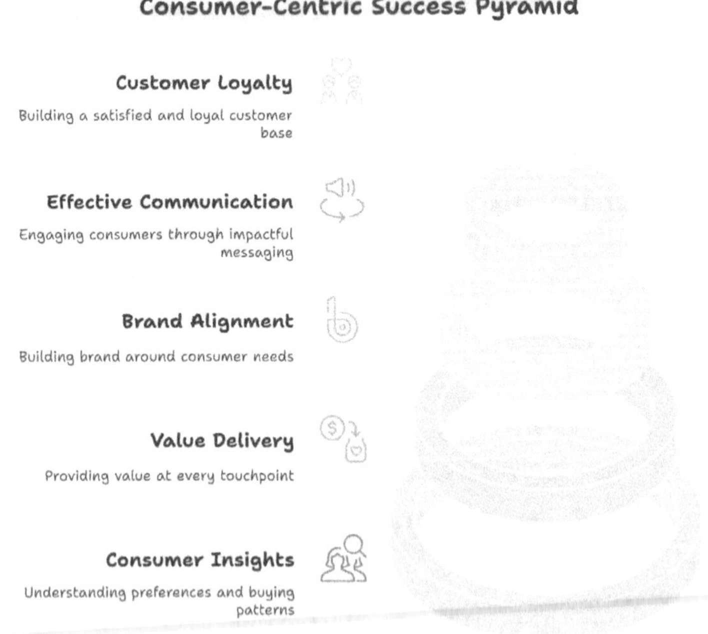

Figure 20 - Consumer-Centric Success Pyramid

The Road Ahead

As you move forward, armed with the ideas and strategies in this book, it's time to chart your path to success. Set clear and ambitious goals for your business. Develop a detailed plan that outlines how you will achieve these goals, and be prepared to adjust and pivot as needed.

Surround yourself with a dedicated team of professionals who share your vision and commitment. Foster a culture of innovation, excellence, and continuous learning within your organization. Stay on top of industry trends, stay open to new ideas, and never stop looking for ways to improve.

The world of wholesale distribution is challenging, but it is also full of opportunities for those who are willing to work. The road ahead will require perseverance, resilience, and a relentless focus on delivering value. But with the right mindset and the right strategies, you can achieve extraordinary success.

Thank you for embarking on this journey with us. We hope that "Wholesale MBA" has provided you with the tools, knowledge, and inspiration you need to take your business to new heights. We look forward to seeing the incredible impact it will have on the world of wholesale distribution. Here's to your success and the exciting journey ahead.

Chapter 32 – Glossary

"No, this is not going to be on the test."

No, this is not going to be on the test. However, it would be best to familiarize yourself with the basic wholesale industry terminology for the MBA part of the book. Without knowing at least what a distributor or durable good is, you'll be mad at me by the third chapter because you can't follow the examples.

What is a Wholesale Distributor?

By definition, you might think wholesalers and distributors are the same, but they're not. They are very different businesses. Some wholesalers can be distributors, but distributors are not usually wholesalers. What?! Don't worry; we have devoted entire chapters to each type of wholesaler and distributor, such as Direct Store Delivery or DSD, Foodservice, Beverage, Wagon Jobbers, and more.

For our first introduction, let's call a wholesale distributor a business that sells products to retailers, including convenience stores, supermarkets, superstores, pharmacies, restaurants, hotels, bars, offices, or natural stores. These retailers sell your products anywhere in the store, including shelves, racks, or even on the counter or checkout.

OK, that's a concise definition of a wholesale distributor, but it's a good one and one we need to get started. Your takeaway from this should be that there are many more wholesalers, distributors, and retailers than the ones you have in your head, so you can grow your distribution channels by targeting new types of wholesalers and distributors. If you're a wholesale distributor, you can target many other retailers, including some you never thought of, such as car washes or delis, hardware stores, roadshows, or street fairs.

You want distributors and wholesalers to carry and sell your product if you're a manufacturer. If you're on the other side of the warehouse and you're the distributor, you're looking for the bestselling products that will give you your 20% to 30% gross margin by just dropping off your products without doing much work.

What is your Sales Retail Channel?

Your sales or retail channel is how you'll sell your product. It includes your retailer and, by necessity, your distributor because you need to get your product to the stores. Let's focus on your retailers for now.

Retailers are stores that will sell your products. Kroger, Supervalu, and Safeway supermarkets are the first ones that come to mind. It also includes pharmacies like Walgreens or CVS, Convenience Stores or C-stores that can be independent, or chains like 7-Eleven or Arco AM/PM. They can be corporate-owned like Circle K. How about superstores like Target and Walmart or club stores like COSTCO or Sam's Club? These are the first that come to mind and the first most people would like to target with their products. But let's not be hasty. You must think outside the mass retail box. Plenty of other stores or categories of stores are waiting for all your products.

Other retailers include department stores like Macy's, Nordstrom, and JCPenney. They may also include car washes, liquor stores, and hardware stores such as Home Depot or Lowes. Or even office supplies retailers like the big national chains led by Office Depot and Staples.

If you only think of supermarkets and convenience stores, you're wasting money. Explore all channels before choosing your perfect distributor, retailer, and consumer.

What is a Consumer Good?

Consumer goods are products that the user purchases for consumption. Raw materials are not consumer goods; products that need altering or production are not considered consumer goods. Consumer goods are what the consumer can purchase at retail, and they could include small products like food or toys and large, durable goods or durable products like cars, televisions, or furniture. Other names are Consumer Packaged Goods, CPG products, or consumer products.

Why is it important to know the different types of consumer goods? If you don't know all kinds of goods, you won't know what to buy and sell or what distributors and retailers are thinking, and you'll be at a disadvantage because of your limited knowledge. And we're all about learning and experience. We need to understand before we make mistakes and experience after we make them!

The following definitions will help you in your wholesale business and understand more about the economy, manufacturing, retailing, world politics, and world economics. You'll be able to identify which country produces what and why, how they export products, and the trade deficits between raw materials and consumer goods exporters.

What is a Consumer Packaged Good or CPG?

This is the product we'll focus on in this book. Consumer Packaged Goods are the products you buy in supermarkets, convenience stores, pharmacies, and superstores or using direct sales or direct response. This includes every category that you see in these stores, such as:

Food
Beverages
Nutritional supplements
Housewares

Cleaning products
Housewares
Cookware
Electronics
Toys
Novelties
Impulse buy
Tools
Auto Accessories
Frozen, refrigerated & dry goods
Snacks & candy
Bakery
Fresh food
Tea & coffee
Canned goods
Spices
Alcoholic beverages

CPCs are also products in catalogs, magazines, or late-night television infomercials, such as oxy-clean detergent or items from chopping channels like QVC.

It doesn't matter if you're a distributor, wholesaler, or retailer; you need to be a manufacturer or brand owner at one time or another. It's very profitable, and it's also fun to own your products. In this case, consumer packaged goods. I'll insist on this time and time again, and hopefully, by the end of the book, you're convinced that you need your private label or full-blown brand.

What is a Fast-Moving Consumer Good?

Durable Good

Also called Durable Products or Hard Goods, Durable Goods are consumer goods that will not wear out quickly; they last longer. Food is not a durable good because it's for immediate consumption. The perfect example of durable goods are products you own that you only buy once in a lifetime or at least every few years, such as your house, computer, furniture, or car. By contrast, non-durable goods are goods that wear out quickly.

Non-Durable Goods

Non-Durable Goods or soft goods are contrary to durable goods. They're products that you, the consumer, use quickly, if not immediately. The perfect example can be a chocolate bar you eat in the supermarket's checkout line. By the time you pay, it's gone. Non-Durable Goods include food and beverage products and toilet paper, office supplies, apparel (unless it's a heritage item or custom-made suit), cigarettes, cleaning products, matches, hair and skin products, vitamins, etc. Think of things you consume or can wear out in less than three years. A T-shirt can be a soft good, but a leather jacket that will last you for years is not. A high-end watch or jewelry would not be a soft good either.

Perishable Goods

Perishable goods are products with a short expiration date. These include milk, meat, fish, poultry, and fruit. Milk is an excellent example because it requires refrigeration, specialized local distributors, rack jobbing or merchandising, and a local supplier to supply the product to distributors or deliver it independently. You might have a perishable product or are thinking of developing one. If so, consider the extra costs of refrigeration, having a refrigerated truck for delivery, and even investing in refrigerators for your accounts, just in case your competitors don't want to let you into their space.

Major Types of Distributors

Many different distributors are selling wholesale products to retailers and other outlets. Here are the ones that control most of the industry:

DSD Direct Store Delivery Distributors = distributors that sell to retailers and provide full service, including merchandising, delivery, and collections, often on the same trip. The words "Full Service" are synonymous with DSD. Many distributors, such as beverage distributors and wagon jobbers, are full-service distributors. You can find large DSD distributors covering vast territories and mom-and-pop, one-person operations selling sunglasses, beef jerky, or novelties from behind their cars.

Wholesalers = are large distributors that don't offer full service to clients, usually drop cases or pallets of merchandise to stores. They sell to larger accounts and often have cash-and-carry in their warehouse. Depending on where you are in the nation, some Wholesalers are only cash-and-carry operators. Remember, this is an industry definition, not a dictionary definition. The largest Wholesalers in the USA deliver products to large convenience store chains nationwide.

Cash and Carry = warehouse where retailers can pick up products for their stores. Some of them are also wholesalers. They only buy well-known products and brands. Major brand name stores now have cash and carry stores. Costco has Cash and Carry only stores servicing retailers and restaurants. Walmart competes with its Cash and Carry, called Sam's Club. Restaurant Depot sells to restaurants using the same business model.

Foodservice distributors = sell fresh, frozen, and dry goods, mainly food, to restaurants, bars, and hotels. They bring the food that you consume to your favorite restaurant.

Beverage distributors = are specialty distributors with specialty trucks that sell beverages, mostly beer and other non-alcoholic products like sodas, energy drinks, water, and more, to retail and foodservice accounts. The largest distributors in the USA are franchises for beer and soda companies.

Wagon Jobbers = are smaller distributors, usually a one-person operation with a van or small truck selling many different products mainly to convenience stores, especially liquor stores and other independently owned stores. Many Wagon Jobbers buy their products from Wholesalers and Cash-and-Carry stores.

Vending operators = own or service vending machines and service offices with snacks and beverages.

Brokers = are not usually distributors but middlemen placing your product with retailers, especially chains. Brokers make a commission on products sold and paid for.

Alcoholic distributors = sell wine and spirits like Tequila, Vodka, and other beverages to retail and foodservice accounts. No, they are not distributors who drink too much, they just call them alcoholic because they distribute alcohol, but you knew that. Many alcohol distributors also sell specialty beer to their food service clients.

Drop-Shippers = We're not talking about companies that ship products to consumers using direct response, eBay.com, or Amazon.com. These companies sell and ship products to all types of retailers, from supermarkets to convenience stores, carwashes, specialty stores, and more.

Many specialty distributors are hybrids or sub-categories of these distributors, such as distributors selling to natural stores, gymnasiums, and vitamin stores, distributors selling frozen products to supermarkets, or even more specialized distributors like milk distributors selling and delivering fresh perishable milk to supermarkets and restaurants.

What is a Manufacturer?

The first thing that comes to mind might be a factory or somebody with a manufacturing plant or in the business of production. This was true when all brands were made by their brand owners. Nowadays, a manufacturer is a brand owner and has nothing to do with the actual production business. Most starting manufacturers or brand owners use co-packers or third-party production facilities to make their products in the USA or other countries, most famously in China. If you're an importer of products, you probably have the same responsibilities as a manufacturer, even if it's not your product. You respond for the brand, get distributors, warehouse the product, go out and search for retailers, and, most importantly, establish relationships with your consumers.

"Enough with the definitions. Give me a story." Yes, I can get carried away with definitions, but I need to remember to include examples and case studies. So I'll mix it around. We need definitions to understand how the machine works and stories so that the information sticks. We can visualize how to apply the knowledge to your business now and in the future. Some of the concepts will immediately impact what you're doing right now. Maybe you're developing a new product or about to go to a trade show. Others will hit home in the future when you're tackling new problems or looking for solutions.

Pick a Retailer

Your retail channels include businesses and people who can sell your product to consumers. For the most part, these are brick-and-mortar or online locations, but they can also include infomercials, magazines, people (direct sales, MLM), catalogs, food service, and many more out-of-the-box sales channels. The most popular retail stores are supermarkets, convenience stores, pharmacies or drug stores, superstores, club stores, department stores, and specialty stores such as appliances, hardware, office supplies, or vitamins. A retailer can also include a food service account for your business as they buy from you at wholesale and sell it at retail. We'll create a new category to separate the two so we don't get them mixed up.

Foodservice or On-premise

What is the difference between Foodservice and On-premise accounts? There is no difference. Food distributors call restaurants, bars, and hotels food services, while beverage distributors such as beer, wine, spirit, and non-alcoholic call the same accounts On-premise. They include all non-traditional retailers where you can consume products. In other words, you don't buy and take it home (unless they have take-out). You consume the food or drink on the premises.

Table of Figures

Index

www.ingramcontent.com/pod-product-compliance
Lightning Source LLC
LaVergne TN
LVHW010050110826
845155LV00028B/278

* 9 7 8 1 9 4 5 1 9 6 3 3 1 *